THE COMMON LAW]

PROFESSIONAL LIABILITY

THE COMMON LAW LIBRARY

JACKSON & POWELL
ON
PROFESSIONAL LIABILITY

Second Supplement
to the
Sixth Edition

Up-to-date until September 2008

SWEET & MAXWELL

Published in 2009 by Thomson Reuters (Legal) Limited
(Registered in England & Wales, Company No. 1679046.
Registered Office and address for service: 100 Avenue Road, London NW3 3PF)
Trading as Sweet & Maxwell

Typeset by Interactive Sciences Ltd, Gloucester
Printed and bound in Great Britain by Athenaeum Press Ltd, Gateshead

For further information on our products and services, visit:
www.sweetandmaxwell.co.uk

ISBN 978-1-84703-297-3

No natural forests were destroyed to make this product:
only farmed timber was used and replanted.

A CIP catalogue record for this book is available from the British Library

All rights reserved. Crown Copyright material is reproduced with the
permission of the Controller of the HMSO and the Queen's Printer for Scotland.
No part of this publication may be reproduced or transmitted, in any form
or by any means, or stored in any retrieval system of any nature,
without prior written permission, except for permitted fair dealing under the
Copyright, Designs and Patents Act 1988, or in accordance with the
terms of a licence issued by the Copyright Licensing Agency in respect of
photocopying and/or reprographic reproduction.
Application for permission for other use of copyright material
including permission to reproduce extracts in other published works
shall be made to the publishers. Full acknowledgement of
author, publisher and source must be given.

Thomson Reuters and the Thomson Reuters Logo are trademarks of Thomson Reuters.
Sweet & Maxwell ® is a registered trademark of Thomson Reuters (Legal) Limited.

©
J.L. Powell & R. Stewart
2009

GENERAL EDITORS

JOHN L. POWELL, Q.C., M.A., LL.B.
Of the Middle Temple

ROGER STEWART, Q.C., M.A., LL.M.
Of the Inner Temple

EDITORS

SCOTT ALLEN, B.A.
Of the Inner Temple, Barrister

MARK CANNON, B.A.
Of the Middle Temple, Barrister

GRAHAM CHAPMAN, B.A.
Of the Inner Temple, Barrister

ANNELIESE DAY, M.A.
Of the Inner Temple, Barrister

BEN ELKINGTON, M.A., LL.M.
Of Gray's Inn and of Lincoln's Inn, Barrister

HUGH L. EVANS, M.A., B.C.L.
Of the Middle Temple, Barrister

DAVID HALPERN, Q.C., M.A.
Of Gray's Inn

GRAEME MCPHERSON, M.A.
Of Gray's Inn, Barrister

SIAN MIRCHANDANI, M.A., Vet, MB.
Of the Inner Temple, Barrister

LEIGH-ANN MULCAHY, M.A., LL.M.; Dip. EC Law
Of the Inner Temple, Barrister

AMANDA SAVAGE, LL.B., BCL, B.A.
Of the Middle Temple, Barrister

FIONA SINCLAIR, M.A., LL.M.
Of the Inner Temple and of Lincoln's Inn, Barrister

PAUL SUTHERLAND, M.A.
Of the Middle Temple, Barrister

DAVID TURNER, M.A.
Of Gray's Inn, Barrister

CONSULTANT EDITOR

SIR RUPERT JACKSON, M.A., LL.B.
*One of Her Majesty's Judges of the
Queen's Bench Division, Of the Middle Temple*

HOW TO USE THIS SUPPLEMENT

This is the Second Supplement to the Sixth Edition of *Jackson and Powell on Professional Liability*, and has been compiled according to the structure of the main volume.

At the beginning of each chapter of this Supplement is a mini table of contents from the main volume. Where a heading in this table of contents has been marked with the symbol ■, the material under that heading has been added to or amended, and should be referred to. Where a heading is marked with the symbol □, the material under that heading was added to or amended in the First Supplement but has not been updated further in this Supplement.

Within each chapter, updating information is referenced to the relevant paragraph in the main volume. New paragraphs which have been introduced in this supplement have been identified as, e.g. **8–085A**.

TABLE OF CASES

3M United Kingdom Plc v Linklaters & Paines (A Firm) [2006] EWCA Civ 530; [2006] P.N.L.R. 30; [2006] 2 E.G.L.R. 53; [2006] 28 E.G. 106; [2006] 20 E.G. 292 (C.S.), CA (Civ Div) 5–080
3464920 Canada Inc v Strother (2007) 281 D.L.R. (4th) 640, SC (Can) 11–025, 11–147, 11–228
A v Hoare; H v Suffolk CC; X v Wandsworth LBC [2008] UKHL 6; [2008] 1 A.C. 844; [2008] 2 W.L.R. 311; [2008] 2 All E.R. 1; [2008] 1 F.L.R. 771; [2008] 1 F.C.R. 507; (2008) 11 C.C.L. Rep. 249; (2008) 100 B.M.L.R. 1; [2008] Fam. Law 402; (2008) 105(6) L.S.G. 27; (2008) 158 N.L.J. 218; (2008) 152(6) S.J.L.B. 28, HL 5–085, 5–091
A Hospital v SW. *See* A Hospital v W
A Hospital v W; sub nom. A Hospital v SW [2007] EWHC 425 (Fam); [2007] LS Law Medical 273, Fam Div 7–071, 13–054
AB v Nugent Care Society [2008] EWCA Civ 795 5–091
ADF Properties Pty Ltd and Kestrel Holdings (No.2) [2007] FCA 1561, Fed Ct (Aus) 10–101
AIG Europe (Ireland) Ltd v Faraday Capital Ltd [2006] EWHC 2707 (Comm); [2007] 1 All E.R. (Comm) 527; [2006] 2 C.L.C. 770; [2007] Lloyd's Rep. I.R. 267, QBD (Comm) 8–020
AK v Central & North West London Mental Health NHS Trust and Kensington & Chelsea LBC [2008] EWHC 1217 7–054
ALE Heavy Lift v MSD (Darlington) Ltd [2006] EWHC 2080 (TCC), QBD 9–354, 9–367
AS v Hungary (4/2004) (2007) 45 E.H.R.R. SE1, UN CEDW 7–061A
AXA Insurance UK Plc v Cunningham Lindsey United Kingdom [2007] EWHC 3023 (TCC) 9–006, 9–304, 9–318, 9–343
Abbott v Will Gannon & Smith Ltd [2005] EWCA Civ 198; [2005] B.L.R. 195; 103 Con. L.R. 92; [2005] P.N.L.R. 30; [2005] 10 E.G. 154 (C.S.); [2005] N.P.C. 30, CA (Civ Div) 5–072
Aer Lingus Plc v Gildacroft Ltd [2006] EWCA Civ 4; [2006] 1 W.L.R. 1173; [2006] 2 All E.R. 290; [2006] C.P. Rep. 21; [2006] P.I.Q.R. P16; (2006) 103(6) L.S.G. 32; (2006) 156 N.L.J. 147; (2006) 150 S.J.L.B. 129; [2006] N.P.C. 4, CA (Civ Div) 4–017
Affordable Medicines Trust & Ors v Minister of Health & Director-General of Health, South Africa High Court, [2006] 5 C.H.R.L.D. 516 (summary) 7–090
Airedale NHS Trust v Bland [1993] A.C. 789; [1993] 2 W.L.R. 316; [1993] 1 All E.R. 821; [1993] 1 F.L.R. 1026; [1994] 1 F.C.R. 485; [1993] 4 Med. L.R. 39; (1993) 12 B.M.L.R. 64; [1993] Fam. Law 473; (1993) 143 N.L.J. 199, HL 13–054
Albonetti v Wirral MBC [2008] EWCA Civ 783 .... 5–087, 5–091
Amaltal Corp Ltd v Maruha Corp [2007] 1 N.Z.L.R. 608, CA (NZ) 2–133, 5–102
Amec Civil Engineering Ltd v Secretary of State for Transport [2005] EWCA Civ 291; [2005] 1 W.L.R. 2339; [2005] B.L.R. 227; 101 Con. L.R. 26; (2005) 21 Const. L.J. 640; [2005] 12 E.G. 219 (C.S.); (2005) 102(20) L.S.G. 30, CA (Civ Div) 9–362
An NHS Trust v MB 260432 [2006] EWHC 507; [2006] 2 F.L.R. 319; (2006) 9 C.C.L. Rep. 568; [2006] Lloyd's Rep. Med. 323; [2006] Fam. Law 445, Fam Div 13–054, 13–056

TABLE OF CASES

Andrews v Barnett Waddingham (A Firm) [2006] EWCA Civ 93; [2006] P.N.L.R. 24; [2006] Pens. L.R. 101, CA (Civ Div) 3–002, 15–069
Anns v Merton LBC; sub nom. Anns v Walcroft Property Co Ltd [1978] A.C. 728; [1977] 2 W.L.R. 1024; [1977] 2 All E.R. 492; 75 L.G.R. 555; (1977) 243 E.G. 523; (1988) 4 Const. L.J. 100; [1977] J.P.L. 514; (1987) 84 L.S.G. 319; (1987) 137 N.L.J. 794; (1977) 121 S.J. 377, HL 2–063A
Aquatec-Maxcon Pty Led v Barwon Regional Water Authority (No.2) [2006] V.S.C. 117 9–115
Arab Monetary Fund v Hashim (No.10), The Times, June 17, 1993 4–004
Arbory Group Ltd v West Craven Insurance Services [2007] Lloyd's Rep. I.R. 491; [2007] P.N.L.R. 23, QBD (Leeds) 16–143A
Armory v Delamirie (1722) 1 Strange 505 .... 16–128A, 16–135
Arthur JS Hall & Co v Simons; Barratt v Woolf Seddon; Cockbone v Atkinson Dacre & Slack; Harris v Scholfield Roberts & Hill; sub nom. Harris v Scholfield Roberts & Hall; Barratt v Ansell (t/a Woolf Seddon) [2002] 1 A.C. 615; [2000] 3 W.L.R. 543; [2000] 3 All E.R. 673; [2000] B.L.R. 407; [2000] E.C.C. 487; [2000] 2 F.L.R. 545; [2000] 2 F.C.R. 673; [2001] P.N.L.R. 6; [2000] Fam. Law 806; [2000] E.G. 99 (C.S.); (2000) 97(32) L.S.G. 38; (2000) 150 N.L.J. 1147; (2000) 144 S.J.L.B. 238; [2000] N.P.C. 87, HL 5–074A, 7–038, 10–053A
Attorney General v X [1992] 2 C.M.L.R. 277, Sup Ct (Irl) 7–054
Aveat Heating Ltd v Jerram Falkus Construction Ltd [2007] EWHC 131 (TCC); [2007] T.C.L.R. 3; 113 Con. L.R. 13, QBD 9–363
Awoyomi v Radford [2007] EWHC 1671 (QB); [2008] 3 W.L.R. 34; [2007] P.N.L.R. 34; (2007) 157 N.L.J. 1046, QBD 5–074A, 7–038, 12–009
B v Reading BC; sub nom. L v Reading BC [2007] EWCA Civ 1313; [2008] 1 F.L.R. 797; [2008] 1 F.C.R. 295; [2008] LS Law Medical 182; [2008] Fam. Law 314, CA (Civ Div) 7–036
BRB (Residuary) Ltd v Connex South Eastern Ltd (fomerly South Eastern Train Co Ltd) [2008] EWHC 1172 (QB); (2008) 105(24) L.S.G. 25 4–003
Bailey v Ministry of Defence [2008] EWCA Civ 883 13–115
Baird Textile Holdings Ltd v Marks & Spencer Plc; sub nom. Baird Textiles Holdings Ltd v Marks & Spencer Plc [2001] EWCA Civ 274; [2002] 1 All E.R. (Comm) 737; [2001] C.L.C. 999, CA (Civ Div) 13–109
Bakker v Austria (2004) 39 E.H.R.R. 26 7–095
Balfour Beatty Construction v Serco Ltd [2004] EWHC 3336, QBD (TCC) 9–359
Bank of Credit and Commerce International (Overseas) Ltd v Akindele; sub nom. BCCI v Chief Labode Onadimaki Akindele [2001] Ch. 437; [2000] 3 W.L.R. 1423; [2000] 4 All E.R. 221; [2000] Lloyd's Rep. Bank. 292; [2000] B.C.C. 968; [2000] W.T.L.R. 1049; (1999–2000) 2 I.T.E.L.R. 788; (2000) 97(26) L.S.G. 36; (2000) 150 N.L.J. 950, CA (Civ Div) 4–006
Bank of Ireland Mortgage Bank v Coleman (p/a Coleman & Co) [2006] IEHC 337; [2007] P.N.L.R. 16, HC (Irl) 11–072
Bartoline Ltd v Royal & Sun Alliance Insurance Plc [2007] Lloyd's Rep.I.R. 423 .... 8–017, 8–019
Baxall Securities Ltd v Sheard Walshaw Partnership; sub nom. Blaxhall Securities Ltd v Sheard Walshaw Partnership [2002] EWCA Civ 9; [2002] B.L.R. 100; [2002] T.C.L.R. 18; 83 Con. L.R. 164; [2002] Lloyd's Rep. P.N. 231; [2002] P.N.L.R. 24; [2002] 1 E.G.L.R. 73; [2002] 17 E.G. 158; (2002) 18 Const. L.J. 481; [2002] 5 E.G. 130 (C.S.), CA (Civ Div) 9–078, 9–281
Bear Stearns Bank Plc v Forum Global Equity Ltd [2007] EWHC 1576 (Comm), QBD 15–072
Benfield (t/a Autoroute Circuits) v Life Racing Ltd [2007] EWHC 1505 (TCC) 9–170

TABLE OF CASES

Beresford v Royal Insurance Co Ltd [1938] A.C. 586, HL 8–078
Biffa Waste Services Ltd v Maschinenfabrik Ernst Hese GmbH [2008] EWHC 6
    (TCC); [2008] B.L.R. 155; [2008] P.N.L.R. 17, QBD 9–060, 9–121, 9–334
Bluck v Information Commissioner (2007) 98 B.M.L.R. 1; [2008] W.T.L.R. 1,
    Information Tr 7–085
Board of Governors of the Hospitals for Sick Children v McLaughlin Harvey Plc
    (1987) 19 Con.L.R. 25 9–304
Board of Trustees of the Tate Gallery, The v Duffy Construction Ltd [2007]
    EWHC 912 (TCC); [2008] Lloyd's Rep. I.R. 159, QBD 8–077
Bolitho (Deceased) v City and Hackney HA [1998] A.C. 232; [1997] 3 W.L.R.
    1151; [1997] 4 All E.R. 771; [1998] P.I.Q.R. P10; [1998] Lloyd's Rep.
    Med.26; (1998) 39 B.M.L.R. 1; [1998] P.N.L.R. 1; (1997) 94(47) L.S.G. 30;
    (1997) 141 S.J.L.B. 238, HL 13–141
Bolton MBC v Municipal Mutual Insurance Ltd [2006] EWCA Civ 50; [2006] 1
    W.L.R. 1492; [2006] 1 C.L.C. 242; [2007] Lloyd's Rep. I.R. 173; (2006)
    103(9) L.S.G. 31; (2006) 150 S.J.L.B. 226, CA (Civ Div) 8–070A
Boodhoo, Re [2007] EWCA Crim 14; [2007] 1 Cr. App. R. 32; [2007] P.N.L.R.
    20, CA (Crim Div) 11–141
Bovingdon v Hergott (2006) 275 D.L.R. (4th) 168, Ontario Superior Court of
    Justice 13–020, 13–021
Brent LBC v K [2007] EWHC 1250 (Fam); [2007] 2 F.L.R. 914; [2008] B.L.G.R.
    37; [2007] Fam. Law 691, Fam Div 7–081
British Racing Drivers Club Ltd v Hextall Erskine & Co [1996] 3 All E.R. 667;
    [1996] B.C.C. 727; [1997] 1 B.C.L.C. 182; [1996] P.N.L.R. 523, ChD 11–319
Brown v Russell Young & Co [2007] EWCA Civ 43; [2008] 1 W.L.R. 525;
    [2007] 2 All E.R. 453; [2007] 4 Costs L.R. 552; (2007) 157 N.L.J. 222;
    (2007) 151 S.J.L.B. 196, CA (Civ Div) 6–005
Browne v Associated Newspapers Ltd [2007] EWCA Civ 295; [2007] 3 W.L.R.
    289; [2007] C.P. Rep. 29; (2007) 157 N.L.J. 671; [2007] E.M.L.R. 20, CA
    (Civ Div) 2–156, 2–173
Bryen & Langley Ltd v Boston [2005] EWCA Civ 973; [2005] B.L.R. 508, CA
    (Civ Div) 5–020
Bunney v Burns Anderson Plc; Cahill v Timothy James & Partners Ltd [2007]
    EWHC 1240 (Ch); [2008] Bus. L.R. 22; [2007] 4 All E.R. 246; [2008] 1
    B.C.L.C. 17; [2008] Lloyd's Rep. I.R. 198; (2007) 104(25) L.S.G. 36,
    ChD 14–117, 14–123A
Byrzykowski v Poland (11562/05) (2008) 46 E.H.R.R. 32; [2006] Lloyd's Rep.
    Med. 505; [2006] Inquest L.R. 125, ECHR 7–054
CA Blackwell (Contracts) Ltd v Gerling Allegemeine Verischerungs-AG; sub
    nom. CA Blackwell (Contracts) Ltd v Gerling General Insurance Co [2007]
    EWHC 94 (Comm); [2007] Lloyd's Rep. I.R. 511, QBD (Comm) 8–077
CGU Insurance v Porthouse [2008] HCA 30 .... 8–082, 8–085
Cantillon Ltd v Urvasco Ltd [2008] EWHC 282 (TCC); [2008] B.L.R. 250;
    [2008] C.I.L.L. 2564, QBD 9–360, 9–362
Carillion Construction Ltd v Devonport Royal Dockyard Ltd [2005] EWCA Civ
    1358; [2006] B.L.R. 15; 104 Con. L.R. 1; (2005) 102(47) L.S.G. 26, CA
    (Civ Div) 9–364
Carr-Glynn v Frearsons [1999] Ch. 326; [1999] 2 W.L.R. 1046; [1998] 4 All E.R.
    225; [1999] 1 F.L.R. 8; [1998] 3 F.C.R. 487; [1999] P.N.L.R. 13; [1998]
    Fam. Law 739; [1998] E.G. 128 (C.S.); (1998) 148 N.L.J. 1487; [1998]
    N.P.C. 136, CA (Civ Div) 11–048
Castravet v Moldova (23393/05), June 13, 2007, ECHR 7–042

TABLE OF CASES

Catholic Care (Diocese of Leeds) v Y (Kevin Raymond); Home Office v Y (Kevin Raymond); sub nom. Y (Kevin Raymond) v Catholic Care (Diocese of Leeds); Y (Kevin Raymond) v South Tyneside MBC [2006] EWCA Civ 1534; [2007] 1 All E.R. 895; [2007] P.I.Q.R. P15; (2006) 103(46) L.S.G. 33; (2006) 156 N.L.J. 1802; (2006) 150 S.J.L.B. 1531; [2007] 2 W.L.R. 1192, CA (Civ Div) 5–091

Cattley v Pollard [2006] EWHC 3130 (Ch); [2007] Ch. 353; [2007] 3 W.L.R. 317; [2007] 2 All E.R. 1086; [2007] P.N.L.R. 19; [2007] W.T.L.R. 245, ChD 5–114A

Charlton v Northern Structural Services Ltd [2008] EWHC 66 (TCC) 9–262, 9–306, 9–318

Charter Plc v City Index Ltd. *See* City Index Ltd v Gawler

Chern v Chern (2006) 263 D.L.R. (4th) 318, Alberta CA 11–030

Cheshire BS v Dunlop Haywards (DHL) Ltd [2008] P.N.L.R. 549 10–011

Chief Constable of Hertfordshire v Van Colle. *See* Van Colle v Chief Constable of Hertfordshire

Childs v Desormeaux (2006) 266 D.L.R. (4th) 641, SC (Can) 2–063A

Chirnside v Fay [2006] N.Z.S.C. 68; [2007] 1 N.Z.L.R. 433 3–019

City Access Ltd v Jackson [1998] 64 Comm. L.R. 84 9–320

City Index Ltd v Gawler; sub nom. Charter Plc v City Index Ltd [2007] EWCA Civ 1382; [2008] Ch. 313; [2008] 2 W.L.R. 950; [2008] 3 All E.R. 126; [2008] 2 All E.R. (Comm) 425; [2007] 2 C.L.C. 968; [2008] P.N.L.R. 16; (2008) 105(2) L.S.G. 27 .... 4–006, 4–014, 17–081

Clef Aquitaine Sarl v Laporte Materials (Barrow) Ltd; sub nom. Clef Aquitaine Sarl v Sovereign Chemical Industries Ltd [2001] Q.B. 488; [2000] 3 W.L.R. 1760; [2000] 3 All E.R. 493, CA (Civ Div) 5–102

Cohen v Davis; sub nom. International Championship Management Ltd, Re; Mall Corporate Events Ltd, Re Cohen v Dubey [2006] EWHC 768 (Ch); [2007] B.C.C. 95; [2007] 2 B.C.L.C. 274; [2006] P.N.L.R. 33, ChD (Companies Ct) 4–006, 4–008

Cohen v Kingsley Napley (A Firm) [2006] EWCA Civ 66; [2006] P.N.L.R. 22; (2006) 103(9) L.S.G. 31, CA (Civ Div) 5–046, 11–298

Collins v Drumgold [2008] EWHC 584 (TCC); [2008] T.C.L.R. 5; [2008] C.I.L.L. 2585; (2008) 158 N.L.J. 521, QBD 9–008

Commercial Union Assurance Co Plc v NRG Victory Reinsurance Ltd; Skandia International Insurance Corp v NRG Victory Reinsurance Ltd [1998] 2 All E.R. 434; [1998] 2 Lloyd's Rep. 600; [1998] C.L.C. 920; [1998] Lloyd's Rep. I.R. 439, CA (Civ Div) 8–024

Commissioner of Inland Revenue v Bhanabhai [2007] 2 N.Z.L.R. 478, CA (NZ) 11–065

Commissioner of Police of the Metropolis v Hurst. *See* R. (on the application of Hurst) v HM Coroner for Northern District London

Conlon v Simms; sub nom. Simms v Conlon [2006] EWCA Civ 1749; [2007] 3 All E.R. 802, CA (Civ Div) 11–103

Contex Drouzhba v Wiseman [2006] EWHC 2708 (QB); [2007] 1 B.C.L.C. 758, QBD 2–093

Cook v Cook [1986] HCA 73; (1986) 162 C.L.R., HC (Aus) 2–067

County Personnel (Employment Agency) Ltd v Alan R Pulver & Co [1987] 1 W.L.R. 916; [1987] 1 All E.R. 289; [1986] 2 E.G.L.R. 246; (1987) 84 L.S.G. 1409; (1986) 136 N.L.J. 1138; (1987) 131 S.J. 474, CA (Civ Div) 10–170

Cowley v Cheshire and Merseyside Strategic HA [2007] EWHC 48 (QB); [2007] LS Law Medical 160; (2007) 94 B.M.L.R. 29, QBD 13–038

Creutzfeldt-Jakob Disease Litigation (No.5), Re. *See* Group B Plaintiffs v Medical Research Council

Table of Cases

Cubitt Building & Interiors Ltd v Richardson Roofing (Industrial) Ltd [2008] EWHC 1020 (TCC); [2008] B.L.R. 354; [2008] C.I.L.L. 2588, QBD 9–356

Cundall Johnson & Partners LLP v Whipps Cross University Hospital NHS Trust [2007] EWHC 2178 (TCC); [2007] B.L.R. 520; [2008] T.C.L.R. 1; 115 Con. L.R. 125; [2007] C.I.L.L. 2516, QBD 9–007

Customs and Excise Commissioners v Barclays Bank Plc [2006] UKHL 28; [2006] 3 W.L.R. 1; [2006] 1 C.L.C. 1096; (2006) 103(27) L.S.G. 33; (2006)156 N.L.J. 1060; (2006) 150 S.J.L.B. 859, HL 17–027

D v Ireland (Admissibility) (26499/02) (2006) 43 E.H.R.R. SE16, ECHR 7–054

DGT Steel & Cladding Ltd v Cubitt Building & Interiors Ltd [2007] EWHC 1584 (TCC); [2008] Bus. L.R. 132; [2007] B.L.R. 371; [2007] T.C.L.R. 8; 116 Con. L.R. 118; [2007] C.I.L.L. 2492; (2007) 104(33) L.S.G. 27, QBD 9–356

DV v General Medical Council [2007] EWHC 1497 (Admin); [2007] LS Law Medical 603, QBD 7–095

DW Moore v Ferrier [1988] 1 W.L.R. 267; [1988] 1 All E.R. 400; (1988) 132 S.J. 227, CA (Civ Div) 5–053

Das v General Medical Council [2003] UKPC 75, PC (UK) 7–095

David Truex (A Firm) v Kitchin [2007] EWCA Civ 618 ; [2007] 4 Costs L.R. 587; [2007] 2 F.L.R. 1203; [2007] P.N.L.R. 33; [2007] Fam. Law 903; (2007) 157 N.L.J. 1011; (2007) 151 S.J.L.B. 926; [2007] N.P.C. 87, CA (Civ Div) 11–176

Demery v Cardiff and Vale NHS Trust [2006] EWCA Civ 1131, CA (Civ Div) 13–133

Derring Land Pty Ltd v Fitzgibbon [2007] V.S.C.A. 79 .... 10–038, 10–122A

Design Services Ltd v The Queen (2008) 293 D.L.R. (4th) 437, SC (Can) 2–063A

Diab v Regent Insurance Co Ltd [2006] UKPC 29; [2007] 1 W.L.R. 797; [2006] 2 All E.R. (Comm) 704; [2006] 1 C.L.C. 1084; [2006] Lloyd's Rep. I.R. 779; [2007] Bus. L.R. 915, PC (Bze) 8–027

Diamond v Mansfield [2006] EWHC 3290; (2007) 104(3) L.S.G. 28, QBD 7–100A

Dickson v United Kingdom (44362/04) [2006] 2 F.L.R. 449; [2006] 2 F.C.R. 1; (2007) 44 E.H.R.R. 21; 21 B.H.R.C. 236; [2006] Fam. Law 532, ECHR 7–060, 7–067

Doheny v New India Assurance Co Ltd [2004] EWCA Civ 1705; [2005] 1 All E.R. (Comm) 382; [2005] Lloyd's Rep. I.R. 251, CA (Civ Div) 8–046

Domsalla (t/a Domsalla Building Services) v Dyason [2007] EWHC 1174 (TCC); 112 Con. L.R. 95, QBD (TCC) 9–360

Dresna Pty Ltd v Linknarf Management Services Pty [2006] FCAFC 193; (2006) 237 A.L.R. 687, FC (Aus) 2–133

Dubai Aluminium Co Ltd v Salaam; Dubai Aluminium Co Ltd v Amhurst Brown Martin & Nicholson [2002] UKHL 48; [2003] 2 A.C. 366; [2002] 3 W.L.R. 1913; [2003] 1 All E.R. 97; [2003] 2 All E.R. (Comm) 451; [2003] 1 Lloyd's Rep. 65; [2003] 1 B.C.L.C. 32; [2003] 1 C.L.C. 1020; [2003] I.R.L.R. 608; [2003] W.T.L.R. 163; (2003) 100(7) L.S.G. 36; (2002) 146 S.J.L.B. 280, HL 4–014

Dudarec v Andrews [2006] EWCA Civ 256; [2006] 1 W.L.R. 3002; [2006] 2 All E.R. 856; [2006] P.N.L.R. 26, CA (Civ Div) 11–289, 11–299

Dunlop Haywards (DHL) Ltd (formerly Dunlop Heywood Lorenz Ltd) v Erinaceous Insurance Services Ltd (formerly Hanover Park Commercial Ltd) [2008] EWHC 520 (Comm); [2008] N.P.C. 40, QBD 16–033, 16–035

Dwyer v Roderick (1983) 80 L.S.G. 3003; (1983) 127 S.J. 806, CA (Civ Div) 13–065

Earl of Malmesbury v Strutt and Parker (A Partnership) [2007] EWHC 999 (QB); 116 Con. L.R. 38; [2007] P.N.L.R. 29; [2007] 3 E.G.L.R. 153; [2007] 21 E.G. 130 (C.S.), QBD 10–053A, 10–129, 10–170

TABLE OF CASES

Edmonds v Donovan [2005] V.S.C.A. 27; [2005] V.S.C.A. 36; (2005) 12 V.R. 513, Victoria CA 5–134
Edmund Nuttall Ltd v RG Carter Ltd (Definition: Dispute) [2002] EWHC 400 (TCC); [2002] B.L.R. 312; [2002] T.C.L.R. 27; 82 Con. L.R. 24, QBD 9–362
Eggertsdóttir v Iceland (31930/04) July 5, 2007 7–011
Eiles v Southwark LBC [2006] EWHC 1411, QBD (TCC) 9–318
Ellis v Counties Manakau District Health Board [2007] 1 N.Z.L.R. 196 13–019
Emms, Petitioner; sub nom. Emms' Application for Judicial Review, Re [2007] CSOH 184; 2008 S.L.T. 2; (2008) 99 B.M.L.R. 116; 2007 G.W.D. 39–674, OH 7–054
Enterprise Oil Ltd v Strand Insurance Co Ltd [2006] EWHC 58; [2006] 1 Lloyd's Rep. 500; [2006] 1 C.L.C. 33, QBD (Comm) 8–020, 8–024
Epping Electrical Co Ltd v Briggs & Forrester (Plumbing Services) Ltd [2007] EWHC 4 (TCC); [2007] B.L.R. 126; [2007] C.I.L.L. 2438, QBD (TCC) 9–363
Evans v United Kingdom (6339/05) [2007] 1 F.L.R. 1990; [2007] 2 F.C.R. 5; (2008) 46 E.H.R.R. 34; 22 B.H.R.C. 190; (2007) 95 B.M.L.R. 107; [2007] Fam. Law 588; (2007) 157 N.L.J. 599, ECHR (Grand Chamber) 7–060
Farah Constructions Pty Ltd v Say-Dee Pty Ltd [2007] HCA 22; (2007) 236 A.L.R. 209, HC (Aus) 2–137
Farmer v Outokumpu Stainless Ltd Unreported, LTL 31/8/06 13–014
Farraj v King's Healthcare NHS Trust [2006] EWHC 1228; [2006] 2 F.C.R. 804; [2006] P.I.Q.R. P29; (2006) 90 B.M.L.R. 21; (2006) 103(25) L.S.G. 29, QBD 13–006, 13–149
Fennell v Johns Elliott (A Firm) [2007] NIQB 72; [2008] P.N.L.R. 12, QBD (NI) 11–121, 11–184
Field v British Coal Corp [2008] EWCA Civ 912 5–091
Financial Services Authority v Fradley (t/a Top Bet Placement Services); Financial Services Authority v Woodward [2005] EWCA Civ 1183; [2006] 2 B.C.L.C. 616, CA (Civ Div) 14–028, 14–088
Financial Services Authority v Martin [2004] EWHC 3255; [2005] 1 B.C.L.C. 495, ChD 14–083, 14–088, 14–091
Financial Services Authority v Matthews [2004] EWHC 2966; [2005] Pens. L.R. 241, ChD 14–083, 14–093
Financial Services Compensation Scheme Ltd v Abbey National Treasury Services Plc [2008] EWHC 1897 (Ch) 14–133
Fisk v Brian Thornhill & Son (A Firm) [2007] EWCA Civ 152; [2007] P.N.L.R. 21; (2007) 151 S.J.L.B. 334, CA (Civ Div) 16–033, 16–035, 16–155
Floyd v John Fairhurst & Co [2004] EWCA Civ 604; [2004] P.N.L.R. 41; (2004) 148 S.J.L.B. 661, CA (Civ Div) 17–065, 17–079
Foglia v Switzerland (35865/04), March 13, 2008, ECHR 7–048A
Football League Ltd v Edge Ellison (A Firm) [2006] EWHC 1462 (Ch); [2007] P.N.L.R. 2; (2006) 150 S.J.L.B. 890, ChD 11–170, 11–264, 11–333
Forster v Outred & Co [1982] 1 W.L.R. 86; [1982] 2 All E.R. 753; (1981) 125 S.J. 309, CA (Civ Div) 5–053
Foster Bryant Surveying Ltd v Bryant [2007] EWCA Civ 200; [2007] 2 B.C.L.C. 239; [2007] I.R.L.R. 425; [2007] 12 E.G. 154 (C.S.); (2007) 104(13) L.S.G. 24, CA (Civ Div) 2–144
Friends Provident Life Office v Hillier Parker May & Rowden [1997] Q.B. 85; [1996] 2 W.L.R. 123; [1995] 4 All E.R. 260; [1995] C.L.C. 592; (1996) 71 P. & C.R. 286; [1995] E.G. 64 (C.S.); [1995] N.P.C. 63, CA (Civ Div) 4–006
Fulham Leisure Holdings Ltd v Nicholson Graham & Jones (A Firm) [2008] EWCA Civ 84; [2008] P.N.L.R. 22; [2008] 9 E.G. 201 (C.S.); (2008) 152(10) S.J.L.B. 32, CA (Civ Div) 11–283

TABLE OF CASES

Funnell v Adams & Remer (A Partnership) [2007] EWHC 2166 (QB); [2008]
B.L.R. 206; (2007) 104(40) L.S.G. 27; [2008] 1 P. & C.R. DG5, QBD 11–279
GE Capital Bank Ltd v Rushton [2005] EWCA Civ 1556; [2006] 1 W.L.R. 899;
[2006] 3 All E.R. 865; [2006] R.T.R. 17, CA (Civ Div) 14–022
Gaelic Inns Pte Ltd v Patric Lee PAC [2007] 2 S.L.R. 147 17–052
Gallaher International Ltd v Tlais Enterprises Ltd; Gallaher International Ltd v
Ptolemeos Tlais [2007] EWHC 464 (Comm), QBD (Comm) 6–020
Galliford Try Infrastructure Ltd (formerly (A) Morrison Construction Ltd & (B)
Morrison Construction Services Ltd) v Mott MacDonald Ltd [2008] EWHC
1570 (TCC) 9–111
Gallop v Abdoulah [2006] 8 W.W.R. 220, Saskatchewan CA 11–166
Garrett v Halton BC. *See* Myatt v National Coal Board
General Medical Council v Hiew [2007] EWCA Civ 369; [2007] 1 W.L.R. 2007;
[2007] 4 All E.R. 473; [2007] LS Law Medical 309, CA (Civ Div) 7–098
General Medical Council v Pembrey [2002] EWHC 1602; [2002] Lloyd's
Rep.Med. 434, QBD (Admin) 7–098
Gillick v West Norfolk and Wisbech AHA [1986] A.C. 112; [1985] 3 W.L.R. 830;
[1985] 3 All E.R. 402; [1986] Crim. L.R. 113; (1985) 82 L.S.G. 3531;
(1985) 135 N.L.J. 1055; (1985) 129 S.J. 738, HL 13–057
Gouldsmith v Mid Staffordshire General Hospitals NHS Trust [2007] EWCA Civ
397, CA (Civ Div) 13–141
Green v Gaul; sub nom. Loftus (Deceased), Re [2006] EWCA Civ 1124; [2007]
1 W.L.R. 591; [2006] 4 All E.R. 1110; [2006] W.T.L.R. 1391; (2006–07) 9
I.T.E.L.R. 107; (2006) 156 N.L.J. 1365; [2007] 1 P. & C.R. DG12, CA (Civ
Div) 5–136
Grieves v FT Everard & Sons Ltd; Quinn v George Clark & Nem Ltd; Mears v
RG Carter Ltd; Jackson v Brock Plc; Rothwell v Chemical & Insulating Co
Ltd; Downey v Charles Evans Shopfitters Ltd; Storey v Clellands Shipbuilders Ltd; Topping v Benchtown Ltd (formerly Jones Bros (Preston) Ltd);
Johnston v NEI International Combustion Ltd; Hindson v Pipe House Wharf
(Swansea) Ltd [2007] UKHL 39; [2008] 1 A.C. 281; [2007] 3 W.L.R. 876;
[2007] 4 All E.R. 1047; [2007] I.C.R. 1745; [2008] P.I.Q.R. P6; [2008] LS
Law Medical 1; (2008) 99 B.M.L.R. 139; (2007) 104(42) L.S.G. 34; (2007)
157 N.L.J. 1542; (2007) 151 S.J.L.B. 1366, HL 13–154
Group B Plaintiffs v Medical Research Council; sub nom. Creutzfeldt-Jakob
Disease Litigation (No.5), Re; CJD Litigation (No.5), Re [2000] Lloyd's
Rep. Med. 161; (1998) 41 B.M.L.R. 157; (2000) 54 B.M.L.R. 92, QBD 13–154
HG Construction Ltd v Ashwell Homes (East Anglia) Ltd [2007] EWHC 144
(TCC); [2007] B.L.R. 175; 112 Con. L.R. 128; [2007] C.I.L.L. 2453, QBD
(TCC) 9–363
HIH Casualty & General Insurance Ltd v JLT Risk Solutions Ltd (formerly Lloyd
Thompson Ltd) [2007] EWCA Civ 710; [2008] Bus. L.R. 180; [2007] 2 All
E.R. (Comm) 1106; [2007] 2 Lloyd's Rep. 278; [2007] 2 C.L.C. 62; [2007]
Lloyd's Rep. I.R. 717; [2008] P.N.L.R. 3; (2007) 104(30) L.S.G. 35, CA
(Civ Div) 16–015A, 16–100, 16–116A
HLB Kidsons (A Firm) v Lloyds Underwriters [2007] EWHC 1951 (Comm),
QBD (Comm); [2008] EWCA Civ 1206; [2008] 1 All E.R. (Comm) 769;
[2008] Lloyd's Rep. I.R. 237; [2008] Bus. L.R. D28, QBD 8–027, 8–081A,
8–082, 8–084, 8–085, 8–085A, 8–085B, 8–085C, 8–085D
HRH Prince of Wales v Associated Newspapers Ltd; sub nom. Associated
Newspapers Ltd v HRH Prince of Wales [2006] EWCA Civ 1776; [2008]
Ch. 57; [2007] 3 W.L.R. 222; [2007] 2 All E.R. 139; (2007) 104(2) L.S.G.
30; (2007) 157 N.L.J. 106; (2007) 151 S.J.L.B. 63; [2007] 3 W.L.R. 222, CA
(Civ Div) 2–173

TABLE OF CASES

Haarvig v Norway (Admissibility) (11187/05) (2008) 46 E.H.R.R. SE12, ECHR 7–087
Halech v State of South Australia [2006] S.A.S.C. 29 13–016
Hammerton v Hammerton [2007] EWCA Civ 248; [2007] 2 F.L.R. 1133; [2007] 3 F.C.R. 107; [2007] Fam. Law 798<, CA (Civ Div) 7–007
Hart Investments Ltd v Fidler (t/a Terence Fidler Partnership) Hart Investments Ltd v Larchpark Ltd (In Liquidation) [2007] EWHC 1058 (TCC); [2007] B.L.R. 526; 112 Con. L.R. 33; [2007] P.N.L.R. 26, QBD (TCC) 9–249
Hart Investments Ltd v Fidler [2006] EWHC 2857 (TCC); [2007] B.L.R. 30; [2007] T.C.L.R. 1; 109 Con. L.R. 67; [2006] C.I.L.L. 2397, QBD (TCC) 9–354, 9–363
Hedrich v Standard Bank London Ltd [2008] EWCA Civ 905 11–140
Heibei Enterprises Ltd v Livasiri & Co [2007] 3 H.K.L.R.D. 723, CA (HK) 11–091, 11–202
Henriques v Luxembourg (60255/00) May 9, 2006; [2006] 5 E.H.R.L.R. 568 7–035
Herschel Engineering Ltd v Breen Property Ltd [2000] B.L.R. 272 9–367
Heslop v Cousins [2007] 3 N.Z.L.R. 679 11–203
Hill v Chief Constable of West Yorkshire [1989] A.C. 53; [1988] 2 W.L.R. 1049; [1988] 2 All E.R. 238; (1988) 152 L.G. Rev. 709; (1988) 85(20) L.S.G. 34; (1988) 138 N.L.J. Rep. 126; (1988) 132 S.J. 700, HL 7–036
Hill v Hamilton-Wentworth Regional Police Services Board (2007) 285 D.L.R. (4th) 621, SC (Can) 2–063A
Holt v Edge [2007] EWCA Civ 602; (2007) 151 S.J.L.B. 854, CA (Civ Div) 13–114
Horton v Evans [2006] EWHC 2808 (QB); [2007] LS Law Medical 212; (2007) 94 B.M.L.R. 60; [2007] P.N.L.R. 17, QBD 13–058, 13–065
Horton v Sadler [2006] UKHL 27; [2007] 1 A.C. 307; [2006] 2 W.L.R. 1346; [2006] 3 All E.R. 1177; [2006] R.T.R. 27; [2006] P.I.Q.R. P30; (2006) 91 B.M.L.R. 60; (2006) 103(26) L.S.G. 27; (2006) 156 N.L.J. 1024; (2006) 150 S.J.L.B. 808, HL 5–094
Humes Building Contracts Ltd v Charlotte Homes (Surrey) Ltd Unreported January 4, 2007, QBD (TCC)9–364, 9–365
Hunt v A [2007] NZSC 332; [2008] 1 NZLR 368, SC (NZ) 2–165
Hunter Kane Ltd v Watkins [2003] EWHC 186, ChD 2–144
Hurstanger Ltd v Wilson [2007] EWCA Civ 299; [2007] 1 W.L.R. 2351; [2008] Bus. L.R. 216; [2007] 4 All E.R. 1118; [2007] 2 All E.R. (Comm) 1037; (2007) 104(16) L.S.G. 23; (2007) 157 N.L.J. 555; (2007) 151 S.J.L.B. 467; [2007] N.P.C. 41, CA (Civ Div) 2–137
Hurter v Switzerland (53146/99) (2007) 44 E.H.R.R. 201 7–095
IFE Fund SA v Goldman Sachs International [2007] EWCA Civ 811; [2007] 2 Lloyd's Rep. 449; [2007] 2 C.L.C. 134; (2007) 104(32) L.S.G. 24, CA (Civ Div) 15–014, 15–016, 15–017A, 15–046, 15–061
Iggleden v Fariview New Homes [2007] EWHC 1573 (TCC) 9–318, 9–320
Imbree v McNeilly [2008] HCA 4, HC (Aus) 2–067
Inertia Partnership LLP, Re [2007] EWHC 539 (Ch); [2007] Bus. L.R. 879; [2007] 1 B.C.L.C. 739, ChD 14–024
Islington LBC v University College London Hospital NHS Trust [2005] EWCA Civ 596; [2006] B.L.G.R. 50; (2005) 8 C.C.L. Rep. 337; [2006] P.I.Q.R. P3; [2005] Lloyd's Rep. Med. 387; (2005) 85 B.M.L.R. 171; [2005] N.P.C. 77, CA (Civ Div) 13–109
J Rothschild Assurance Plc v Collyear [1998] C.L.C. 1697; [1999] Lloyd's Rep. I.R. 6; [1999] Pens. L.R. 77, QBD (Comm) 8–027, 8–085D
JD Wetherspoon Plc v Van De Berg & Co Ltd [2007] EWHC 1044 (Ch); [2007] P.N.L.R. 28, ChD 2–133

TABLE OF CASES

JP Morgan Bank (formerly Chase Manhattan Bank) v Springwell Navigation Corp [2008] EWHC 1186 (Comm) 15–017A, 15–032A, 15–043, 15–079

JP Morgan Chase Bank v Springwell Navigation Corp (Application to Strike Out) [2006] EWHC 2755 (Comm); [2007] 1 All E.R. (Comm) 549, QBD (Comm) 6–012, 15–020, 15–072

JSI Shipping (S) Pte Ltd v Teofoongwonglchong [2007] 1 S.L.R. 821; [2006] S.G.H.C. 223 .... 17–052, 17–057

Jain v Trent Strategic HA [2007] EWCA Civ 1186; [2008] Q.B. 246; [2008] 2 W.L.R. 456; (2008) 11 C.C.L. Rep. 79; [2008] LS Law Medical 139, CA (Civ Div) 2–070, 2–086

Jarvis, Re; sub nom. Edge v Jarvis [1958] 1 W.L.R. 815; [1958] 2 All E.R. 336; (1958) 102 S.J. 546, ChD 5–134

Jassi v Gallagher [2006] EWCA Civ 1065; [2007] P.N.L.R. 4; [2006] 31 E.G. 88 (C.S.); [2006] N.P.C. 91, CA (Civ Div) 12–008, 12–023, 12–033

Jessup v Wetherell [2006] EWHC 2582 (QB); [2007] P.N.L.R. 10; [2007] W.T.L.R. 515, QBD 5–046, 5–101

John F Hunt Demolition Ltd v Asme Engineering Ltd [2007] EWHC 1507 (TCC); [2008] Bus. L.R. 558; [2008] 1 All E.R. 180; [2008] 1 All E.R. (Comm) 473; [2008] B.L.R. 115; [2007] T.C.L.R. 6; 114 Con. L.R. 105; [2007] C.I.L.L. 2496, QBD 9–343

Johnson v Havering LBC. *See* L v Birmingham City Council

Johnston v NEI International Combustion Ltd. *See* Grieves v FT Everard & Sons Ltd

KOO Golden East Mongolia v Bank of Nova Scotia [2008] EWHC 1120 (Admin) 11–137

KR v Bryn Alyn Community (Holdings) Ltd (In Liquidation); sub nom. Various Claimants v Bryn Alyn Community (Holdings) Ltd (In Liquidation); Various Claimants v BACHL [2003] EWCA Civ 85; [2003] Q.B. 1441; [2003] 3 W.L.R. 107; [2004] 2 All E.R. 716; [2003] 1 F.L.R. 1203; [2003] 1 F.C.R. 385; [2003] Lloyd's Rep. Med. 175; [2003] Fam. Law 482, CA (Civ Div) 5–091

KR v Royal & Sun Alliance Plc [2006] EWCA Civ 1454; [2007] Bus. L.R. 139; [2007] 1 All E.R. (Comm) 161; [2007] Lloyd's Rep. I.R. 368; [2007] P.I.Q.R. P14; (2006) 150 S.J.L.B. 1467; [2007] B.C.C. 522, CA (Civ Div) 8–078

Kajima UK Engineering Ltd v Underwriter Insurance Co Ltd [2008] EWHC 83 (TCC); [2008] 1 All E.R. (Comm) 855; [2008] Lloyd's Rep. I.R. 391; [2008] C.I.L.L. 2567, QBD 8–081A, 8–085C

Kallinicos v Hunt [2005] N.S.W.S.C. 1181; (2006) 64 N.S.W.L.R. 561 11–032

Keisner v Terrus Group Ltd; Evolution Trading Group Ltd v Baris (UK) Ltd [2006] EWHC 2765 (Ch); [2007] 1 B.C.L.C. 303, ChD (Manchester) 2–176

Kennedy v Lord Advocate; Black v Lord Advocate [2008] CSOH 21; 2008 S.L.T. 195; (2008) 100 B.M.L.R. 158; 2008 G.W.D. 5–77, OH 7–054

Khairule v North West Strategic Health Authority [2008] EWHC 1537 (QB) 5–091

Kier Regional Ltd (t/a Wallis) v City & General (Holborn) Ltd [2006] EWHC 848 (TCC); [2006] B.L.R. 315; [2006] C.I.L.L. 2353, QBD (TCC) 9–364

Kosmar Villa Holidays Plc v Trustees of Syndicate 1 2 3 4 [2008] EWCA Civ 147; [2008] Bus. L.R. 931; [2008] 2 All E.R. (Comm) 14; [2008] 1 C.L.C. 307; [2008] Lloyd's Rep. I.R. 489; (2008) 105(11) L.S.G. 24, CA (Civ Div) 8–070A

Kyprianou v Cyprus (73797/01) (2007) 44 E.H.R.R. 27, ECHR 7–041, 7–048A

Table of Cases

L v Birmingham City Council; YL v Birmingham City Council; sub nom. Johnson v Havering LBC; R. (on the application of Johnson) v Havering LBC; [2007] UKHL 27; [2008] 1 A.C. 95; [2007] 3 W.L.R. 112; [2007] 3 All E.R. 957; (2007) 96 B.M.L.R. 1; (2007) 104(27) L.S.G. 29; (2007) 157 N.L.J. 938; (2007) 151 S.J.L.B. 860; [2007] N.P.C. 75, HL 7–001, 7–060
L v Law Society [2008] EWCA Civ 811 7–095
Lai v Chamberlains [2006] N.Z.S.C. 70; [2007] N.Z.L.R. 7 12–009
Laing v Taylor Walton (A Firm); sub nom. Taylor Walton (A Firm) v Laing [2007] EWCA Civ 1146; [2008] B.L.R. 65; [2008] P.N.L.R. 11; [2007] 47 E.G. 169 (C.S.); (2007) 104(46) L.S.G. 27, CA (Civ Div) 11–116
Larkin v Great Western (Nepean) Gravel Ltd [1940] HCA 37; (1940) 64 C.L.R. 221 5–029
Law Society v Sephton & Co [2006] UKHL 22; [2006] 2 A.C. 543; [2006] 2 W.L.R. 1091; [2006] 3 All E.R. 401; [2006] P.N.L.R. 31; (2006) 156 N.L.J. 844; (2006) 150 S.J.L.B. 669; [2006] N.P.C. 56, HL 5–042, 5–046, 5–053
Law Society v Shah; sub nom. Aziz, Re; Law Society v Earp (Official Receiver) [2007] EWHC 2841 (Ch); [2007] B.P.I.R. 1595; [2008] Lloyd's Rep. I.R. 442, Ch d 8–106
Lawrence v Pembrokeshire CC; sub nom. L v Pembrokeshire CC; SL v Pembrokeshire CC [2007] EWCA Civ 446; [2007] 1 W.L.R. 2991; [2007] 2 F.L.R. 705; [2007] 2 F.C.R. 329; [2007] H.R.L.R. 30; (2007) 10 C.C.L. Rep. 367; (2007) 96 B.M.L.R. 158; [2007] Fam. Law 804; (2007) 104(22) L.S.G. 24, CA (Civ Div) 7–036
Lead Technical Services Ltd v CMS Medical Ltd [2007] EWCA Civ 316; [2007] B.L.R. 251; 116 Con. L.R. 192; (2007) 23 Const. L.J. 547, CA (Civ Div) 9–354, 9–363
Leeson v Marsden [2008] EWHC 1011 (QB) 5–094
Lennie v Royal Victoria Infirmary and Associated Hospitals NHS Trust [2006] EWCA Civ 975 13–037
Lillywhite v University College London Hospitals NHS Trust [2005] EWCA Civ 1466; [2006] Lloyd's Rep. Med. 268, CA (Civ Div) 13–100
Littler v Price [2004] Q.C.A. 383; [2005] 1 Qd.R. 275, Queensland CA 11–170
Loftus (Deceased), Re. See Green v Gaul
London Fire and Emergency Planning Authority (LFEPA) v Halcrow Gilbert Associates Ltd [2007] EWHC 2546 (TCC); (2008) 24 Const. L.J. 103, QBD 9–038, 9–203, 9–299
Lord Browne of Madingley v Associated Newspapers Ltd. See Browne of Madingley v Associated Newspapers Ltd
Luke v Kingsley Smith & Co (A Firm) [2004] P.N.L.R. 12 11–241
M&S Tarpaulins v Green [2008] 6MA 70030 .... 17–059A, 17–064, 17–080
MDIS Ltd (formerly McDonnell Information Systems Ltd) v Swinbank; sub nom. McDonnell Information Systems Ltd v Swinbank [1999] 2 All E.R. (Comm) 722; [1999] C.L.C. 1800, CA (Civ Div) 8–024
McConnell Dowell Constructors (Aust) Pty Ltd v National Grid Gas Plc (formerly Transco Plc) [2006] EWHC 2551 (TCC); [2007] B.L.R. 92, QBD (TCC) 9–367
McCoubrey v Ministry of Defence [2007] EWCA Civ 17; [2007] 1 W.L.R. 1544; [2007] LS Law Medical 150; (2007) 151 S.J.L.B. 159; [2007] 1 W.L.R. 1544, CA (Civ Div) 5–080, 5–091
McGlinn v Waltham Contractors Ltd [2007] EWHC 149 (TCC); 111 Con. L.R. 1; [2007] C.I.L.L. 2441, QBD (TCC) 9–239, 9–241, 9–253, 9–304
McKennitt v Ash; sub nom. Ash v McKennitt [2006] EWCA Civ 1714; [2007] 3 W.L.R. 194; [2007] E.M.L.R. 4; (2007) 151 S.J.L.B. 27; [2007] 3 W.L.R. 194, CA (Civ Div) 2–156, 2–173

TABLE OF CASES

McKerr's Application for Judicial Review, Re; sub nom. McKerr, Re [2004] UKHL 12; [2004] 1 W.L.R. 807; [2004] 2 All E.R. 409; [2004] N.I. 212; [2004] H.R.L.R. 26; [2004] U.K.H.R.R. 385; [2004] Lloyd's Rep. Med. 263; (2004) 101(13) L.S.G. 33; (2004) 148 S.J.L.B. 355, HL (NI) 7–054
McNamara Business & Property Law v Kasmeridis [2007] 97 S.A.S.R. 129, South Australia CA 11–176
Maguire v Makaronis [1997] HCA 23; (1997) 188 C.L.R. 449, HC (Aus) 2–137
Makers UK Ltd v Camden LBC [2008] EWHC 1836 (TCC) 9–365
Man Nutzfahrzeuge AG v Freightliner Ltd; sub nom. Man Nutzfahrzeuge AG v Ernst & Young [2007] EWCA Civ 910; [2007] B.C.C. 986; [2008] 2 B.C.L.C. 22; [2007] 2 C.L.C. 455; [2008] P.N.L.R. 6; (2007) 104(37) L.S.G. 35; (2007) 151 S.J.L.B. 1229, CA (Civ Div) 17–027, 17–039, 17–040, 17–064, 17–080
Mannai Investment Co Ltd v Eagle Star Life Assurance Co Ltd [1997] A.C. 749; [1997] 2 W.L.R. 945; [1997] 3 All E.R. 352; [1997] C.L.C. 1124; [1997] 1 E.G.L.R. 57; [1997] 25 E.G. 138; [1997] 24 E.G. 122; (1997) 16 Tr. L.R. 432; [1997] E.G. 82 (C.S.); (1997) 94(30) L.S.G. 30; (1997) 147 N.L.J. 846; (1997) 141 S.J.L.B. 130; [1997] N.P.C. 81, HL 8–085
Mantella v Mantella (2006) 267 D.L.R. (4th) 532, Ontario Superior Court 11–058
Marplace (Number 512) Ltd v Chaffe Street (A Firm) [2006] EWHC 1919 (Ch), ChD 5–016A
Mast Electrical Services v Kendall Cross Holdings General [2007] EWHC 1296 (TCC); [2007] N.P.C. 70, QBD (TCC) 9–354
Matthews v Hunter & Robertson Ltd [2008] CSOH 88; 2008 S.L.T. 634; 2008 Rep. L.R. 78; 2008 G.W.D. 20–342, OH 11–048
Meadow v General Medical Council; sub nom. General Medical Council v Meadow [2006] EWCA Civ 1390; [2007] Q.B. 462; [2007] 2 W.L.R. 286; [2007] 1 All E.R. 1; [2007] I.C.R. 701; [2007] 1 F.L.R. 1398; [2006] 3 F.C.R. 447; [2007] LS Law Medical 1; (2006) 92 B.M.L.R. 51; [2007] Fam. Law 214; [2006] 44 E.G. 196 (C.S.); (2006) 103(43) L.S.G. 28; (2006) 156 N.L.J. 1686; [2007] Q.B. 462, CA (Civ Div) 2–100, 2–102, 13–011
Mersey Care NHS Trust v Ackroyd (No.2); sub nom. Ackroyd v Mersey Care NHS Trust (No.2) [2007] EWCA Civ 101; [2007] H.R.L.R. 19; (2007) 94 B.M.L.R. 84; (2007) 104(10) L.S.G. 31; (2007) 151 S.J.L.B. 298, CA (Civ Div) 7–081
Midland Bank Plc v Cox McQueen (A Firm) [1999] Lloyd's Rep. Bank. 78; [1999] 1 F.L.R. 1002; [1999] Lloyd's Rep. P.N. 223; [1999] P.N.L.R. 593; [1999] Fam. Law 310; [1999] E.G. 12 (C.S.); (1999) 96(6) L.S.G. 36; (1999) 149 N.L.J. 164; [1999] N.P.C. 11, CA (Civ Div) 10–019A
Miller v Garton Shires (formerly Gartons) [2006] EWCA Civ 1386; [2007] C.P. Rep. 9; [2007] R.T.R. 24; [2007] P.N.L.R. 11, CA (Civ Div) 11–293
Mirant Asia-Pacific Construction (Hong Kong) Ltd v Ove Arup & Partners International Ltd [2007] EWHC 918 (TCC); [2007] C.I.L.L. 2480; [2008] Bus. L.R. D1, QBD (TCC) 9–279, 9–340
Mitchells (A Firm) v Funkwerk Information Technologies York Ltd [2008] P.N.L.R. 29, EAT 11–135
Mott MacDonald Ltd v London & Regional Properties Ltd [2007] EWHC 1055 (TCC); [2007] C.I.L.L. 2481, QBD (TCC) 9–354, 9–363
Moy v Pettman Smith (A Firm) [2005] UKHL 7; [2005] 1 W.L.R. 581; [2005] 1 All E.R. 903; [2005] Lloyd's Rep. Med. 293; [2005] P.N.L.R. 24; (2005) 102(11) L.S.G. 31; (2005) 155 N.L.J. 218; (2005) 149 S.J.L.B. 180; [2005] N.P.C. 15, HL 12–008

TABLE OF CASES

Multiplex Constructions (UK) Ltd v Cleveland Bridge UK; sub nom. Cleveland Bridge UK Ltd v Multiplex [2007] EWCA Civ 443, CA (Civ Div) 9–323
Multiplex Constructions (UK) Ltd v Cleveland Bridge UK Ltd [2008] EWHC 2220 (TCC) 6–007
Murad v Al-Saraj; Murad v Westwood Business Inc [2005] EWCA Civ 959; [2005] W.T.L.R. 1573; (2005) 102(32) L.S.G. 31, CA (Civ Div) 3–019
Myatt v National Coal Board; Garrett v Halton BC [2006] EWCA Civ 1017; [2007] 1 W.L.R. 554; [2007] 1 All E.R. 147; [2006] 5 Costs L.R. 798; (2006) 103(31) L.S.G. 26; (2006) 150 S.J.L.B. 1190, CA (Civ Div) 11–176
Myatt v National Coal Board [2007] EWCA Civ 307; [2007] 1 W.L.R. 1559; [2007] P.N.L.R. 25, CA (Civ Div) 11–126, 11–136
NHS Trust A v M; NHS Trust B v H [2001] Fam. 348; [2001] 2 W.L.R. 942; [2001] 1 All E.R. 801; [2001] 2 F.L.R. 367; [2001] 1 F.C.R. 406; [2001] H.R.L.R. 12; [2001] Lloyd's Rep. Med. 28; (2001) 58 B.M.L.R. 87; [2001] Fam. Law 501, Fam Div 7–071
Nam Tai Electronics Inc v Pricewaterhouse Coopers [2008] 1 H.K.L.R.D. 666 17–025
National Notary Chamber v Albania (17029/05) (2008) 47 E.H.R.R. SE11, ECHR 7–048B
Ndri v Moorfields Eye Hospital NHS Trust [2006] EWHC 3652 (QB), QBD 13–114
Nesbitt v Holt [2007] EWCA Civ 249; [2007] P.N.L.R. 24; (2007) 151 S.J.L.B. 430, CA (Civ Div) 11–116
New Islington and Hackney Housing Association Ltd v Pollard Thomas and Edwards Ltd [2001] B.L.R. 74; (2001) 3 T.C.L.R. 25; 85 Con. L.R. 194; [2001] Lloyd's Rep. P.N. 243; [2001] P.N.L.R. 20; (2001) 17 Const. L.J. 55, QBD (TCC) 5–030
Newline Corporate Name Ltd v Morgan Cole (A Firm) [2007] EWHC 1628 (Comm); [2008] P.N.L.R. 2, QBD 11–264
Nicholson v Knox Ukiwa & Co (A Firm) [2008] EWHC 1222 (QB) 11–294, 11–300
Noblebright Ltd v Sirius International Corp [2007] Lloyd's Rep. I.R. 30 8–046
OBG Ltd v Allan; sub nom. Douglas v Hello! Ltd; Mainstream Properties Ltd v Young [2007] UKHL 21; [2007] 2 W.L.R. 920; [2007] I.R.L.R. 608; [2007] E.M.L.R. 12; (2007) 30(6) I.P.D. 30037; [2007] 19 E.G. 165 (C.S.); (2007) 151 S.J.L.B. 674; [2007] N.P.C. 54, HL .2–156, 2–168
Odhavji Estate v Woodhouse (2003) 233 D.L.R. (4th) 193, SC (Can) 2–063A
Orange Personal Communications Services Ltd v Hoare Lea (A Firm) [2008] EWHC 223 (TCC) 9–007
Otter v Church, Adams, Tatham & Co [1953] Ch. 280; [1953] 1 W.L.R. 156; [1953] 1 All E.R. 168; (1953) 97 S.J. 48, Ch D 11–048
Oxford Architects Partnership v Cheltenham Ladies College [2006] EWHC 3156 (TCC); [2007] B.L.R. 293; [2007] P.N.L.R. 18; [2007] Bus. L.R. D25, QBD (TCC) 5–030, 5–072, 9–020, 9–039
P&M Construction Ltd v Husar Estate (2007) 281 D.L.R. (4th) 305, CA (Ontario) 5–134
P&O Nedlloyd BV v Arab Metals Co (The UB Tiger); P&O Nedlloyd BV v Arab Metals Co (No.2) [2006] EWCA Civ 1717; [2007] 1 W.L.R. 2288; [2007] 2 All E.R. (Comm) 401; [2006] 2 C.L.C. 985, CA (Civ Div) 5–124
Page v Smith [1996] A.C. 155; [1995] 2 W.L.R. 644; [1995] 2 All E.R. 736; [1995] 2 Lloyd's Rep. 95; [1995] R.T.R. 210; [1995] P.I.Q.R. P329; (1995) 92(23) L.S.G. 33; (1995) 145 N.L.J. 723; (1995) 139 S.J.L.B. 173, HL 13–154
Paper Reclaim Ltd v Aotearoa International Ltd [2007] NZSC 26; [2007] 3 N.Z.L.R. 169 2–133

TABLE OF CASES

Pearce v European Reinsurance Consultants & Run-Off Ltd [2005] EWHC 1493 (Ch); [2005] 2 B.C.L.C. 366; [2006] P.N.L.R. 8, ChD 17–064
Pearson Education Ltd v Charter Partnership Ltd; sub nom. Pearson Education Ltd v The Charter Partnership Ltd [2007] EWCA Civ 130; [2007] 21 E.G. 132; [2007] 9 E.G. 203 (C.S.); (2007) 104(10) L.S.G. 31; (2007) 151 S.J.L.B. 300, CA (Civ Div) 9–078, 9–281
Peekay Intermark Ltd v Australia & New Zealand Banking Group Ltd [2006] EWCA Civ 386; [2006] 2 Lloyd's Rep. 511; [2006] 1 C.L.C. 582, CA (Civ Div) 15–014
Pereira v Inner South London Coroner [2007] EWHC 1723 (Admin); [2007] 1 W.L.R. 3256; [2007] Inquest L.R. 160, DC 7–054
Perkin v Lupton Fawcett (A Firm) [2008] EWCA Civ 418; [2008] P.N.L.R. 30; (2008) 152(18) S.J.L.B. 29, CA (Civ Div) 11–264
Phelps v Stewarts (A Firm) [2007] EWHC 1561 (Ch); [2007] P.N.L.R. 32; [2007] W.T.L.R. 1267; [2007] N.P.C. 86, ChD 11–175
Phillips & Co v Whatley; Phillips v Whatley [2007] UKPC 28; [2008] Lloyd's Rep. I.R. 111; [2007] P.N.L.R. 27; (2007) 104(20) L.S.G. 28; (2007) 151 S.J.L.B. 612, PC (Gib) 11–297, 16–128A, 16–135
Platform Funding Ltd v Bank of Scotland Plc (formerly Halifax Plc) [2008] EWCA Civ 930; [2008] 32 E.G. 83 (C.S.) 2–010, 10–019A, 10–075
Preferred Mortgages Ltd v Shanks [2008] CSOH 23; [2008] P.N.L.R. 20; 2008 G.W.D. 8–144, OH 10–116, 11–304
PricewaterhouseCoopers Legal v Perpetual Trustees Victoria Ltd [2007] NSWCA 388, CA (NSW) 10–100, 10–175
Pritchard Joyce & Hinds (A Firm) v Batcup [2008] EWHC 20 (QB); [2008] P.N.L.R. 18; [2008] 3 E.G. 179 (C.S.), QBD 12–037, 12–046
Pulvers (A Firm) v Chan [2007] EWHC 2406 (Ch); [2008] P.N.L.R. 9, Ch D 4–014, 11–342

Quietfield Ltd v Vascroft Contractors Ltd; sub nom. Quietfield Ltd v Vascroft Construction Ltd [2006] EWCA Civ 1737; [2007] B.L.R. 67; [2007] C.I.L.L. 2425; [2007] Bus. L.R. D1, CA (Civ Div) 9–363

R. (on the application of Andrew Jones) v Legal Services Commission [2007] EWHC 2106 (Admin) 7–058
R. (on the application of Axon) v Secretary of State for Health [2006] EWHC 37 (Admin); [2006] Q.B. 539; [2006] 2 W.L.R. 1130; [2006] 2 F.L.R. 206; [2006] 1 F.C.R. 175; [2006] H.R.L.R. 12; (2006) 88 B.M.L.R. 96; [2006] A.C.D. 58; [2006] Fam. Law 272; (2006) 103(8) L.S.G. 25, QBD (Admin) 13–057
R. (on the application of B) v S (Responsible Medical Officer, Broadmoor Hospital [2006] EWCA Civ 28; [2006] 1 W.L.R. 810; [2006] H.R.L.R. 14; [2006] U.K.H.R.R. 432; (2006) 9 C.C.L. Rep. 280; (2006) 90 B.M.L.R. 1; (2006) 103(7) L.S.G. 24; (2006) 150 S.J.L.B. 163, CA (Civ Div) 13–047
R. (on the application of Burke) v General Medical Council [2005] EWCA Civ1003; [2006] Q.B. 273; [2005] 3 W.L.R. 1132; [2005] 2 F.L.R. 1223; [2005]3 F.C.R. 169; [2005] H.R.L.R. 35; [2006] U.K.H.R.R. 509; (2005) 8 C.C.L. Rep. 463; [2005] Lloyd's Rep. Med. 403; (2005) 85 B.M.L.R. 1; [2006]A.C.D. 27; [2005] Fam. Law 776; (2005) 155 N.L.J. 1457, CA (Civ Div) 7–071
R. (on the application of Cash) v HM Coroner for Northamptonshire [2007] EWHC 1354 (Admin); [2007] 4 All E.R. 903; [2007] U.K.H.R.R. 1037; [2007] Inquest L.R. 147; (2007) 157 N.L.J. 895, QBD (Admin) 7–054

TABLE OF CASES

R. (on the application of Countryside Alliance) v Attorney General; R. (on the application of Derwin) v Attorney General; R. (on the application of Friend) v Attorney General [2006] EWCA Civ 817; [2007] Q.B. 305; [2006] 3 W.L.R. 1017; [2007] Eu. L.R. 139; [2006] H.R.L.R. 33; [2006] U.K.H.R.R. 927; (2006) 150 S.J.L.B. 886; [2006] N.P.C. 73, CA (Civ Div) 7–090
R. (on the application of Garrison Investment Analysis) v Financial Ombudsman Service [2006] EWHC 2466, QBD (Admin) 14–117
R. (on the application of H) v Mental Health Review Tribunal [2007] EWHC 884 (Admin); (2007) 10 C.C.L. Rep. 306, QBD (Admin) 7–055
R. (on the application of Heather) v Leonard Cheshire [2002] EWCA Civ 366; [2002] 2 All E.R. 936; [2002] H.R.L.R. 30; [2002] U.K.H.R.R. 883; [2002] H.L.R. 49; (2002) 5 C.C.L. Rep. 317; (2003) 69 B.M.L.R. 22; [2002] A.C.D. 43, CA (Civ Div) 7–001
R. (on the application of Heather Moor & Edgecomb Ltd) v Financial Ombudsman Service [2008] EWCA Civ 642; (2008) 158 N.L.J. 897, CA (Civ Div) 14–116, 14–117
R. (on the application of Hide) v Staffordshire CC [2007] EWHC 2441 (Admin); [2008] P.N.L.R. 13; [2008] A.C.D. 3; (2007) 157 N.L.J. 1543, QBD 11–133
R. (on the application of Hurst) v HM Coroner for Northern District London; sub nom. Commissioner of Police of the Metropolis v Hurst; R. (on the application of Hurst) v Northern District of London Coroner; R. (on the application of Hurst) v London Northern District Coroner [2007] UKHL 13; [2007] 2 W.L.R. 726; [2007] 2 All E.R. 1025; (2007) 157 N.L.J. 519; (2007) 151 S.J.L.B. 466; [2007] H.R.L.R. 23, HL 7–054
R. (on the application of JL) v Secretary of State for the Home Department [2007] EWCA Civ 767; [2008] 1 W.L.R. 158; [2007] H.R.L.R. 39; [2007] A.C.D. 95, CA (Civ Div) 7–054
R. (on the application of Johnson) v Professional Conduct Committee of the Nursing and Midwifery Council [2008] EWHC 885 (Admin) 7–094
R. (on the application of Keith Williams) v Financial Services Ombudsman Serives [2008] EWHC 2142 (Admin) 14–117
R. (on the application of L (A Patient) (by the Official Solicitor as a litigation friend)) v Secretary of State for the Home Department [2008] 1 W.L.R. 158, CA (Civ Div) 7–054
R. (on the application of Main) v Minister for Legal Aid [2007] EWCA Civ 1147; [2008] H.R.L.R. 8; [2008] U.K.H.R.R. 52; (2008) 99 B.M.L.R. 34; [2008] A.C.D. 12; (2007) 104(47) L.S.G. 27, CA (Civ Div) 7–099
R. (on the application of Malik) v Waltham Forest Primary Care Trust [2007] EWCA Civ 265; [2007] 1 W.L.R. 2092; [2007] I.C.R. 1101; [2007] I.R.L.R. 529; [2007] H.R.L.R. 24, CA (Civ Div) 7–090
R. (on the application of Middleton) v HM Coroner for Western Somerset; sub nom. R. v HM Coroner for Western Somerset Ex p. Middleton; R. (on the application of Middleton) v West Somerset Coroner [2004] UKHL 10; [2004] 2 A.C. 182; [2004] 2 W.L.R. 800; [2004] 2 All E.R. 465; (2004) 168 J.P. 329; [2004] H.R.L.R. 29; [2004] U.K.H.R.R. 501; 17 B.H.R.C. 49; [2004] Lloyd's Rep. Med. 288; (2004) 79 B.M.L.R. 51; (2004) 168 J.P.N. 479; (2004) 101(15) L.S.G. 27; (2004) 154 N.L.J. 417; (2004) 148 S.J.L.B. 354, HL 7–054
R. (on the application of Scholes) v Secretary of State for the Home Department; sub nom. Scholes v Secretary of State for the Home Department [2006] EWCA Civ 1343; [2006] H.R.L.R. 44; [2007] U.K.H.R.R. 112 ; [2006] Inquest L.R. 180; (2007) 93 B.M.L.R. 136; [2007] A.C.D. 24, CA (Civ Div) 7–054

Table of Cases

R. (on the application of Sinha) v General Medical Council [2008] EWHC 1732 (Admin) 7–099A
R. (on the application of Wright) v Secretary of State for Health; R. (on the application of Jummun) v Secretary of State for Health; R. (on the application of Quinn) v Secretary of State for Health; R. (on the application of Gambier) v Secretary of State for Health [2007] EWCA Civ 999; [2008] Q.B. 422; [2008] 2 W.L.R. 536; [2008] 1 All E.R. 886; [2008] H.R.L.R. 4; [2008] U.K.H.R.R. 294; (2008) 11 C.C.L. Rep. 31, CA (Civ Div) 7–100
RJ Knapman Ltd v Richards [2006] EWHC 2518; 108 Con. L.R. 64; [2006] C.I.L.L. 2400, QBD (TCC) 9–359
Ramco Ltd v Weller Russell & Laws Insurance Brokers Ltd [2008] EWHC 2202 (QB) 16–054, 16–058, 16–135, 16–144
Ramwade v WJ Emson & Co [1987] R.T.R. 72; (1986) 83 L.S.G. 2996; (1986) 130 S.J. 804, CA (Civ Div)16–143A
Ratiu v Conway; sub nom. Conway v Ratiu [2005] EWCA Civ 1302; [2006] 1 All E.R. 571; [2006] 1 E.G.L.R. 125; [2006] W.T.L.R. 101; [2005] 46 E.G. 177 (C.S.), CA (Civ Div) 11–018, 11–021
Reader v Molesworths Bright Clegg Solicitors; sub nom. Reader v Molesworths Bright Clegg (A Firm) [2007] EWCA Civ 169; [2007] 1 W.L.R. 1082; [2007] 3 All E.R. 107; [2007] P.N.L.R. 22; (2007) 157 N.L.J. 367; [2007] C.P. Rep. 25, CA (Civ Div) 11–045
Redbus LMDS Ltd v Jeffrey Green & Russell (A Firm) [2006] EWHC 2938 (Ch); [2007] P.N.L.R. 12, ChD 11–239, 11–319
Regent Leisuretime Ltd v Skerrett [2006] EWCA Civ 1184; [2007] P.N.L.R. 9, CA (Civ Div) 11–121
Richardson v Watson [2006] EWCA Civ 1662; [2007] C.P. Rep. 13; [2007] R.T.R. 21; [2007] P.I.Q.R. P18, CA (Civ Div) 5–094
Rickard Constructions Pty Ltd v Rickard Hails Moretti Pty Ltd [2006] N.S.W.C.A. 356 9–115
Rind v Theodore Goddard (A Firm) [2008] EWHC 459 (Ch); [2008] P.N.L.R. 24; [2008] W.T.L.R. 699, Ch D 11–048
Ringway Infrastructure Services Ltd v Vauxhall Motors Ltd [2007] EWHC 2507 (TCC); [2008] T.C.L.R. 2; 115 Con. L.R. 149; [2007] C.I.L.L. 2532, QBD 9–357, 9–362
Ristimaki v Cooper (2006) 268 D.L.R. (4th) 155, Ontario CA 11–080
Roberts v Nottinghamshire Healthcare NHS Trust [2008] EWHC 1934 (QB) 7–085
Rok Build Ltd v Harris Wharf Development Co Ltd [2006] EWHC 3573 (TCC), QBD 9–351
Royal Brompton Hospital NHS Trust v Hammond (No.3) [2002] UKHL 14; [2002] 1 W.L.R. 1397; [2002] 2 All E.R. 801; [2002] 1 All E.R. (Comm) 897; [2003] 1 C.L.C. 11; [2002] B.L.R. 255; [2002] T.C.L.R. 14; 81 Con. L.R. 1; [2002] P.N.L.R. 37, HL 4–006
Sallinen v Finland (50882/99) (2007) 44 E.H.R.R. 18, ECHR 7–043
Satnam Investments Ltd v Dunlop Heywood & Co Ltd [1999] 3 All E.R. 652; [1999] 1 B.C.L.C. 385; [1999] F.S.R. 722; [1999] Lloyd's Rep. P.N. 201; [1998] E.G. 190 (C.S.); (1999) 96(6) L.S.G. 33; (1999) 96(2) L.S.G. 30; [1998] N.P.C. 169, CA (Civ Div) 2–133
Savage v South Essex Partnership NHS Foundation Trust [2007] EWCA Civ 1375; [2008] 1 W.L.R. 1667; [2008] H.R.L.R. 15; [2008] U.K.H.R.R. 330; (2008) 11 C.C.L. Rep. 65; [2008] LS Law Medical 66; (2008) 100 B.M.L.R. 98; (2008) 105(1) L.S.G. 25; (2008) 152(2) S.J.L.B. 33, CA (Civ Div) < 7–054
Sayers v Smithkline Beecham Plc [2007] EWHC 1346 (QB), QBD 7–085
Seavision Investment SA v Evennett (The Tiburon) [1992] 2 Lloyd's Rep. 26, CA (Civ Div) 16–144

Table of Cases

Sempra Metals Ltd (formerly Metallgesellschaft Ltd) v Inland Revenue Commissioners [2007] UKHL 34; [2008] 1 A.C. 561; [2007] 3 W.L.R. 354; [2008] Bus. L.R. 49; [2007] 4 All E.R. 657; [2007] S.T.C. 1559; [2008] Eu. L.R. 1; [2007] B.T.C. 509; [2007] S.T.I. 1865; (2007) 104(31) L.S.G. 25; (2007) 157 N.L.J. 1082; (2007) 151 S.J.L.B. 985, HL 16–143

Shepherds Investments Ltd v Walters [2006] EWHC 836 (Ch); [2007] 2 B.C.L.C. 202; [2007] I.R.L.R. 110; [2007] F.S.R. 15; (2006) 150 S.J.L.B. 536, ChD 2–144

Shore v Sedgwick Financial Services Ltd [2008] EWCA Civ 863; (2008) 152(30) S.J.L.B. 31, CA (Civ Div) 5–036, 5–053, 5–080, 14–077

Sifri v Clough & Willis (A Firm) [2007] EWHC 985 (Ch); [2007] W.T.L.R. 1453, Ch D 11–319

Simpson v Harwood Hutton (A Firm) [2008] EWHC 1376 (QB) 17–024

Smirnov v Russia (71362/01) June 7, 2007, ECHR 7–043

Smith v Southampton University Hospitals NHS [2007] EWCA Civ 387; (2007) 96 B.M.L.R. 79, CA (Civ Div) 13–024

Spreadex Ltd v Sekhon [2008] EWHC 1136 (Ch); (2008) 105(24) L.S.G. 26, Ch D 14–077, 15–056A, 15–079

Standard Life Assurance Ltd v Oak Dedicated Ltd [2008] EWHC 222 (Comm); [2008] 1 C.L.C. 59; [2008] P.N.L.R. 26, QBD 8–101A, 16–049, 16–053, 16–054, 16–055, 16–058, 16–150

Stefaniu v Ahmed (2007) 275 D.L.R. (4th) 101 13–019

Stingel v Clark [2006] HCA 37; (2006) 228 A.L.R. 229; (2006) C.L.R. 442 5–085

Stone Heritage Developments Ltd v Davis Blank Furniss [2007] EWCA Civ 765, CA (Civ Div) 11–162

Stone and Rolls Ltd (In Liquidation) v Moore Stephens (A Firm) [2008] EWCA Civ 644; (2008) 105(25) L.S.G. 26, CA (Civ Div) <x917–027, 17–064, 17–081

Stuart v Goldberg; sub nom. Stuart v Goldberg Linde (A Firm) [2008] EWCA Civ 2; [2008] 1 W.L.R. 823; [2008] C.P. Rep. 18; (2008) 152(4) S.J.L.B. 28, CA (Civ Div) 11–117

Stubbings v Webb [1993] A.C. 498; [1993] 2 W.L.R. 120; [1993] 1 All E.R. 322; [1993] 1 F.L.R. 714; [1993] P.I.Q.R. P86; [1993] Fam. Law 342; (1993) 137 S.J.L.B. 32, HL 5–085

Sutcliffe v BMI Healthcare Ltd [2007] EWCA Civ 476; (2007) 98 B.M.L.R. 211, CA (Civ Div) 13–139

Sutradhar v Natural Environment Research Council [2006] UKHL 33; [2006] 4 All E.R. 490; [2007] Env. L.R. 10; [2006] P.N.L.R. 36; (2006) 150 S.J.L.B. 922, HL 2–077

T v BBC [2007] EWHC 1683 (QB); [2008] 1 F.L.R. 281; [2008] 2 F.C.R. 497; (2007) 10 C.C.L. Rep. 737; [2007] Fam. Law 904, QBD 7–060

TFW Printers Ltd v Interserve Project Services Ltd [2006] EWCA Civ 875; [2006] 2 C.L.C. 106; [2006] B.L.R. 299; 109 Con. L.R. 1; (2006) 22 Const. L.J. 481; [2006] C.I.L.L. 2376; (2006) 103(28) L.S.G. 27, CA (Civ Div) 9–121, 9–334

TJ Brent Ltd v Black & Veatch Consulting Ltd [2008] EWHC 1497 (TCC) 9–007

Templeton Insurance Ltd v Penningtons Solicitors [2006] EWHC 685 (Ch); [2007] W.T.L.R. 1103, ChD 11–068

Tesco Stores Ltd v David Constable [2008] EWCA Civ 362; [2008] 1 C.L.C. 727; [2008] C.I.L.L. 2593; (2008) 105(17) L.S.G. 28, CA (Civ Div) 8–017

Thai Trading Co v Taylor [1998] Q.B. 781; [1998] 2 W.L.R. 893; [1998] 3 All E.R. 65; [1998] 1 Costs L.R. 122; [1998] 2 F.L.R. 430; [1998] 3 F.C.R. 606; [1998] P.N.L.R. 698; [1998] Fam. Law 586; (1998) 95(15) L.S.G. 30; (1998) 142 S.J.L.B. 125, CA (Civ Div) 11–095

TABLE OF CASES

Thornton Springer v NEM Insurance Co Ltd [2000] 2 All E.R. 489; [2000] 1 All E.R. (Comm) 486; [2000] C.L.C. 975; [2000] Lloyd's Rep. I.R. 590; (2000) 97(13) L.S.G. 42; (2000) 144 S.J.L.B. 147, QBD (Comm) 8–024
Tiburon, The. *See* Seavision Investment SA v Evennett
Toth v Jarman [2006] EWCA Civ 1028; [2006] 4 All E.R. 1276 (Note); [2006] C.P. Rep. 44; [2006] Lloyd's Rep. Med. 397; (2006) 91 B.M.L.R. 121, CA (Civ Div) 13–038
Treasure & Son Ltd v Dawes [2007] EWHC 2420 (TCC); [2008] B.L.R. 24; [2007] C.I.L.L. 2533; [2007] 44 E.G. 181 (C.S.), QBD 9–354
Turner Page Music v Torres Design Associates Ltd, *The Times*, August 3, 1998, CA (Civ Div) 9–323
Tyco Fire & Integrated Solutions (UK) Ltd (formerly Wormald Ansul (UK) Ltd) v Rolls Royce Motor Cars Ltd (formerly Hireus Ltd) [2008] EWCA Civ 286; [2008] 1 C.L.C. 625; [2008] B.L.R. 285; [2008] 14 E.G. 100 (C.S.); (2008) 105(15) L.S.G. 25; (2008) 152(14) S.J.L.B. 31, CA (Civ Div) 9–121, 9–334
Tysiac v Poland (5410/03) [2007] 1 F.C.R. 666; 22 B.H.R.C. 155, ECHR 7–054
United Project Consultants Pte Ltd v Leon Kwok Onn [2005] S.L.R. 214 17–027
Vaidya v General Medical Council [2007] EWHC 1497 (Admin), QBD (Admin) 7–095
Van Colle v Chief Constable of Hertfordshire; sub nom. Chief Constable of Hertfordshire v Van Colle; Smith v Chief Constable of Sussex [2008] UKHL 50; [2008] 3 W.L.R. 593; [2008] 3 All E.R. 977; (2008) 152(32) S.J.L.B. 31, HL 7–036
Veitch v Avery [2007] EWCA Civ 711; 115 Con. L.R. 70; [2008] P.N.L.R. 7; [2007] N.P.C. 89, CA (Civ Div) 11–255, 11–266
Verderame v Commercial Union Assurance Co Plc [1992] B.C.L.C. 793; [2000] Lloyd's Rep. P.N. 557; [1955–95] P.N.L.R. 612, CA (Civ Div) 16–143A
Vo v France (53924/00) [2004] 2 F.C.R. 577; (2005) 40 E.H.R.R. 12; 17 B.H.R.C. 1; (2004) 79 B.M.L.R. 71, ECHR (Grand Chamber) 7–054
Vranicki v Architects Registration Board [2007] EWHC 506 (Admin); [2007] 13 E.G. 254 (C.S.), QBD (Admin) 9–002
Wakefield v Channel Four Television Corp [2006] EWHC 3289 (QB); (2007) 94 B.M.L.R. 1; (2007) 104(5) L.S.G. 28, QBD 7–085
Walker v Inter-Alliance Group Plc (In Administration) [2007] EWHC 1858 (Ch) 15–011, 15–017, 15–023, 15–049A, 15–070
Warman International Ltd v Dwyer (1995) 182 C.L.R. 544 5–134
Wasa International Insurance Co Ltd v Lexington Insurance Co; AGF Insurance Ltd v Lexington Insurance Co [2008] EWCA Civ 150; [2008] Bus. L.R. 1029; [2008] 1 All E.R. (Comm) 1085; [2008] 1 C.L.C. 340; [2008] Env. L.R. 39; [2008] Lloyd's Rep. I.R. 510, CA (Civ Div) 8–024
Watkins v Jones Maidment Wilson (A Firm) [2008] EWCA Civ 134; [2008] P.N.L.R. 23; [2008] 10 E.G. 166 (C.S.); [2008] N.P.C. 27, CA (Civ Div) 5–042
Watts v Bell & Scott WS [2007] CSOH 108; 2007 S.L.T. 665; [2007] P.N.L.R. 30; 2007 G.W.D. 21–364, OH 11–252, 11–281
West Bromwich Albion Football Club Ltd v El-Safty [2006] EWCA Civ 1299; [2007] P.I.Q.R. P7; [2007] LS Law Medical 50; (2006) 92 B.M.L.R. 179; (2006) 103(41) L.S.G. 34; (2006) 150 S.J.L.B. 1428, CA (Civ Div) 13–109
Whitehead v Searle; sub nom. Hibbert Pownall & Newton (A Firm) v Whitehead; McLeish (Deceased), Re [2008] EWCA Civ 285; [2008] P.N.L.R. 25; (2008) 152(16) S.J.L.B. 32, CA (Civ Div) 11–299, 13–021
Whiteley Insurance Consultants (A Firm), Re [2008] EWHC 1782 (Ch) 14–073, 14–097, 14–098, 14–099

TABLE OF CASES

Wieser v Austria (74336/01); sub nom. Bicos Beteiligungen GmbH v Austria (74336/01) (2008) 46 E.H.R.R. 54, ECHR 7–043
William Verry Ltd v Camden LBC [2006] EWHC 761 (TCC), QBD 9–359
Williams v General Medical Council [2007] EWHC 2603 (Admin); (2008) 99 B.M.L.R. 59, QBD 7–098
Winnote Pty Ltd v Page [2006] NSWCA 287; (2006) 68 N.S.W.L.R. 531, CA (NSW) 5–029, 5–042, 11–012
Woolcock Street Investments Pty Ltd v CDG Pty Ltd (formerly Cardno & Davies Australia Pty Ltd) [2005] B.L.R. 92; 101 Con. L.R. 113; (2005) 21 Const. L.J. 141, HC (Aus) 9–115
Wright v Hampton Winter & Glynn [2008] 2 H.K.L.R.D. 341 11–030
Wright v Paton Farrell, 2006 S.C. 404; 2006 S.L.T. 269; 2006 S.C.L.R. 371; [2007] P.N.L.R. 7; 2006 G.W.D. 8–139, IH (1 Div) 2–100, 12–009
Young v Borzoni (2007) 277 D.L.R. (4th) 685, British Columbia CA 11–062
Young v Tyneside MBC. *See* Catholic Care (Diocese of Leeds) v Y (Kevin Raymond)
Zarb v Odetoyinbo [2006] EWHC 2880; (2007) 93 B.M.L.R. 166, QBD 13–139
Zeller v British Caymanian Insurance Co Ltd [2008] UKPC 4, PC (CI) 8–044
Zurich GSG Ltd v Gray & Kellas (A Firm) [2007] CSOH 91; 2007 S.L.T. 917; [2008] P.N.L.R. 1; 2007 G.W.D. 26–460, OH 11–147
Zurich Professional Ltd v Karim [2006] EWHC 3355, QB 8–079

TABLE OF STATUTES

1890	Partnership Act (53 & 54 Vict. c.39)	11–147
1948	National Assistance Act (11 & 12 Geo.6 c.29)	
	s.21	7–001
	s.26	7–001
1975	Policy Holders Protection Act (c.75)	15–069
1976	Fatal Accidents and Sudden Deaths Inquiry (Scotland) Act (c.14)	7–054
	Fatal Accidents Act (c.30)	11–045
1978	Civil Liability (Contribution) Act (c.47)	
	s.6	17–081
	(1)	4–004, 4–006
1980	Limitation Act (c.58)	5–134, 5–136, 9–020
	s.14	5–080, 5–085, 5–087
	s.14A	5–080
	s.21	5–114A
	(3)	5–114A
	s.33	5–080, 5–085, 5–094
1983	Mental Health Act (c.20)	7–054, 7–055
	s.58	13–047
1985	Companies Act (c.6)	17–008, 17–013
	s.156	17–059A
1986	Latent Damage Act (c.37)	5–046
	Insolvency Act (c.45)	
	s.214	4–006
	s.238	4–006
	s.239	4–006
	Financial Services Act (c.60)	15–023
	s.5(3)	14–098
	s.62	15–023
	s.132(3)	14–098
	Sch.1 para.15	15–023, 15–049A
1995	Regulation of Information (Services outside the State for Termination of Pregnancies) Act (No.5/1995) (Irl)	
	s.5	7–054
	s.8	7–054
1996	Housing Grants, Construction and Regeneration Act (c.53)	9–360
	s.107	9–354
	(5)	9–354
	s.108	9–363
1998	Human Rights Act (c.42)	7–036
	s.6(3)(b)	7–001, 7–060
1999	Access to Justice Act (c.22)	7–058
2000	Financial Services and Markets Act (c.8)	14–088, 14–133
	Pt 6	14–077
	s.90A	14–081
	s.90B	14–081A
	s.150	14–077
	Freedom of Information Act (c.36)	
	s.44	7–085
2006	Companies Act (c.46)	
	Pt 15	17–008
	Pt 16	17–013
	ss.485—488	17–013
	ss.532—538	17–013
	Legislative and Regulatory Reform Act (c.51)	14–004

TABLE OF STATUTORY INSTRUMENTS

1994	Construction (Design and Management) Regulations (SI 2004/3140) 9–048	2005	Financial Services and Markets Act 2000 (Financial Promotion) Order (SI 2005/1529) ("FPO")	
1998	Civil Procedure Rules (SI 1998/3132)		art.12 14–009	
	r.5.4C(2) 7–085		art.20B 14–009	
	Pt 20 ..... 10–011, 17–064, 17–081		art.26A 14–027	
2001	Financial Services and Markets Act 2000 (Regulated Activities) Order (SI 2001/544) ("RAO") 14–024		art.26B 14–027	
			arts 30—33 14–009	
			Sch.1 14–027	
		2007	Construction (Design and Management) Regulations (SI 2007/320) 9–048	
	art.25 .... 14–015, 14–024			
	art.25A 14–015			
	art.25B 14–015, 14–024		Financial Services and Markets Act 2000 (Ombudsman Scheme) Order (SI 2007/383) 14–106	
	art.25C 14–015, 14–024			
	art.25D 14–024			
	art.39A 14–015			
	art.40 14–015		Money Laundering Regulations (SI 2007/2157) 14–086	
	art.52B 14–015			
	art.53 14–015			
	art.53A 14–015		Legislative and Regulatory Reform (Regulatory Functions) Order (SI 2007/3544) 14–004	
	art.53B 14–015, 14–024			
	art.53C 14–015, 14–024			
	art.63B 14–024, 14–027			
	art.63F 14–024, 14–027			
	art.64 14–015			

Chapter 2

DUTIES AND OBLIGATIONS

	Para.
1. Professional Liability	2–001
(a) Positive Duties	2–001
(b) Restrictions and Inhibitions	2–005
2. Contractual Liability	2–007
3. Tortious Liability	2–013
(a) The Tort of Negligence	2–013
(b) Theoretical Basis for the Duty of Care	2–022
(i) Lord Atkin's Approach	2–022
(ii) *Hedley Byrne*	2–024
(iii) The Inclusive Approach	2–026
(iv) The Threefold Test	2–030
(v) The Exclusive Approach	2–036
(vi) Extensions of *Hedley Byrne*	2–044
(vii) The Co-existence of Different Approaches	2–049
(viii) Commonwealth Approaches to Duty of Care Issues	2–054
(ix) Analysis	2–068
(c) Particular Situations	2–081
(i) Public and Local Authorities: Duty of Care and Statute	2–081
(ii) Directors and Employees	2–089
(iii) Sub-agents and Sub-contractors	2–096
(iv) Immunity	2–100
(d) Concurrent Liability, Contracts and Tortious Duties of Care	2–103
(i) Competing Considerations	2–104
(ii) Authority	2–105
(iii) *Henderson v Merrett*	2–108
(iv) The Scope of the Concurrent Duty	2–109
(v) Can the Concurrent Duty in Tort be More Extensive than the Contractual Obligations?	2–110
(vi) Further Significance of the Contract	2–111

	Para.
(e) Liability to Third Parties	2–112
(i) Denning L.J.'s Dissenting Judgment	2–113
(ii) Analysis of Denning L.J.'s Dissenting Judgment	2–114
(iii) Intended Beneficiaries	2–117
(iv) Particular Professions	2–118
4. The Standard of Skill and Care	2–119
(a) The Meaning of Reasonable Skill and Care	2–119
(b) Relevance of Defendant's Qualifications and Experience	2–121
(c) Formulation of the Standard	2–123
(d) Organisation Offering Professional Services	2–124
(e) Undertaking Work of Other Professions	2–125
(f) New Techniques	2–126
(g) Changes in the Standard Required	2–127
5. Fiduciary Obligations	2–128
(a) The Nature of Fiduciary Obligations	2–128
(b) Dealing with the Principal	2–137
(c) Unauthorised Profits and Diversion of Opportunities	2–144
(d) Undue Influence	2–145
(i) *Royal Bank of Scotland Plc v Etridge (No.2)* and Undue Influence	2–145
(ii) Undue Influence and the Burden of Proof	2–147
(iii) Discharging the Burden of Proof	2–154
6. Confidentiality	2–155
(a) Introduction	2–155
(b) Origins of the Duty of Confidence	2–157
(c) Elements of the Cause of Action	2–167
(d) The Continuing Duty to Former Clients	2–176

2. Contractual Liability

2–010 Add: However, in *Platform Funding Limited v Bank of Scotland PLC* [2008] EWCA Civ 930, the Court of Appeal (Rix and Moore-Bick L.JJ., Clarke M.R. dissenting) held that a valuer who certified that he had inspected the relevant property was subject to a strict obligation to inspect that property. Moore-Bick L.J. (with whom Rix L.J. agreed) reviewed the authorities and observed that "although there is a presumption that those who provide professional services normally do no more than undertake to exercise the degree of care and skill to be expected of a competent professional in the relevant field, there is nothing to prevent them from assuming an unqualified obligation in relation to particular aspects of their work". When deciding whether a particular obligation is qualified or unqualified the question to ask is "whether, having regard to the facts and matters known to both parties when the instructions were accepted, the professional person assumed an unqualified obligation in relation to the particular matter in question". Moreover, where the language was clear, there was no reason not to give effect to it. This decision on its particular facts is discussed in para.**10–019A** below.

3. Tortious Liability

(b) *Theoretical Basis for the Duty of Care*

(viii) *Commonwealth Approaches to Duty of Care Issues*

Add new para.**2–063A** after para.**2–063**:

2–063A The first stage is not limited to reasonable forseeability, but includes consideration of the specific relationship between the parties: proximity. This was acknowledged by Iacobucci J. giving the judgment of the Supreme Court of Canada in *Odhavji Estate v Woodhouse* (2003) 233 D.L.R. (4th) 193. He explained that to establish a duty of care the following had to be shown:

> (i) that the harm complained of is a reasonably foreseeable consequence of the alleged breach; (ii) that there is sufficient proximity between the parties that it would not be unjust or unfair to impose a duty of care on the defendants; and (iii) that there exist no policy reasons to negative or otherwise restrict that duty.

The recognition of reasonable forseeability and proximity as separate questions was confirmed in *Childs v Desormeaux* (2006) 266 D.L.R. (4th) 641, where McLachlin C.J., with whom other members of the Supreme Court agreed, said:

> "Some cases speak of forseeability being an element of proximity where 'proximity' is used in the sense of establishing a relationship sufficient to give rise to a duty of care: see, e.g., *Kamloops*. *Odhavji*, by contrast, sees forseeability and proximity as separate elements at the first stage; 'proximity' is here used in the narrower sense of features of the relationship other than

foreseeability. There is no suggestion that *Odhavji* was intended to change the *Anns* test; rather, it merely clarified that proximity will not always be satisfied by reasonable foreseeability. What is clear is that at stage one, foreseeability and factors going to the relationship between the parties must be considered with a view to determining whether a *prima facie* duty of care arises. At stage two, the issue is whether this duty is negated by other, broader policy considerations."

A similar approach, breaking down the first stage of *Anns* to two sub-stages, reasonable foreseeability and "other considerations relevant to proximity", was adopted by the Supreme Court in *Hill v Hamilton-Wentworth Regional Police Services Board* (2007) 285 D.L.R. (4th) 621 and in *Design Services Ltd v The Queen* (2008) 293 D.L.R. (4th) 437.

Add to NOTE 3: Indeed, so firm is the rejection of "proximity" that in *Imbree v McNeilly* [2008] HCA 40 the High Court of Australia overturned its earlier decision in *Cook v Cook* [1986] HCA 73; (1986) 162 C.L.R. 376, which has been based upon "proximity", observing that it was based upon "reasoning that does not accord with subsequent decisions of this Court denying the utility of that concept as a determinant of duty".   2–067

(ix) *Analysis*

Add to NOTE 17: See also *Jain v Trent Strategic Health Authority* [2007] EWCA Civ 1186; [2008] Q.B. 246, at [30] per Arden L.J.   2–070

Add to NOTE 42: The decision of the Court of Appeal was upheld by the House of Lords: [2006] UKHL 33; [2006] 4 All E.R. 490.   2–077

(c) *Particular Situations*

(i) *Public and Local Authorities: Duty of Care and Statute*

Add to NOTE 5: See also *Jain v Trent Strategic Health Authority* [2007] EWCA Civ 1186; [2008] Q.B. 246, where Arden L.J., with whom Hughes L.J. agreed, when finding that no duty of care was owed, identified a "broad category of cases in which public authorities have powers and duties to protect a class of persons, and, in the course of exercising those powers, cause a loss to third parties".   2–086

(ii) *Directors and Employees*

Add to NOTE 41: See also the decision of Irwin J. in *Contex Drouzhba Ltd v Wiseman* [2006] EWHC 2708, QBD; [2007] 1 B.C.L.C. 758, where the correct result was achieved despite some confusion as to the principles and relevant authorities.   2–093

(iv) *Immunity*

Add to NOTE 62: For the position of advocates in Scotland, see now *Wright v Paton Farrell* [2006] C.S.I.H. 7; [2007] P.N.L.R. 7 where it was held, *obiter*, that advocates for the defence in criminal trials should enjoy immunity. Two members   2–100 of the Court of Session, Inner House, First Division, considered that immunity might well no longer extend to advocates in civil proceedings.

Add to NOTE 64: The immunity of witnesses, including expert witnesses, could in principle extend to professional disciplinary hearings, but does not extend to "fitness to practise" hearings concerning medical practitioners because the purpose of such hearings is to protect the public: *Meadow v General Medical Council* [2006] EWCA Civ 1390; [2007] Q.B. 462.

2–102 Add new NOTE 72A at the end of the paragraph: The courts are reluctant to extend immunity: see *Meadow v General Medical Council* [2006] EWCA Civ 1390; [2007] Q.B. 462 at [17], per Sir Anthony Clarke M.R.

5. FIDUCIARY OBLIGATIONS

(a) *The Nature of Fiduciary Obligations*

2–133 Add to NOTE 75: See also *Paper Reclaim Ltd v Aotearoa International Ltd* [2007] NZSC 26; [2007] 3 N.Z.L.R. 169 at [31]:

"It is not enough to attract an obligation of loyalty that one party may have given up more that the other in entering into the contract or that the contract may be more advantageous for one party than the other. Nor is a relationship fiduciary in nature merely because the parties may be depending upon one another to perform the contract in its terms. That would be true of many commercial contracts which require cooperation. A fiduciary relationship will be found when one party is entitled to repose and does repose trust and confidence in the other. The existence of an agreement, express or implied, to act on behalf of another and thus to put the interests of the other before one's own is a frequent manifestation of a situation in which fiduciary obligations are owed. Partners are a classic example of parties in that situation. Their position is different from that of parties to a contract who may have to cooperate but are doing so for their separate advantages."

See also *Amaltal Corporation Ltd v Maruha Corporation* [2007] NZSC 40; [2007] 3 N.Z.L.R. 192, at [19]–[21].

Add to NOTE 76: It follows that the directors of a company which is a fiduciary may themselves be subject to fiduciary obligations if there is the requisite kind of reliance or trust and confidence in them personally: see *JD Wetherspoon Plc v Van de Berg & Co Ltd* [2007] EWHC 1044 (Ch); [2007] P.N.L.R. 28 (Lewison J.), applying *Satnam Investments Ltd v Dunlop Hayward Ltd* [1999] 3 All E.R. 652, CA.

Add to NOTE 77: See also *Dresna Pty Ltd v Linknarf Management Services Pty* [2006] FCAFC 193; (2006) 237 A.L.R. 687 where the Federal Court of Australia held that an arrangement between vendor and purchaser of a lease of a supermarket to pursue litigation to obtain the consent of the landlord to the assignment did not give rise to any fiduciary obligation.

Fiduciary Obligations

(b) *Dealing with the Principal*

Add: What constitutes full advice and disclosure will depend in part upon the knowledge, ability and understanding of the beneficiary. So, in *Farah Constructions Pty Ltd v Say-Dee Pty Ltd* [2007] HCA 22; (2007) 236 A.L.R. 209 the High Court of Australia held that piecemeal disclosure over a period of time was sufficient. Given the business experience and intelligence of the beneficiaries, it did not matter that there was no single occasion on which the fiduciary had explained the position. In so finding, the Court followed its earlier decision in *Maguire v Makaronis* [1997] HCA 23; (1997) 188 C.L.R. 449 that: **2–137**

> "What is required for a fully informed consent is a question of fact in all the circumstances of each case and there is no precise formula which will determine in all cases if fully informed consent has been given."

By the same token, a credit broker dealing with borrowers who are vulnerable and unsophisticated will have to disclose the detail of the commission he is to receive, not just that he is to receive commission: *Wilson v Hurstanger Ltd* [2007] EWCA Civ 299; [2007] 1 W.L.R. 2351.

(c) *Unauthorised Profits and Diversion of Opportunities*

Add to Note 22: A helpful statement of the principles which apply where a fiduciary resigns from his position (in the context of a director resigning from a company) was given by Bernard Livesey Q.C. sitting as a Deputy Judge of the High Court in *Hunter Kane Ltd v Watkins* [2003] EWHC 186 (Ch). This summary was endorsed by the Court of Appeal in *Foster Bryant Surveying Ltd v Bryant* [2007] EWCA Civ 200; [2007] 2 B.C.L.C. 239, where, after a full review of the authorities, Rix L.J., with whom Moses and Buxton L.JJ. agreed, described it as "perceptive and useful". A director will not be in breach of his fiduciary obligation if the business opportunity which he exploits after resigning is not a "maturing business opportunity" and the company was not pursuing further business orders or where his resignation was not prompted or influenced by the wish to aquire that business opportunity himself. There is a need to balance the proper enforcement of the fiduciary obligation of loyalty with the fiduciary's right to earn a living in his chosen field. For another recent decision concerning the fiduciary obligations of directors who resigned from their company, see *Shepherds Investments Ltd v Walters* [2006] EWHC 836 (Ch); [2007] 2 B.C.L.C. 202 (Etherton J.). **2–144**

6. Confidentiality

(a) *Introduction*

Add to Note 62: See also *OBG Ltd v Allan* [2007] UKHL 21; [2007] 2 W.L.R. 920 at [118], per Lord Hoffmann; *McKennitt v Ash* [2006] EWCA Civ 1714; [2007] 3 W.L.R. 194 and *Lord Browne of Madingley v Associated Newspapers Ltd* [2007] EWCA Civ 295; [2007] 3 W.L.R. 289. **2–156**

2–165   Chapter 2—Duties and Obligations

(b) *Origins of the Duty of Confidence*

2–165 Add to Note 86: See also the decision of the New Zealand Supreme Court in *Hunt v A* [2007] NZSC 332; [2008] 1 N.Z.L.R. 368 at [92].

(c) *Elements of the Cause of Action*

2–168 In *OBG Ltd v Allan* [2007] UKHL 21; [2007] 2 W.L.R. 920 the House of Lords, by a majority, held that there was sufficient confidentiality in photographs of a celebrity wedding.

2–173 Add to Note 14: On the need to balance Arts 8 and 10 of the Convention, see also *McKennitt v Ash* [2006] EWCA Civ 1714; [2007] 3 W.L.R. 194; *HRH Prince of Wales v Associated Newspapers Ltd* [2006] EWHC 522 (Ch); [2006] EWCA Civ 1776; [2007] 3 W.L.R. 222 and *Lord Browne of Madingley v Associated Newspapers Ltd* [2007] EWCA Civ 295; [2007] 3 W.L.R. 289.

(d) *The Continuing Duty to Former Clients*

2–176 Add to Note 30: See also *Keisner v Terrus Group Ltd* [2006] EWHC 2765 (Ch); [2007] 1 B.C.L.C. 303 at [127]–[128] (Patten J.).

Chapter 3

REMEDIES

	Para.		Para.
1. Damages	3–001	(i) General	3–021
2. Loss of Remuneration	3–008	(ii) Clinical Negligence: Claims for Personal Injuries	3–022
3. Equitable Remedies	3–011		
(a) Rescission	3–011		
(b) Equitable Compensation	3–013	(iii) Damages for Inconvenience and Discomfort	3–023
(i) Compensation for Loss caused by Breach of Fiduciary Obligation	3–013	(iv) Interest on Damages for Pecuniary Losses in Solicitors' and Surveyors' Negligence Actions	3–024
(ii) Equitable Compensation for Breach of Confidence	3–017		
(c) Account of Profits	3–019	(b) Interest under the Civil Procedure Rules	3–025
(d) Injunction	3–020		
4. Interest	3–021	(c) Interest in Equity	3–026
(a) Interest under the Supreme Court Act 1981	3–021		

1. Damages

Add new Note 12A at the end of the paragraph: For an example of how this works in practice, see the decision of the Court of Appeal in *Andrews v Barnett Waddingham (a firm)* [2006] EWCA Civ 83; [2006] P.N.L.R. 432, discussed in para.**18–039** below. **3–002**

3. Equitable Remedies

(c) *Account of Profits*

Add: A defaulting fiduciary cannot rely upon the fact that the principal would not or might not have realised the profit himself: *Chirnside v Fay* [2006] NZSC 68; [2007] 1 N.Z.L.R. 433, following, among other cases, *Murad v Al-Saraj* [2005] EWCA Civ 959. **3–019**

[7]

Chapter 4

CONTRIBUTION BETWEEN DEFENDANTS

	Para.		Para.
1. Introduction	4–001	(b) Matters which can be raised in Defence to a Claim	4–012
2. Entitlement to Contribution	4–002	(c) Basis of Assessment of Contribution	4–013
■ 3. Liability of the Person Claiming Contribution	4–003	(d) Time for Bringing a Claim for Contribution	4–017
■ (a) Basis of Liability	4–006 □		
□ (b) Meaning of "the same damage"	4–007		
4. The Claim	4–011		
(a) Matters which cannot be raised in Defence to a Claim	4–011		

3. Liability of the Person Claiming Contribution

4–003 Add to Note 7: See also *BRB (Residuary) Ltd v Connex South Eastern Ltd* [2008] EWHC 1172 (Q.B.) (Cranston J.) where the liability arose from a judgment entered against the person seeking to recover contribution. At that stage the person against whom judgment was entered mistakenly believed it was liable.

4–004 Add new Note 8A at the end of the paragraph: The wording of the proviso in s.1(4) of the Civil Liability (Contribution) Act 1978 ("provided, however, that he would have been liable assuming that the factual basis of the claim against him could be established") is wide enough to allow a person against whom contribution is sought to dispute that claim not only on the basis that the person seeking to recover compensation would not have been liable had the factual basis of the claim advanced against him been made good, but also on the basis that the person seeking to recover contribution had a collateral defence which it would have been for him, and not the original claimant, to establish: *BRB (Residuary) Ltd v Connex South Eastern Ltd* [2008] EWHC 1172 (Q.B.) (Cranston J.), following *Arab Monetary Fund v Hashim*, *The Times*, June 17, 1993 (Chadwick J.). Cranston J. considered himself bound to follow this decision.

(a) *Basis of Liability*

4–006 Add to Note 13: See now the decision of the Court of Appeal in *City Index Ltd v Gawler* [2007] EWCA Civ 1382; [2008] Ch. 313, affirming the decision Sir Andrew Morritt C. in *Charter Plc v City Index Ltd* [2006] EWHC 2508 (Ch); [2007] 1 W.L.R. 26. In both decisions the authorities discussed in this note are authoritatively reviewed. *Friends' Provident Life Office v Hiller Parker May & Rowden* [1997] Q.B. 85 remains binding authority. Carnwath L.J., with whom

4–006   CHAPTER 4—CONTRIBUTION BETWEEN DEFENDANTS

Mummery L.J. agreed, resolved the question as follows. A disposition of property in breach of trust can give rise both to a claim for damages for breach of trust and a claim in restitution to restore the trust property. A claim for "knowing receipt" was fault based, as had been made clear in *Bank of Credit and Commerce International (Overseas) Ltd v Akindele* [2001] Ch. 437. Adopting a "wide view" of the Civil Liability (Contribution) Act 1978, a knowing recipient is liable to make good loss in a way which can be referred to as "compensatory". It does not necessarily follow that all claims in restitution have the necessary compensatory characteristic. This was emphasised by Arden L.J., who agreed with the result, but not the reasoning of Carnwath L.J. on this point. She distinguished between "claims for unjust enrichment based on the wrongful conduct of the defendant (known as knowing receipt) and claims for unjust enrichment based on innocent receipt (often called claims for money had and received)". She also drew attention to the need "to distinguish between a claim that a person should pay damages to make good the claimant's loss and a claim that a person should account for profits which he has made by use of the claimant's property". The latter is not compensatory and Arden L.J. considered that it was to that type of claim that the comments of Lord Steyn in *Royal Brompton Hospital National Heath Service Trust v Hammond* [2002] UKHL 14; [2002] 1 W.L.R. 1397 were directed.

Add to NOTE 15: See also *Cohen v Davies* [2006] EWHC 768 (Ch); [2007] 2 B.C.L.C. 274 (Richard Sheldon Q.C., sitting as a Deputy Judge of the High Court): Claims by liquidator against former directors of a company under ss.214, 238 and 239 of the Insolvency Act 1986 were brought by him as liquidator. It followed that a claim for contribution by defendants to such claims against a person who was allegedly liable to the company but not the liquidator should be struck out.

(b) *Meaning of "the same damage"*

4–008   Add to NOTE 23: See also *Cohen v Davies* [2006] EWHC 768 (Ch); [2007] 2 B.C.L.C. 274 (Richard Sheldon Q.C., sitting as a Deputy Judge of the High Court): the damage suffered by a company when money is wrongly paid away is different from the damage represented by the loss of the opportunity to bring proceedings to recover that money earlier than they were in fact taken.

(c) *Basis of Assessment of Contribution*

4–014   Add new NOTE 37A at the end of the paragraph: This aspect of the decision of the House of Lords in *Dubai Aluminium Co Ltd v Salaam* [2002] UKHL 48; [2002] 2 A.C. 366 was applied by Morgan J. in *Pulvers (a firm) v Chan* [2007] EWHC 2406 (Ch); [2008] P.N.L.R. 9. However, where a party has received money which represented the original loss, but no longer holds it, it does not follow that the recipient will be liable to contribute 100 per cent of the amount he had received: *City Index Ltd v Gawler* [2007] EWCA Civ 1382; [2008] Ch. 313.

4. The Claim

(d) *Time for Bringing a Claim for Contribution*

Add: When judgment is given on liability with damages to be assessed, time runs **4–017** not from then, but from the date on which damages are subsequently assessed: *Aer Lingus Plc v Gildacroft Ltd* [2006] EWCA Civ 4; [2006] 1 W.L.R. 1173.

Chapter 5

DEFENCES

	Para.		Para.
1. Exclusion or Restriction of Liability	5–001	(f) Fraud or Concealment	5–099
(a) The Position at Common Law	5–003	3. Limitation in Equity	5–105
(b) The Statutory Framework	5–009	(a) Express Application of the Limitation Act 1980	5–107
(c) Exclusion of Liability to Third Parties	5–021	(b) Application of the Limitation Act 1980 by Analogy	5–115
2. Limitation in Contract and Tort	5–025	(c) Where there is No Analogy or Correspondence	5–124
(a) The Limitation Period	5–025	4. Other Equitable Defences: Laches and Acquiescence	5–126
(b) Date when Cause of Action in Contract Accrues	5–029	(a) Laches	5–127
(c) Date when Cause of Action in Tort Accrues	5–031	(i) Unreasonable Delay	5–131
(i) Claims against Solicitors	5–037	(ii) Prejudice to the Defendant or Third Party	5–134
(ii) Claims against Surveyors	5–049	(iii) Relationship between Laches and the Limitation Act 1980	5–136
(iii) Claims against Insurance Brokers	5–051	(b) Acquiescence	5–137
(iv) Claims against Financial Advisers	5–053	5. Contributory Negligence	5–141
(v) Claims against Accountants	5–054	(a) Contributory Negligence and Contract	5–143
(vi) Claims against Construction Professionals	5–056	(b) Application to Professional Negligence	5–145
(vii) Claims against Barristers	5–074A	(c) Methods by which Claimants might seek to Circumvent a Plea of Contributory Negligence	5–147
(d) Effect of the Latent Damage Act 1986	5–075	(d) Attribution	5–148
(e) Special Rules re Personal Injury and Death	5–085		
(i) Primary Limitation Periods	5–085		
(ii) Discretionary Exclusion of Time Limit	5–093		

1. Exclusion or Restriction of Liability

(b) *The Statutory Framework*

Add new paragraph **5–016A**:

In *Marplace (No.512) Ltd v Chaffe Street (a firm)* [2006] EWHC 1919 (Ch) Laurence Collins J. addressed the question whether a clause in the defendant solicitors' retainer limiting liability to £20 million satisfied the test of reasonableness. He held that the test would have been satisfied had the issue arisen (he had found that the solicitors were not in breach of duty so that his decision on this point was *obiter*). The clients were sophisticated and wealthy consumers who had accepted another party's limitation of its liability without demur. They had been aware of the term which was not put forward as non-negotiable. The limit

5–016A

5–016A

of £20 million had been determined on reasonable commercial principles, taking into account the availability and cost of professional indemnity insurance and the circumstances of the transaction. This decision provides a helpful indication as to the approach of the Courts to limitation clauses in the retainers of professional firms and individuals.

5–020 Add to Note 57: See also *Bryen & Langley Ltd v Martin Boston* [2005] EWCA Civ 973; [2005] B.L.R. 508.

2. Limitation in Contract and Tort

(b) *Date when Cause of Action in Contract Accrues*

5–029 Add to Note 7: See also *Winnote Pty Ltd v Page* [2006] NSWCA 287; (2006) 68 N.S.W.L.R. 531, where it was held that a firm of solicitors was not under a continuing duty to provide advice about a transaction which they had already negligently executed for their client. In so finding, the New South Wales Court of Appeal applied a dictum of Dixon J. in *Larkin v Great Western (Nepean) Gravel Ltd* [1940] HCA 37; (1940) 64 C.L.R. 221, at 236:

> "If a covenantor undertakes that he will do a definite act and omits to do it within the time allowed for the purpose, he has broken his covenant finally and his continued failure to do the act is nothing but a failure to remedy his past breach and not the commission of any further breach of his covenant. His duty is not considered as persisting and, so to speak, being forever renewed until he actually does that which he promised. On the other hand, if his covenant is to maintain a state or condition of affairs, as, for instance, maintaining a building in repair, keeping the insurance of a life on foot, or affording a particular kind of lateral or vertical support to a tenement, then a further breach arises in every successive moment of time during which the state or condition is not as promised, during which, to pursue the examples, the building is out of repair, the life uninsured, or the particular support unprovided.
>
> The distinction may be difficult of application in a given case, but it must regarded as one depending upon the meaning of the covenant."

5–030 Add to Note 14: This aspect of the decision of Dyson J. in *New Islington and Hackney Housing Association Ltd v Pollard Thomas & Edwards Ltd* [2001] P.N.L.R. 515 was followed by Ramsey J. in *Oxford Architects Partnership v Cheltenham Ladies College* [2006] EWHC 3156 (TCC); [2007] P.N.L.R. 18.

(c) *Date when Cause of Action in Tort Accrues*

5–036 Add new Note 27A at the end of the paragraph: See, for example, *Shore v Sedgwick Financial Services Ltd* [2008] EWCA Civ 863, discussed in para. **5–053**, below.

(i) Claims against Solicitors

Add to NOTE 49: See also *Winnote Pty Ltd v Page* [2006] NSWCA 287; (2006) 68 N.S.W.L.R. 531 (cause of actions against solicitors accrued when they negligently advised their client to obtain a lease from the landowner to extract peat rather than a mining lease from the Crown and not several years later when someone else acquired a mining lease). The judgment of Mason P., with whom Tobias J.A. agreed, contains a helpful review of Australian and English authority. It is clear from the decision of the Court of Appeal in *Watkins v. Jones Maidment Wilson (a firm)* [2008] EWCA Civ 134; [2008] P.N.L.R. 23 that the English authorities remain good law following the decision of the House of Lords in *Law Society v Sephton* [2006] UKHL 22; [2006] 2 A.C. 453.

5–042

Replace NOTE 62 with: [2006] EWCA Civ 66; [2006] P.N.L.R. 22, where the principle established in the earlier cases was not doubted, but, on the facts, it was arguable that the defendant to the original claim might not have applied to strike it out at the relevant time. In *Cohen* the Court of Appeal was considering an application to strike out. In *Jessup v Wetherell* [2006] EWHC 2582 (QB); [2007] P.N.L.R. 259 Silber J. reviewed the authorities considered in paras **5–045** and **5–046** in the light of the speeches of the House of Lords in *Law Society v Sephton* [2006] UKHL 22; [2006] 2 A.C. 453. He concluded at [42] that:

5–046

> "a claimant's cause of action against defendant solicitor for failing to pursue expeditiously an earlier claim accrues when that earlier action is *'doomed to failure'* (*per* Lord Walker) or *'liable to be struck out for want of prosecution (thereby obviously eliminating or reducing the value of any claim)'* (*per* Lord Mance) or *'there was an inevitability or at least a very serious risk that they would be struck out at any time'* (*per* Sir Murray Stuart Smith) or has suffered *'relevant damage'* (*per* Chadwick L.J.) or *'it would have been struck out had an application been made'* (*per* Pill L.J.)."

On the facts before Silber J. the action was statute-barred on any of these formulations.

(iv) Claims against Financial Advisers

Add: Where the complaint is that the breach of duty by the financial adviser caused the claimant to make an investment which carried a greater degree of risk than was appropriate, damage is suffered when that investment is made and the claimant is exposed to the risk, even if the risk does not materialise at that point and there is a chance that the investment actually made will outperform that which should or would have been made: *Shore v Sedgwick Financial Services Ltd* [2008] EWCA Civ 863. In that case the claimant had transferred from his occupational pension scheme to a more risky scheme in reliance on the defendant's advice. Relying on the decision of the House of Lords in *Law Society v Sephton* [2006] UKHL 22; [2006] 2 A.C. 453 (as to which see para.**5–055**), the claimant argued that mere exposure to risk was not itself loss, but was equivalent to the exposure to a contingency. Rejecting that argument, Dyson L.J., with whom the other members of the Court of Appeal agreed, held that *Law Society v Sephton* was a "pure contingent liability case", to be contrasted with "transaction" cases such as those discussed in para.**5–042**. In such "transaction" cases it

5–053

5–053 was always possible that the risk against which the defendant had failed to secure adequate protection, might not materialise. For example, on this analysis in *D.W. Moore v Ferrier* [1988] 1 W.L.R. 267, the risk was that the director would leave the plaintiff's employment and compete with it in circumstances in which the claimant did not have the benefit of an enforceable restrictive covenant. Dyson L.J. said that "it is the possibility of actual financial harm that constitutes the loss". This is not the conventional analysis of the "transaction" cases, which is that the claimant suffers actual loss by receiving less valuable rights than it should have done as a result of the defendant's breach of duty (in *D.W. Moore v Ferrier* an enforceable restrictive covenant). It is right to say that the reason why the rights are less valuable may be that the claimant is exposed to a risk or contingency against which he should have been protected, but that is not the same as saying that the risk or contingency itself constitutes the loss. *Shore v Sedgwick Financial Services Ltd* appears to lean towards the wider interpretation of *Forster v Outred & Co* [1982] 1 W.L.R. 86 which was rejected by the House of Lords in *Law Society v Sephton*.

(vi) *Claims against Construction Professionals*

5–072 Add to NOTE 60: The decision of the Court of Appeal in *Abbott v Will Gannon & Smith Ltd* [2005] EWCA Civ 198 was followed by Ramsey J. in *Oxford Architects Partnership v Cheltenham Ladies College* [2006] EWHC 3156 (TCC); [2007] P.N.L.R. 18.

Add new subheading and paragraph **5–074A**:

(vii) *Claims against Barristers*

5–074A The decision of the House of Lords in *Arthur JS Hall & Co (a firm) v Simons* [2002] 1 A.C. 615 ended barristers' immunity from suit. In *Awoyomi v Radford* [2007] EWHC 1671 (Q.B.); [2008] 3 W.L.R. 34 Lloyd Jones J. had to decide whether a claim which, absent any issue of immunity, would have become statute barred in 2001, was not statute barred because the defendant was immune from suit until the decision of the House of Lords on July 20, 2000. He held that the effect of the decision of the House of Lords was that immunity had not been a defence to barristers from at least 1991 so that the claim was statute barred.

(d) *Effect of the Latent Damage Act 1986*

5–080 Add to NOTE 95: However, to the extent that the courts approach s.14 on the basis that it should be relatively narrowly construed because of the availability of relief under s.33 (as to which see *McCoubrey v Ministry of Defence* [2007] EWCA Civ 17; [2007] 1 W.L.R. 1544 at [45], per Neuberger L.J., with whom the other members of the Court of Appeal agreed), care is needed in applying their decisions on that provision to s.14A where there is no equivalent to s.33.

5–081 Add: In the same way, it is sufficient that the claimant knows that he has lost valuable rights as a result of the acts or omissions of the defendant, even if there is an outside chance that the rights may be retrieved or the position remedied by further action: the damage has still be suffered so that time runs: *3M United*

Kingdom Plc v Linklaters & Paines (a firm) [2006] EWCA Civ 530; [2006] P.N.L.R. 30 (options to terminate could not be exercised because of solicitors' alleged negligence. The possibility that they could be reinstated through negotiation did not prevent the claimant having the requisite knowledge.). If an investor is aware of what advice he has and has not been given about an investment and he knows that that investment is worth less than it would have been had he acted differently and that there was a real possibility that the difference in his position was the result of the advice he received, then time will run under s.14A: see *Shore v Sedgwick Financial Services Ltd* [2008] EWCA Civ 863, at [61] per Dyson L.J. with whom the other members of the Court of Appeal agreed.

(e) *Special Rules re Personal Injury and Death*

(i) *Primary Limitation Periods*

Add to NOTE 17: In *A v Hoare* [2008] UKHL 6; [2008] 1 A.C. 844 the House of Lords reversed the decision of the Court of Appeal in [2006] EWCA Civ 395; [2006] 1 W.L.R. 2320 and its own decision in *Stubbings v Webb* [1993] A.C. 498 and held that the limitation period for a claim for damages for trespass to the person was within the scope of both s.14 and s.33 of the Limitation Act 1980. This brought English law into line with Australian law: see *Stingel v Clark* [2006] H.C.A. 37; (2006) 228 A.L.R. 229.   5–085

Add to NOTE 29: See also *Albonetti v Wirral Metropolitan Borough Council* [2008] EWCA Civ 783 (the victim of a rape must be taken to have known she had suffered a significant injury for the purposes of s.14).   5–087

Add to NOTE 44: See now *A v Hoare* [2008] UKHL 6; [2008] 1 A.C. 844. Decisions such as *KR v Bryn Alyn Community (Holdings) Ltd (in liquidation)* [2003] EWCA Civ 85; [2003] Q.B. 1441, *Young v Tyneside Metropolitan Borough Council* [2006] EWCA Civ 1534l; [2007] 2 W.L.R. 1193 and *McCoubrey v Ministry of Defence* [2007] EWCA Civ 17; [2007] 1 W.L.R. 1544 need to be read in the light of *A v Hoare*. See also *AB and Others v The Nugent Care Society* [2008] EWCA Civ 795, *Khairule v North West Strategic Health Authority* [2008] EWHC 1537 (QB) (Cox J.), *Albonetti v Wirral Metropolitan Borough Council* [2008] EWCA Civ 783 and *Field v British Coal Corporation* [2008] EWCA Civ 912.   5–091

(ii) *Discretionary Exclusion of Time Limit*

Add to NOTE 49: In *Leeson v Marsden* [2008] EWHC 1011 (QB) (Cox J.), a clinical negligence claim, the second set of proceedings was issued only after the decision of the House of Lords in *Horton v Sadler* [2006] UKHL 27; [2007] 1 A.C. 307. It was held, following *Richardson v Watson* [2006] EWCA Civ 1662; [2007] R.T.R. 21, that the delay pending the decision in *Horton v Sadler* should not be attributed to the claimant and that, overall, the s.33 discretion should be exercised in her favour.   5–094

5–101 CHAPTER 5—DEFENCES

(f) *Fraud or Concealment*

5–101 Add: There also has to be some deliberate concealment of a relevant fact. So the proper exercise by a firm of solicitors of their lien over their papers until their fees were paid does not of itself amount to deliberate concealment: see the decision of Silber J. in *Jessup v Wetherell* [2006] EWHC 2582 (QB); [2007] P.N.L.R. 259.

5–102 Add to NOTE 81: See also the helpful review of the authorities, including *Clef Aquitaine Sarl v Laporte Materials (Barrow) Ltd (sued as Sovereign Chemicals Industries Ltd)* [2000] 3 All E.R. 493, CA in *Amaltal Corp Ltd v Maruha Corp* [2007] 1 N.Z.L.R. 608 (New Zealand Court of Appeal) at [147]–[161].

3. LIMITATION IN EQUITY

(a) *Express Application of the Limitation Act 1980*

Add new paragraph **5–114A**:

5–114A Section 21(3) of the Limitation Act 1980 concludes that for the purposes of that subsection, "the right of action shall not be treated as having accrued to any beneficiary entitled to a future interest in the trust property until the interest fell into possession". For the purposes of this provision, it matters not whether the claim is brought by the trustees or the beneficiaries. In so far as a claim is brought on behalf of the beneficiaries, time only begins to run under s.21 when their interests fall into possession: *Cattley v Pollard* [2006] EWHC 3130 (Ch); [2007] Ch. 353 (Richard Sheldon Q.C. sitting as a Deputy High Court Judge) at [94]–[104].

(c) *Where there is no Analogy or Correspondence*

5–124 Add: So, there is no limitation period for the equitable remedy of specific performance, for which there was no correspondent remedy or action at law: *P&O Nedlloyd BV v Arab Metals Co (No.2)* [2006] EWCA Civ 1717; [2007] 1 W.L.R. 2288.

4. OTHER EQUITABLE DEFENCES: LACHES AND ACQUIESCENCE

(a) *Laches*

(ii) *Prejudice to the Defendant or a Third Party*

5–134 Add to NOTE 70: See also *Edmonds v Donovan* [2005] V.S.C.A. 27; [2005] V.S.C.A. 36; (2005) 12 V.R. 513 (Victoria Court of Appeal), where *Re Jarvis (deceased)* [1958] 1 W.L.R. 815, at 820–821 and *Warman International Ltd v Dwyer* (1995) 182 C.L.R. 544 at 559, were followed and it was held to be inequitable to stand by while the defendants ran the business before deciding to

OTHER EQUITABLE DEFENCES: LACHES AND ACQUIESCENCE **5–136**

seek to recover the profits of that business. The same result was reached on similar facts in *P&M Construction Ltd v. Husar Estate* (2007) 281 D.L.R. (4th) 305 (Ontario Court of Appeal).

(iii) *Relationship between Laches and the Limitation Act 1980*

Delete the last sentence and replace with: Where no period of limitation is prescribed by the Limitation Act 1980 then the doctrine of laches may apply: *Re Loftus decd* [2006] EWCA Civ 1124; [2007] 1 W.L.R. 591 at [40], per Chadwick L.J., with whom the other members of the Court of Appeal agreed. **5–136**

Chapter 6

LITIGATION

	Para.		Para.
1. Group Actions	6–001	(d) Relevance and Admissibility of Expert Evidence	6–013
(a) General	6–001	(i) The Appropriate Discipline	6–014
(b) Professional Negligence	6–002	(ii) The Appropriate Questions	6–015
(c) Procedure	6–003	(iii) Appropriate Qualifications and Experience	6–016
□ (d) Costs	6–005	(iv) Impartiality	6–017
2. Expert Evidence	6–006	(e) The Single Joint Expert	6–021
■ (a) The Functions of the Expert Witness	6–006	(f) Experts' Immunity from Suit	6–025
(b) Cases where Expert Evidence is Not Required	6–008		
■ (c) The Civil Procedure Rules	6–012		

1. Group Actions

(d) *Costs*

6–005 Add to Note 26: In *Brown v Russell Young & Co* [2007] 2 All E.R. 453, CA, claims were settled before proceedings had begun and there had been no opportunity for a costs-sharing order to be made. However, the claimants could recover generic costs under the terms of a conditional fee agreement, which were wide enough to encompass such costs, without any specific additional agreement relating to them.

2. Expert Evidence

(a) *The Functions of the Expert Witness*

6–007 Add to Note 32: For an example, see *Multiplex Constructions (UK) Ltd v Cleveland Bridge UK Ltd* [2008] EWHC 2220 (TCC), where Jackson J. held that in construction litigation an engineer who is giving factual evidence may also proffer (a) statements of opinion which are reasonably related to the facts within his knowledge and (b) relevant comments based upon his own experience.

(c) *The Civil Procedure Rules*

6–012 Add to Note 52: For an example of the manner in which the Court will restrict expert evidence to that which is reasonably necessary to determine the issues before it, see *JP Morgan Chase Bank v Springwell Navigation Corporation* [2006] EWHC 2755 (Comm).

[21]

6–020

(d) *Relevance and Admissibility of Expert Evidence*

(iv) *Impartiality*

6–020 Add: That an expert witness is an employee of the party by whom he instructed does not automatically disqualify him from giving expert evidence. In *Gallaher International Ltd v Tlais Enterprises Ltd* [2007] EWHC 464 (Comm), Aikens J. held that the critical tests were whether the expert had the requisite expertise and understood his duty as an expert to the court, although his status might go to the weight to be accorded to his evidence.

Chapter 7

HUMAN RIGHTS AND PROFESSIONALS

	Para.		Para.
1. Introduction	7–001	(ii) Article 3	7–055
2. Relevant Convention Rights	7–003	(iii) Article 6	7–056
(a) Article 6	7–004	(iv) Article 8	7–059
(b) Article 8	7–013	(v) Article 9	7–061
(c) Article 10	7–014	(v)(a) Article 10	7–061A
(d) Article 11	7–018	(vi) Article 12	7–062
(e) Article 1 of Protocol No.1	7–021	7. Particular Issues Arising under the HRA in Relation to Medical Practitioners	7–063
3. Negligence and Duty of Care	7–026		
(a) Z v United Kingdom	7–028		
(b) Striking Out	7–029	(a) Clinical Negligence and the Bolam Test	7–063
(c) Switch from Article 6(1) to Article 13	7–030	(b) Right to Treatment	7–064
(d) Tort or Convention?	7–032	(c) Withdrawal of Treatment	7–069
(e) Claims not Governed by the HRA	7–034	(d) Consent to Treatment	7–073
		(e) Right of Access to Confidential Information	7–076
(f) Further Developments since Z.	7–035		
4. Immunities	7–037	(f) Disclosure of Confidential Information	7–079
5. Lawyers	7–040		
(a) Wasted Costs Orders	7–041	(g) Disclosure of Medical Records and Confidentiality	7–082
(b) Lawyer/Client Confidentiality and the Convention	7–042	(h) Patients' Complaints Procedures	7–086
(c) Freedom of Expression/Association	7–046	8. Professional Disciplinary Proceedings	7–087
6. Medical Practitioners	7–049		
(a) Introduction	7–049	(a) Introduction	7–087
(b) Relevant Articles in relation to Medical Practitioners	7–051	(b) Procedural Guarantees	7–091
		(c) Law Society Interventions and Investigations	7–102
(i) Article 2	7–052		

1. Introduction

Add to Note 1: In *Johnson v Havering London Borough Council; YL (by her litigation friend the Official Solicitor) (FC) v Birmingham City Council and others* [2007] UKHL 27; [2008] 1 A.C. 95; [2007] 3 W.L.R. 112; [2007] 3 All E.R. 957, the majority of the House of Lords held that a private care home providing accommodation and care to a resident pursuant to arrangements made with a local authority under ss.21 and 26 of the National Assistance Act 1948 was not performing "functions of a public nature" for the purpose of s.6(3)(b) HRA because, *inter alia*, the actual provision (as opposed to arrangement) of care and accommodation for those unable to arrange it themselves was not an inherently governmental function and the private and commercial motivation behind the care home's operations pointed against treating the care home as a person with a function of a public nature. Lord Bingham and Baroness Hale

7–001

7–001 CHAPTER 7—HUMAN RIGHTS AND PROFESSIONALS

powerfully dissented, holding that this was a function performed for the appellants pursuant to statutory arrangements, at public expense, and in the public interest and that the Court of Appeal had been wrong to reach a different conclusion in *R. (Heather) v Leonard Cheshire Foundation* [2002] 2 All E.R. 936.

2. RELEVANT CONVENTION RIGHTS

(a) *Article 6*

7–007 Add to NOTE 23: See *Hammerton v Hammerton* [2007] EWCA Civ 248; *The Times*, April 12, 2007, on the right to the additional guarantees for a criminal charge including the right to legal representation.

7–011 Add to NOTE 27: The European Court has recognised that the lack of neutrality of a court-appointed expert may in certain circumstances give rise to a breach of the principle of equality of arms inherent in the concept of a fair trial and also to the objective impartiality of the court or tribunal. Regard must be had in particular to the expert's procedural position and role in the relevant proceedings: *Eggertsdóttir v Iceland* Application No.31930/04, July 5, 2007, para.47.

7–013 Add new NOTE 27a after the first sentence following the Art.8 quote: The case-law of the European Court of Human Rights in interpreting Art.8 is comprehensively analysed in N.A. Moreham, "The Right to Respect for Private Life in the European Convention on Human Rights: a Re-examination" [2008] E.H.R.L.R. 44.

3. NEGLIGENCE AND DUTY OF CARE

(f) *Further Developments since Z*

7–035 Add: The distinction between substantive and procedural bars to proceedings is proving a problematic one. In *Henriques v Luxembourg* (Application No.60255/00, May 9, 2006; [2006] 5 E.H.R.L.R. 568, the European Court rejected an argument that a bar was procedural even though the right to sue had once existed and had been removed. The court found it was substantive by focusing solely on the domestic law at the relevant time, a time at which the right to sue no longer existed. As is argued by the editor of the Case Comment in the E.H.R.L.R. report of *Henriques*, such an approach appears to be blurring the distinction between substantive and procedural bars to access to court and if the court leans too far in favour of treating all bars as substantive ones, this could substantially reduce the protection afforded by Art.6.

7–036 Add: The approach in *D* was followed by the Court of Appeal in *Lawrence v Pembrokeshire County Council* [2007] EWCA Civ 446; [2007] 1 W.L.R. 2991 on similar facts where the issue was whether, as a result of the HRA, a local authority could owe a duty of care to a parent of a child when exercising, through social workers, its duties to protect children from their parents and whether the common law should recognise that such authorities owed a duty of care to parents when investigating or taking steps to protect children. The court dismissed the appeal against the striking out of the claim and stated that when the interests of parent and child were in conflict, Art.8 did not so enhance the status of family life as to require the development of the common law by the introduction of a duty of care. See also *B v Reading Borough Council, Wokingham Borough Council and Chief Constable of Thames Valley* [2007] EWCA Civ 1313; (2008) 1 F.L.R. 797 which again applied *D*. In *Chief Constable of Hertfordshire v Van Colle (Administrator of the Estate of GC, Deceased); Smith v Chief Constable of Sussex* [2008] UKHL 50; [2008] 3 W.L.R. 593; [2008] 3 All E.R. 977, the House of Lords applied the *Osman* test to an Art.2 claim under the HRA against the police but in respect of a common law claim re-affirmed the principle established in *Hill v Chief Constable of West Yorkshire* that police, in the absence of special circumstances, owe no common law duty of care to protect individuals against harm caused by criminals.

4. IMMUNITIES

Add: In *Awoyomi v Radford* [2007] EWHC 1671; [2007] P.N.L.R. 34; *The Times*, July 23, 2007, Lloyd Jones J. held that the abolition of advocates' immunity did have retrospective effect. He based this on an analysis of the *Arthur JS Hall v Simons* judgment and there was no reference to human rights arguments.

7–038

Add new NOTE 81A: For an article on whether absolute judicial immunity should survive and whether it is compatible with human rights and Art.6(1), see A. Nicol, "Judicial Immunity and Human Rights" [2006] 5 E.H.R.L.R. 558.

7–039

5. LAWYERS

(a) *Wasted Costs Orders*

Add: Assuming Art.6(1) applies, there may be issues of compatibility of the summary procedure for determination of wasted costs and the Art.6(1) requirement for an independent and impartial tribunal when determining a wasted costs application, particularly if such a determination is judge-initiated or relates to conduct in which the judge is a witness: see by analogy *Kyprianou v Cyprus* Application No.73797/01, December 15, 2005; (2007) 44 E.H.R.R. 27 which related to an allegation and summary determination of a contempt charge by the same tribunal before whom the issue arose. The European Court held that the confusion of roles between complainant, witness, prosecutor and judge meant that the impartiality of the court was capable of appearing open to doubt and that there had been a violation of Art.6(1) (paras 127–128).

7–041

7–042 CHAPTER 7—HUMAN RIGHTS AND PROFESSIONALS

(b) *Lawyer/Client Confidentiality and the Convention*

7–042   Add a NOTE 94a after the quote from *Campbell v United Kingdom*: The European Court has reaffirmed the importance of the principle of confidentiality of information exchanged between lawyers and clients as an important safeguard in the right to defence in *Castravet v Moldova* Application No.23393/05, June 13, 2007, paras [49]–[55]. The Court applied the test of whether an objective, fair-minded and informed observer would have grounds for believing that the exchange of information between lawyer and client was not confidential.

7–043   Add to NOTE 96: In *Smirnov v Russia* Application No.71362/01, June 7, 2007, the European Court further held that a search order in respect of a lawyer's place of residence in connection with a criminal investigation into various of his clients which was drafted in extremely broad terms and did not provide any safeguard against interference with "professional secrecy" was disproportionate to whatever legitimate aim was pursued. Accordingly, it violated Art.8. See also *Sallinen v Finland* Application No.50882/99, September 27, 2005; (2007) 44 E.H.R.R. 18, where the lack of clarity of domestic law which had given rise to different views on the extent of the protection afforded to privileged material meant that the search and seizure of privileged material relating the office of a lawyer who was suspected of aiding and abetting his clients who were under criminal investigation was not "in accordance with the law" and violated Art.8. In *Wieser and Bicos Beteiligungen GMBH v Austria* Application No.74336/01, October 16, 2007; (2008) 46 E.H.R.R. 54, the European Court found a violation of Art.8 where a police search of a lawyer's offices failed to comply with some of the procedural safeguards designed to prevent abuse or arbitrariness and to protect the lawyer's duty of professional secrecy.

(c) *Freedom of Expression/Association*

Add new paras **7–048A** and **7–048B**:

7–048A   In *Kyprianou v Cyprus* Application No.73797/01, December 15, 2005; (2007) 44 E.H.R.R. 27; [2006] 2 E.H.R.L.R. 220, the European Court found a violation of Art.10 in circumstances where a lawyer was found guilty of contempt and sentenced to five days' imprisonment following his objection to a judicial remark regarding the manner of his cross-examination which he found offensive and his refusal to proceed with the cross-examination. The court stated that the imposition of a disproportionately severe and immediate sentence of imprisonment where a lawyer, acting in the best interests of his client, objected or complained about the conduct of the court would result in lawyers feeling constrained in making such representations and have a chilling effect on the profession as a whole.

Add a NOTE 11a to the end of para.**7–048A**: See also *Foglia v Switzerland* Application No.35865/04, March 13, 2008, where the European Court found a breach of Art.10 where a lawyer had been disciplined with a fine for alleged unprofessional conduct in giving comments and access to trial documents to the press.

In *National Notary Chamber v Albania* Application No.17029/05, May 6, 2008; (2008) 47 E.H.R.R. SE11, the European Court dismissed a complaint that the compulsory requirement for membership by notaries of the National Notary Chamber, a body established by the legislature to exercise a form of public control over the practice of the notary profession, was contrary to Art.11. The Court held that Art.11 was inapplicable and compulsory membership did not infringe the right to freedom of association because the National Notary Chamber and district notary chambers were not "associations" within the meaning of the Article.

7–048B

6. MEDICAL PRACTITIONERS

(b) *Relevant Articles in relation to Medical Practitioners*

(i) *Article 2*

Add in (a) *Abortion*, after the discussion of *Vo v France*: The European Court again sought to sidestep the issue of dealing substantively with the issue of the compatibility of abortion and Convention rights in *D v Ireland* Application No.26499/02; (2006) 43 E.H.R.R. SE16. The applicant sought to complain to the ECHR about the lack of abortion services in Ireland in the case of lethal foetal abnormality, and in particular in respect of ss.5 and 8 of the Regulation of Information (Services outside the State for Termination of Pregnancies) Act 1995 which limited what a doctor could tell a pregnant woman with a lethal foetal abnormality and prohibited a doctor from making proper arrangements, or a full referral, for a therapeutic abortion abroad. At that time, the only recognised exception to the constitutional prohibition in Ireland on abortion was "a real and substantial risk to the life of the mother" including one of suicide (*Attorney General v X*, 1992). The applicant asserted that she had been discriminated against as a pregnant woman with a lethal foetal abnormality. However, the case was declared to be inadmissible by the court as a result of the applicant's failure to exhaust domestic remedies. The court relied on the *X* case as showing that the constitutional courts could develop the protection of individual rights by way of interpretation and emphasised the importance of providing those courts with the opportunity to do so. It stated that the presumption in the *X* case was that the foetus had a normal life expectancy and there was feasible argument to be made that the constitutionally enshrined balance between the right to life of the mother and of the foetus could have shifted in favour of the mother when the "unborn" suffered from an abnormality incompatible with life.

7–054

This decision can be contrasted with that reached by the court in *Tysiac v Poland* Application No.5410/03; [2007] E.H.R.L.R. 463; (2007) 45 E.H.R.R 42. The applicant in this case suffered from a pregnancy-related illness which resulted in a significant deterioration in her eyesight. Despite this, her treating doctors refused to certify that her pregnancy should be terminated on therapeutic grounds. The court held that there had been no breach of Art.3 but that there had been a breach of Art.8 given the failure of Polish law to provide an effective mechanism capable of determining whether the conditions for obtaining a lawful abortion had been met or for resolving disputes either between the woman and

7–054 CHAPTER 7—HUMAN RIGHTS AND PROFESSIONALS

the doctors or between the doctors themselves. Judge Borrego's strong dissenting opinion highlights the inconsistencies between this decision and that in *D v Ireland*.

Add in (e) *Inquests*, after the end of the first sentence: The European Court is also frequently asked to consider these issues, and Turkey, France, Poland, Ukraine and Luxembourg have all recently been found to have violated Art.2 as a result of failures in the State's investigative process. Of direct relevance to medical practitioners is the decision in *Byrzykowski v Poland* Application No.11562/05; [2006] E.H.R.L.R. 588; (2008) 46 E.H.R.R. 32. In this case the court held that there had been a violation of Art.2 in circumstances where a mother had died during childbirth but seven years later the criminal, disciplinary and civil investigations into her death had yet to be concluded (despite all such proceedings having been commenced reasonably soon after her death). While the State was found to have made adequate provision for securing high professional standards amongst health professionals, it was held that the obligations of the State under Art.2 would not be satisfied if the protection afforded by domestic law existed only in theory. Above all, the court emphasised that the relevant provisions must operate effectively in practice within a time frame such that the courts could complete their examination of the merits of each individual case. There was also stated to be a need for prompt consideration of cases concerning death in a hospital setting.

After the reference to *Commissioner of Police for the Metropolis v Christine Hurst* add the following: The Court of Appeal's attempt to retrospectively apply Art.2 through Art.3 has now been overruled by the House of Lords: see *R. (on the application of Hurst) v Commissioner of Police for the Metropolis* [2007] UKHL 13; [2007] 2 W.L.R. 726. The principles set out in *Re McKerr* therefore apply without qualification.

Add at the end: Following *Middleton*, the flurry of case law in respect of the interrelationship between the Convention and inquests has continued. See, for example:

Alessandro Pereira v Inner South London Coroner [2007] EWHC 1723 (Admin) in which it was held that a coroner has a discretion to adjourn an inquest at the request of the Director of Public Prosecutions where there were reasons not to accede to the request, and if he exercised that discretion rationally in light of all relevant matters including the State's duty under Art.2 of the European Convention on Human Rights, his decision could not be impugned by judicial review;

R. (on the application of Helen Cash) v HM Coroner for Northamptonshire & Chief Constable of Northamptonshire [2007] EWHC 1354 (Admin) in which the failure by a jury to determine whether or not force used by police officers on the deceased had been justified, combined with the coroner's decision not to include a verdict of unlawful killing was held to be fatal to the inquest's legitimacy given the provisions of Art.2;

R. (on the application of Yvonne Scholes) v Secretary of State for the Home Department (2006) H.R.L.R. 44 in which the UK's duty to investigate a suicide at a young offender's institution had been held to have been discharged despite a full public inquiry not having been held;

R. (on the application of JL) v Secretary of State for the Home Department [2006] EWHC 2558 in which the Administrative Court stated that whilst it would not be appropriate to propound a general test aimed at identifying the circumstances in which the State should conduct an investigation into a death in custody, the simple fact of an unexpected death or life-threatening injury in custody would usually cross the threshold of circumstances requiring an investigation sufficient to satisfy the State's obligations under Art.2. This decision has now been upheld by the Court of Appeal (at [2007] EWCA Civ 767) in which it was emphasised that a death or serious injury in custody gave rise to an obligation to carry out an enhanced investigation. The extent of the investigation would depend on the facts of the case, but the state was accountable in the sense of having to explain how the death in custody occurred (and the burden being on them to do so);

R (L (A Patient) (by the Official Solicitor as a litigation friend)) v Secretary of State for the Home Department [2008] 1 W.L.R. 158 in which the Court of Appeal again emphasised this duty. The Court of Appeal stated that where a person died or was seriously injured while in state custody, the State was not only accountable for a substantive breach of Art.2 duty but was also required to investigate the facts and explain how the death or the serious injury had occurred. Therefore the mere fact of such death or serious injury gave rise to an obligation on the State to commence an investigation by a person independent of those implicated in the facts. In these circumstances, the internal inquiry held by the prison service was held to lack the required degree of independence.

The above decisions can be contrasted with the attitude adopted in Scotland. See in particular:

Alice Emms, Petitioner (2008) 99 B.M.L.R. 116 in which Lady Smith held that there was no obligation in Scotland to hold a judicial inquiry into a hospital death, even if it raised a question of public interest, where there was no reasonable possibility of the death having been caused by breach of criminal or civil law or of relevant disciplinary rules. She stated that to hold otherwise would be to impose an enormous burden on the State, in the absence of any concern that the domestic laws, which were designed to protect life, had not been observed.

Rosaleen Kennedy v Lord Advocate [2008] CSOH 21 in which Lord Mackay held that the Lord Advocate was not obliged to order fatal accident inquiries into the circumstances of deaths following infection with Hepatitis C received during the course of receiving blood products and blood transfusions unless and until the conclusion had been reached that the statutory criteria set out in the Fatal Accidents and Sudden Deaths Inquiry (Scotland) Act 1976 had been met.

Add a new sub-heading: *(f) Duty of care in relation to patients detained under the Mental Health Act*: In *Savage v South Essex Partnership NHS Foundation*

7–054

Trust (2007) L.S. Law Medical 291 the daughter of a patient who had been detained under the Mental Health Act 1983 for paranoid schizophrenia on an open acute psychiatric ward and who had committed suicide by jumping in front of a train, sought to bring a claim against the NHS trust pursuant to Arts 2 and/or 8 of the Convention. The court held at first instance that the correct test for such a claim under Art.2 was whether or not there was gross negligence on the part of the hospital staff treating the detained patient (which duty was not significantly altered or added to by the provisions of Art.8). The proposed claim was therefore struck out as it was common ground that the failures and inadequacies in the deceased's treatment were not sufficient to constitute gross negligence. However, the Court of Appeal has now overturned these findings: see [2007] EWCA Civ 1375. Applying *Osman*, the Court of Appeal emphasised that it was not necessary for the claimant to establish gross negligence or something more serious. In order to establish a breach of Art.2, on the assumed facts, the claimant had to show that the material time the defendant knew or ought to have known of the existence of a real and immediate risk to life of the deceased from self-harm and failed to take measures within the scope of its powers which, judged reasonably, might have been expected to avoid that risk.

See also *A K v (1) Central & North West London Mental Health NHS Trust (2) Kensington & Chelsea London Royal Borough Council* [2008] EWHC 1217 in which a claim was sought to be made against a health trust and a local authority in respect of the death of a schizophrenic man who had jumped from a second-storey window while living in bed and breakfast accommodation. King J. held that the Master had been correct to strike out a claim based on Art.2 but wrong to strike out claims based on Arts 3 and 8 as it could not be said that such claims were bound to fail and they should therefore be allowed to be fully argued at trial.

(ii) *Article 3*

7–055   Add: See also *R. (on the application of H) v Mental Health Review Tribunal* [2007] EWHC 884 (Admin) in which a condition imposed on an individual subject to a conditional discharge under the Mental Health Act that he "shall comply" with medication prescribed by a doctor was held not to amount to a compulsion that interfered with his right of absolute choice as to whether or not to accept or refuse medical treatment.

(iii) *Article 6*

7–058   Add: By contrast, in *R. (on the application of Andrew Jones) v Legal Services Commission* [2007] EWHC 2106 the approach of the Legal Services Commission in refusing a request for funding of legal representation at an inquest under the Access to Justice Act 1999 was held to not be irrational since there were no exceptional circumstances to justify such funding.

(iv) *Article 8*

7–060   The decision in *Evans v United Kingdom* has now been considered by the Grand Chamber at (2008) 46 E.H.R.R. 34 which upheld the previous ruling.

Add a new sub-paragraph (i): In *Dickson v UK* Application No.44362/04 (2007) 44 E.H.R.R. 21; (2008) 46 E.H.R.R. 41 the European Court held that there had been no violation of Arts 8 or 12 where the Secretary of State had refused a couple's request for access to artificial insemination facilities to enable them to have a child. The husband had been convicted of murder in 1994 and sentenced to life imprisonment with a 15-year tariff. Thereafter he had met his wife in 1999 while she was also imprisoned. The couple argued that without artificial insemination it would not otherwise be possible for them to have a child, given the husband's earliest release date and his wife's age. The court held that the Secretary of State had given careful consideration to the couple's circumstances, including the unlikely event of their being able to conceive after the husband's release from prison, before concluding that those factors were outweighed by other factors and in particular the gravity of the husband's crime, the welfare of any child who might be conceived in light of the absence of its father for prolonged periods of its childhood and the apparent lack of sufficient provision and immediate support network in place for mother and child. In these circumstances, the majority of the court held that it had not been shown that the decision to refuse facilities for artificial insemination was arbitrary or unreasonable or that it failed to strike a fair balance between the general interest of the community and the interests of the individual. However in their joint dissenting opinion, Judges Casadevall and Garlicki rejected the majority's acceptance of the "maintenance of public confidence in the penal system" argument and objected to what they described as the "paternalistic" reasons for the Secretary of State's policy, stating that "it is not for the State to decide who may have children and when". A similar dissenting opinion was expressed by Judge Borrego.

Add a new sub-paragraph (j): In *Johnson v Havering London Borough Council; YL (by her litigation friend the Official Solicitor) (FC) v Birmingham City Council* [2007] UKHL 27; [2007] 3 W.L.R. 112; [2007] 3 All E.R. 957 the House of Lords held that a privately owned care home was not performing functions of a public nature within the meaning of s.6(3)(b) of the Human Rights Act 1998 and therefore was not a public authority obliged to act compatibly with Convention rights. In these circumstances the applicability of Art.8 to decisions taken by the home was not able to be considered.

Add a new subparagraph (k): In *T (by her litigation friend the Official Solicitor) v British Broadcasting Corp* [2007] EWHC 1683 the Art.8 rights of a vulnerable mother who was the subject of a television programme about adoption were held to have been infringed by the programme and an injunction was granted to prevent her identification in the broadcast. The mother's Art.8 rights were said to outweigh the broadcaster's Art.10 right to freedom of expression and the public interest could be satisfied without identification of mother or child.

Add new heading and para.**7–061A**:

(v)(a) *Article 10*

Art.10(h) (access to specific educational information to help to ensure the health and well-being of families, including information and advice on family

7–061A   CHAPTER 7—HUMAN RIGHTS AND PROFESSIONALS

planning) was recently successfully invoked against Hungary by a woman who asserted she had been subjected to coerced sterilisation by medical staff at a Hungarian hospital: see *A.S. v Hungary* (2007) 45 E.H.R.R. SE1. It was emphasised by the Committee on the Elimination of Discrimination against Women that there was a right protected by Art.10(h) of the Convention to specific information on sterilisation and alternative procedures for family planning in order to guard against such intervention being carried out without her having made a fully informed choice.

7. PARTICULAR ISSUES ARISING UNDER THE HRA IN RELATION TO MEDICAL PRACTITIONERS

(b) *Right to Treatment*

7–067   Add: For an example of where the right to refuse artificial insemination was found to be justified, see *Dickson v UK* Application No.44362/04; [2006] E.H.R.L.R. 488, at para.**7–060** above.

(c) *Withdrawal of Treatment*

7–071   After the reference to the *Burke* decision, add a new NOTE 80A: For a detailed commentary on this case and related issues, see Catherine Dupre's article *Human Dignity and the Withdrawal of Medical Treatment: A Missed Opportunity* [2006] E.H.R.L.R. 678.

Add at the end: In *A Hospital v SW (represented by the Official Solicitor as litigation friend) & A PCT (Interested Party)* (2007) L.S. Law Medical 273 the principles set out in *NHS Trust A v M* were applied and the legality of discontinuing life-sustaining medical treatment for a patient in a persistent vegetative state and lack of any breach of Arts 2 or 3 in such circumstances confirmed.

(f) *Disclosure of Confidential Information*

7–081   Add: In *Mersey Care NHS Trust v Robin Ackroyd* (2007) H.R.L.R. 19 the Court of Appeal held that although an order against a newspaper for disclosure of a source, who had supplied confidential information in relation to a patient, had been made in earlier proceedings that resulted in the disclosure of the name of a journalist, a judge in later proceedings against the journalist for disclosure of the source's name had been entitled to refuse to order disclosure because his findings were based on different facts due to new evidence and the passage of time. See also *Brent London Borough Council v SK* [2007] EWHC 1250 in which a local authority was permitted to disclose to another local authority and a care home that a care worker looking after vulnerable adults had been found by the

PARTICULAR ISSUES 7–085

court to have carried out an assault on a child, as there was a real risk of harm to vulnerable adults if disclosure was not ordered.

(g) *Disclosure of Medical Records and Confidentiality*

Add: In *Wakefield v (1) Channel Four Television Corp (2) Twenty Twenty Productions Ltd (3) Brian Deer* (2007) 94 B.M.L.R. 1, the applicant broadcasters applied to inspect confidential documents in the hands of the respondent gastro-enterologist that had been served upon him by the General Medical Council in the course of preparation for disciplinary proceedings against him. The GMC sought to prevent such documents being disclosed on the grounds that documents obtained under compulsory powers should be used only for the purposes intended and disclosure should not interfere with the operations of public investigative bodies. However, the court held that any assurances of confidentiality of medical records given to patients by the GMC when it was investigating serious criticisms of a doctor could not be regarded as absolute, since such assurances might be subject to overriding requirement that other considerations be given priority, the determinative factor being where the interests of justice lay. The documents were therefore required to be disclosed where the broadcasters required them in order to defend themselves against defamation proceedings. See also *Paul Sayers v Smithkline Beecham* [2007] EWHC 1346 in which it was held to be appropriate in the public interest and the interests of justice to grant the Secretary of the Department of Health and Human Services of the United States of America permission under CPR r.5.4C(2) to obtain from the court records copies of expert reports filed by the defendants in the MMR/MR vaccine litigation so as to use those documents in analogous litigation in the United States, providing that those reports were redacted so as to prevent the persons from whom medical specimens had been taken from being identified. 7–085

Contrast the above decisions with the more restrictive approach taken in:

(a) *Bluck v Information Commissioner* (2007) 98 BMLR 1 in which it was doubted, *obiter*, that Art.8 should be translated into a specific form of prohibition to which s.44 of the Freedom of Information Act 2000 should be applied. The view of the Information Tribunal was that if a person was to be prohibited from taking a particular step he must be able to establish clearly whether or not his proposed actions fall within the scope of the prohibition. The language of Art.8 was not thought to be capable of providing the required degree of certainty.

(b) *Clive Roberts v Nottinghamshire Healthcare NHS Trust* [2008] EWHC 1934 in which Cranston J. refused to provide full disclosure of a psychology report to a patient at a high security psychiatric hospital who was suffering from mental illness. It was held that there were clear and compelling reasons based on cogent evidence to support the decision not to disclose: no injustice had been caused to the patient as the Trust did not intend to rely on the report at the hearing and in any event the patient had had a fair opportunity of presenting his own psychological evidence. The court emphasised that a party's right to fair trial under Art.6 of the

7–085

Convention did not mean that he had an absolute or unqualified right to see every document.

8. Professional Disciplinary Proceedings

(a) *Introduction*

7–087 Add to Note 11: In *Haarvig v Norway* Application No.11187/05, December 11, 2007; (2008) 46 E.H.R.R. SE12, the European Court declined to find that proceedings withdrawing the applicant's licence to practise medicine for a period of ten and a half months following his conviction for various offences unrelated to his occupation amounted to a "criminal" matter for the purposes of Art. 4 of Protocol No.7 to the Convention.

7–090 Add: The first instance decision in *R. (on the application of Malik) v Waltham Forest NHS Primary Care Trust* was overturned on appeal: [2007] EWCA Civ 265; [2007] 1 W.L.R. 2092. The Court of Appeal stated that the judge had erred in holding that the personal right of a person to practise in the NHS that flowed from his inclusion in the performers' list was a "possession" within the meaning of Art.1 of Protocol No.1 and held that a person's livelihood in the sense of a future right to income, unless based on loss of some professional or business goodwill or other present legal entitlement, could not amount to a possession that attracted the protection of Art.1 of Protocol No.1 (applying *R. (on the application of the Countryside Alliance) v Attorney General* [2006] EWCA Civ 817; [2007] Q.B. 305).

In South Africa, s.22 of the Constitution provides for a right to choose and a right to practise in a chosen profession, but this does not exclude the regulation of the practice of the profession provided it is rationally connected to the achievement of a legitimate purpose and does not infringe any other constitutional provision: *The Affordable Medicines Trust v Minister of Health & Director-General of Health*, High Court, Ngcobo J., March 11, 2005, reported in summary at [2006] 5 C.H.R.L.D. 516.

(b) *Procedural Guarantees*

7–091 Add to list: (vii) conduct of proceedings

7–094 Add at end of paragraph: In *R. (on the application of Sarah Johnson and Lynette Maggs v Professional Conduct Committee of the Nursing & Midwifery Council* [2008] EWHC 885 (Admin), Beatson J. held that while Art.6(1) was applicable to disciplinary bodies, the issue of whether facilities for preparing a defence were adequate was fact-specific and there was no freestanding positive duty on those who brought disciplinary proceedings to gather evidence in favour of those accused of misconduct who had not been at a disadvantage in obtaining the relevant documents themselves.

7–095 Add after discussion of *Bakker v Austria*: In *Hurter v Switzerland* Application No.53146/99, December 15, 2005; (2007) 44 E.H.R.R. 201, the European Court

PROFESSIONAL DISCIPLINARY PROCEEDINGS   7–099A

again held that there was a violation of Art.6(1) where the applicant, who was a lawyer, had been disciplined for charging excessive fees and other unprofessional actions and the matter was dealt with by way of written submissions and his request for a public hearing was rejected both by the disciplinary tribunal and the appeal court.

Add after first paragraph: In *L v Law Society* [2008] EWCA Civ 811, the Court of Appeal held that an appeal against a decision by the Law Society to cancel the enrolment of a student member was to be heard in public notwithstanding L's application for it to be heard in private. The fact that the hearing would involve the consideration of the student's spent convictions did not amount to exceptional circumstances requiring a hearing in private and did not infringe L's rights under Art.6 because, while it might have an adverse effect on the work he did, that would not amount to a loss of livelihood.

Add after discussion of *Das v General Medical Council*: A similar approach was taken in *DV v General Medical Council* [2007] EWHC 1497 (Admin); (2007) LS Law Medical 603 in which Bennett J. held that a Fitness to Practise Panel was entitled to conduct the hearing of professional misconduct charges against a doctor in his absence. The doctor concerned had known of the dates of the hearing for many months and had no reason not to attend. By not attending or instructing a representative to attend on his behalf, he had chosen not to exercise his right to defend himself under Art.6(3)(c) and had thereby waived it.

Add after reference to *General Medical Council v Pembrey*: The Court of Appeal gave guidance on the approach that the court should take to an application to extend an interim suspension order in *General Medical Council v Hiew* [2007] EWCA Civ 369; [2007] 1 W.L.R. 2007.   7–098

Add at end of paragraph: In *Selvarajan v General Medical Council* [2008] EWHC 182 (Admin); (2008) LS Law Medical 193 Blake J. held that a delay in bringing proceedings against a doctor for misconduct was relevant to mitigation of the sanction to be imposed and that a panel of the General Medical Council had misdirected itself in finding otherwise. A challenge to the fairness of disciplinary proceedings based on Art.6 where the notice of inquiry had not necessarily been served "as soon as may be" as required by the General Medical Council procedural rules failed in *Williams v General Medical Council* [2007] EWHC 2603 (Admin); (2008) 99 B.M.L.R. 59.

Add NOTE 62a at end of paragraph: It might be noted, by way of analogy, that the Court of Appeal declined to find that Art.2 required the provision of funding for an interested party to have full legal representation at an inquest: *R. (on the application of Tobias Main) v Minister for Legal Aid* [2007] EWCA Civ 1147; (2008) H.R.L.R. 8; (2008) U.K.H.R.R. 52; (2008) 99 B.M.L.R. 34.   7–099

Add new paragraph **7–099A**:

Art.6 is not in issue when considering the judgments exercised by advocates and accordingly, an advocate's failure to make a coherent application for a stay   7–099A

[35]

7–099A CHAPTER 7—HUMAN RIGHTS AND PROFESSIONALS

of proceedings at a disciplinary hearing of the General Medical Council did not provide a basis for a successful appeal: *R. (on the application of Shyam Sinha) v General Medical Council* [2008] EWHC 1732 (Admin).

7–100 Add at end of paragraph: In *R. (Wright) v Secretary of State for Health* [2007] EWCA Civ 999; [2008] Q.B. 422, the Court of Appeal held that Art.6 was engaged where care workers were provisionally included in a list of persons precluded from working with vulnerable adults and further that Art.6(1) was breached where there was a denial of a right to make representations before inclusion on such a list. That denial was not made good by the fact that there was an opportunity to seek to persuade the Secretary of State to remove the worker from the list or to seek judicial review of or appeal the decision.

Add new paragraph **7–100A**:

7–100A **Conduct of proceedings.** It is not a breach of Art.6(1) for a professional disciplinary body to withdraw a complaint in circumstances where there was no longer a prima facie case of misconduct: *Diamond v Mansfield* [2006] EWHC 3290.

Chapter 8

PROFESSIONAL INDEMNITY INSURANCE

	Para.		Para.
1. Introduction	8–001	9. Classification of Terms/Consequences of Breach	8–060
2. Regulatory Requirements	8–002	(a) Warranties	8–061
(a) Insurance Brokers	8–003	(b) Conditions Precedent to Cover	8–068
(b) Surveyors	8–004	(c) Condition Precedent to Liability	8–069
(c) Architects	8–007	(d) Collateral Promise and Innominate Terms	8–071
(d) Accountants	8–008	10. The Continuing Duty of Utmost Good Faith and the Rule Against Fraudulent Claims	8–072
(e) Solicitors	8–011	11. Policy Response to the Insured's Liability for Fraud or Illegality	8–076
(f) Barristers	8–016	12. Claims Notification & Co-operation Clauses	8–080
3. The Nature/Scope of Professional Indemnity Insurance	8–017	(a) Generally	8–080
4. Policy Trigger—Claims Made/Circumstances Notified	8–026	(b) Solicitors	8–087
5. Composite and Joint Policies	8–030	(c) Accountants	8–088
6. Contract Formation in the Lloyd's and Companies' Markets	8–031	13. Q.C. Clauses	8–090
(a) Generally	8–031	14. Deductibles and Limits of Indemnity; Aggregation of Claims	8–094
(b) Leading Underwriter Clauses	8–037	(a) Generally	8–094
7. The Pre-contractual Duty of Utmost Good Faith	8–039	(b) Solicitors	8–102
(a) The Duty	8–039	15. Limitation	8–103
(b) The Scope of the Duty	8–044	16. Third Party Rights	8–105
(c) Avoidance	8–047		
8. Rules of Construction	8–054		
(a) Generally	8–054		
(b) Exclusion Clauses and Insuring Clauses	8–058		

2. Regulatory Requirements

(e) *Solicitors*

8–011 Add: From September 1, 2007 SIF also started to provide extended run-off cover for firms which ceased to practise on or after September 1, 2000 without a successor practice, following the completion of the six-year run-off period provided by their qualifying insurance.

3. The Nature/Scope of Professional Indemnity Insurance

8–017 Add: Conversely, should the policy be worded so as to provide an indemnity against "legal liability for damages..." then it is likely to respond only to liability for compensatory damages and will not extend to cover liabilities

8-017 CHAPTER 8—PROFESSIONAL INDEMNITY INSURANCE

imposed by statute or regulatory process.[27a] Furthermore, it is possible that a policy which is not expressly limited to tortious liability and which even contains an extension in respect of liability assumed under a contract or agreement may nevertheless be construed as providing an indemnity only where the Insured either is or would have been liable in tort.[27b]

8-019 Add: This is so even where (in abstract at least) the Insured would or might have come under a legal liability to a third party if it had not incurred such expense.[36a]

8-020 Add: In *AIG Europe (Ireland) Ltd v Faraday Capital Ltd* [2007] Lloyd's Rep. I.R. 267 at [68]–[71], Morison J. sided, *obiter*, with the approach of Aikens J. in *Enterprise Oil*.

8-024 Revise NOTE 48 to read: *Commercial Union v NRG Victory Re* [1998] 2 Lloyd's Rep. 600 (this was a reinsurance case, and there has been some uncertainty as to the extent to which contracts of reinsurance are to be equated to liability policies, although Longmore L.J.'s reasoning in *Wasa International Insurance Co v Lexington Insurance Co* [2008] EWCA Civ 150 at [34] provides strong support for the view that the two are analogous); *MDIS v Swinbank* [1999] Lloyd's Rep. I.R. 516; *Enterprise Oil v Strand Insurance* [2006] 1 Lloyd's Rep. 500 at [74]–[82].

Add new NOTE 48a at end of paragraph: See *Thornton Springer v NEM Insurance* [2000] Lloyd's Rep. I.R. 590 (a case concerning the ICAEW minimum wording) at [47]–[48] *per* Colman J.

4. POLICY TRIGGER: CLAIMS MADE/CIRCUMSTANCES NOTIFIED

8-027 Add: The deeming provision ordinarily follows a term prescribing when and how notification of a "circumstance" should be made, and typically starts with the words "Such notice having been given . . . ". In *Diab v Regent Insurance Co Ltd (Belize)* [2006] Lloyd's Rep. I.R. 779, the Privy Council contemplated[53a] that stipulations as to the form of the notice within a condition precedent might be directory rather than mandatory. However, in *HLB Kidsons v Lloyd's Underwriters* [2008] EWCA Civ 1206, the Court of Appeal[53b] held that the words "such notice" had the effect of elevating the stipulated requirements as to the giving of notice to the status of a condition precedent to the operation of the deeming provision—in particular, the stipulation as to the timing of the notice could not be divorced from the requirement that the notice be in writing so

---

[27a] *Bartoline v Royal & Sun Alliance* [2007] Lloyd's Rep. I.R. 423 at [105]–[117].
[27b] *Tesco Stores Limited v David Constable and others* [2008] Lloyd's Rep. I.R. 302 *per* Field J. at [26]–[34], [37]–[38]; [2008] Lloyd's Rep. I.R. Plus 25 at [18]–[27] *per* Tuckey L.J.
[36a] *Bartoline* (supra) at [130]–[132].
[53a] At [15]–[16].
[53b] Upholding the decision of Gloster J. at [2008] Lloyd's Rep. I.R. 237 at [30], [67].

POLICY TRIGGER: CLAIMS MADE/CIRCUMSTANCES NOTIFIED   8–077

that both requirements had to be satisfied before the insured could bring itself within the extension.[53c]

7. THE PRE-CONTRACTUAL DUTY OF UTMOST GOOD FAITH

(b) *The Scope of the Duty*

Add to NOTE 84: See also *Zeller v British Caymanian Insurance Company Ltd* [2008] UKPC 4 at [18]–[22].   8–044

Add to NOTE 93: In *Doheny*, Potter L.J. indicated, at [37], that the appropriate test was whether a reasonable man reading the proposal form would be justified in thinking that the insurer had consented to the non-disclosure of the fact in question. In *Noblebright Ltd v Sirius International Corporation* [2007] Lloyd's Rep. I.R. 584 at [54], H.H. Judge Hegarty Q.C. applied Potter L.J.'s formulation of the test in rejecting the insured's plea of waiver.   8–046

9. CLASSIFICATION OF TERMS; CONSEQUENCES OF BREACH

(c) *Condition Precedent to Liability*

Add new para.**8–070A**:

In *Kosmar Villa Holidays plc v Trustees of Syndicate 1234* [2008] Lloyd's Rep. I.R. 43, however, Gross J. held[49a] that breach of such a condition gave rise to a right of election which could therefore be waived unilaterally. The Court of Appeal, however, overturned Gross J.'s decision, holding ([2008] Lloyd's Rep. I.R. 489[49b]) that breach of a condition precedent operated automatically (in a manner equivalent to a breach of warranty[49c]) to discharge Insurers from liability, so that breach could only be waived by equitable estoppel.[49d]

11. POLICY RESPONSE TO THE INSURED'S LIABILITY FOR FRAUD OR ILLEGALITY

Add: An act which falls short of subjective recklessness on the part of the Insured should not be characterised as wilful.[69a]   8–077

Add to NOTE 69: See also *The Board of Trustees of the Tate Gallery v Duffy Construction Ltd* [2008] Lloyd's Rep. I.R. 159 at [26].

[53c] See [114] *per* Rix L.J.
[49a] At [65]–[74].
[49b] At [65]–[70] *per* Rix L.J.
[49c] See para.**8–065** above.
[49d] At [43], the Court of Appeal disapproved comments in *Bolton MBC v Municipal Mutual Insurance Ltd* [2006] 1 W.L.R. 1492 at [27]–[34] where Longmore L.J. had assumed (obiter and without reference to *The Good Luck* or *HIH v Axa*) that breach of a condition precedent gave rise to a right of election.
[69a] *CA Blackwell (Contracts) Ltd v Gerling General Ins Co* [2007] Lloyd's Rep. I.R. 511 at [49]–[52].

8–078 Add: However, this approach was rejected by the Court of Appeal in *KR v Royal & Sun Alliance* [2007] Lloyd's Rep. I.R. 368, which held[71a] that where the perpetrator "is to be regarded as, in effect the Company" then a policy exception in respect of the deliberate acts of the Insured would be triggered.[71b]

8–079 Add new NOTE 71c at end of penultimate sentence: Although cl.6.9 of the Law Society's Contract of Assigned Risks Pool Insurance will exclude cover where the Insured has condoned the dishonesty of the perpetrator—for the purposes of the exclusion it matters not whether the specific act or omission has been condoned if (at the very least) general and persistent dishonesty has been condoned: see *Zurich Professional Limited v Karim* [2006] EWHC 3355 (QBD) at [103]–[109]. It is suggested that the facts in this case would have been sufficient to establish wilful conduct on the part of the relevant Insureds, so that they would not have been entitled to any indemnity in any event—see para.**8–076** above—so that whether the subordinate clauses to cl.6.9 were conjunctive or disjunctive should not have affected the overall outcome.

12. CLAIMS NOTIFICATION & CO-OPERATION CLAUSES

(a) *Generally*

8–080 Add end of paragraph: In the absence of any express contractual provision on point, there is no inflexible rule that a notification can only be communicated to the claims side of Insurers.[72a]

8–081A In *Kajima UK Engineering Ltd v The Underwriter Insurance Co* [2008] Lloyd's Rep. I.R. 391 Akenhead J. held[74a] that a notification should be construed as relating only to matters of which the insured was aware at the time of notification. In similar vein, in *HLB Kidsons v Lloyd's Underwriters* [2008] EWCA Civ 1206, Insurers contended that a notification was to be circumscribed by reference to the Insured's actual belief at the time in relation to the merits of concerns expressed by an employee. This approach was rejected by the Court of Appeal: while an unreasoned and internalised concern did not amount to "awareness" of a circumstance,[74b] the expression of concern by another person[74c] of which the Insured was aware could itself amount to a circumstance which was sufficient to trigger an entitlement or obligation to notify.[74d] *Obiter*, Toulson L.J.

[71a] At [65]. The Court of Appeal took into account the well-known dictum of Lord Atkin in *Beresford v Royal Insurance Co Ltd* [1938] AC 586, 595 set out in para.**8–076**.

[71b] It is implicit in the Court of Appeal's reasoning that the policy would not have responded, even if the exception had been absent, for the reasons given by Lord Atkin in the *Beresford* case.

[72a] See *HLB Kidsons v Lloyd's Underwriters* [2008] EWCA Civ 1206 at [18]; *Friends Provident v Sirius* [2005] 1 Lloyd's Rep. I.R. 45 at [135].

[74a] See [99]–[111].

[74b] See [73].

[74c] Including an employee.

[74d] See [78].

also recognised[74e] that the making of a notification involved questions of judgment on which there might be a range of opinion. Where there is an obligation to notify circumstances, it is limited to those circumstances which are either notified or which a reasonable person in the insured's position would recognise as something which might give rise to a claim.[74f]

Add to NOTE 74: See also *CGU Insurance v Porthouse* [2008] HCA 30 at [75].   **8–082**

Add to end: *HLB Kidsons*, the Court of Appeal also confirmed that a notification was generally to be construed objectively,[75a] although the possibility that intention might be taken into account in exceptional cases (for example, where there was a conscious attempt to mislead underwriters) was left open.[75b] However, no real guidance was given as to when or on what reasoned basis a notification might be "invalidated" by any subjective design on the part of the insured: any argument that a notification should be treated as invalid may, in truth, be hard to distinguish from an argument that the Insured is in breach of the post-contractual duty of good faith, in which case any remedy must probably be found within the terms of the contract itself.[75c]

Add to NOTE 77: *HLB Kidsons v Lloyd's Underwriters* [2008] EWCA Civ 1206 at [91], [144].   **8–084**

Add to NOTE 78: Even if a specific circumstance has not been notified prior to inception (as part of the placing process) and expressly excluded, professional indemnity policies will typically exclude liability for any claim arising out of facts known to the insured prior to inception the awareness of which would cause a reasonable person to believe that such facts *could* give rise to a claim—the High Court of Australia has held that such an exclusion is wide in its effect, since it imposes "an objective standard, and [involves] a question of fact to be determined independently of the insured's state of mind": see *CGU Insurance v Porthouse* [2008] HCA 30 at [75].   **8–085**

Add to end of paragraph: In *HLB Kidsons v Lloyd's Underwriters* [2008] EWCA Civ 1206, the Court of Appeal disapproved a more rigorous approach to the question of when a circumstance had been notified effectively which had been adopted by Gloster J. at first instance.[79a] Rix L.J. observed that the authorities did not seem to demand great specificity, and effectively rejected the suggestion (which had been accepted at first instance) that the principles governing the giving of contractual notices set out in *Mannai Investment Co Ltd v Eagle Star Life Assurance Co Ltd* [1999] A.C. 749 should be applied.[79b]

[74e] At [138–41].
[74f] See [142]. This approach is consistent with that of the High Court of Australia in *CGU Insurance v Porthouse* [2008] HCA 30 at [75].
[75a] See [65].
[75b] See [64], [147].
[75c] See *The Mercandian Continent* [2001] Lloyd's Rep. I.R. 802 at [40].
[79a] See [2008] Lloyd's Rep. I.R. 237 at [70]–[79].
[79b] [2008] EWCA Civ 1206 at [86–7].

8–101A   CHAPTER 8—PROFESSIONAL INDEMNITY INSURANCE

14. DEDUCTIBLES AND LIMITS OF INDEMNITY; AGGREGATION OF CLAIMS

(a) *Generally*

Add new paragraphs **8–101A** and **8–101B**:

8–101A   In *Standard Life Assurance v Oak Dedicated Ltd* [2008] EWHC 222 (Comm), the policy deductible was expressed as being £25 million "each and every claim and/or claimant". The policy also provided that:

> "each Claim or series of Claims (whether by one or more than one Claimant) arising from or in connection with or attributable to any one act, error, omission or originating cause or source or dishonesty of any one person or group of persons acting together and any such series of Claims shall be deemed to be one Claim for all purposes under this Policy."

8–101B   Standard Life incurred endowment mis-selling liabilities exceeding £100 million in the aggregate to some 97,000 individual claimants. Insurers contended that the presence of the words "and/or claimant" within the definition of the policy deductible meant that, for the purposes of determining the applicable deductible, claims by one claimant could not be aggregated with claims by any other.[1a] Tomlinson J. acknowledged the force of Standard Life's submissions that a deductible of £25 million did not "wear the air of a per claimant deductible" and concluded that "No properly informed market professional would have regarded it as appropriate to introduce a per claimant deductible which applied across the board, as opposed to one targeted at a specific category of claim". He nevertheless concluded that the only tenable construction of the clause was that it prevented the aggregation of related claims by different claimants.[1b]

16. THIRD-PARTY RIGHTS

8–106   Add after penultimate sentence: In *Law Society v Shah* [2007] EWHC 2841 (Ch), Floyd J. held[11a] that a third party claim against a bankrupt is to be treated as "established" once it is admitted in the insured's bankruptcy; thereafter a claim can be maintained under the 1930 Act even where the insured is discharged from bankruptcy.

[1a] They also denied that Standard Life's liabilities could be attributed to any single aggregating cause or source of the claims. That aspect of the case was not encompassed within the preliminary issues determined by Tomlinson J.

[1b] See particularly [98]–[100] of Tomlinson J.'s judgment.

[11a] See [44]–[49].

CHAPTER 9

CONSTRUCTION PROFESSIONALS

	Para.
1. Introduction	9–001
(a) The Construction Professions	9–001
(b) Claims against Construction Professionals	9–007
(c) Forms of Building Contract	9–010
(i) The "Traditional" Building Contract	9–011
(ii) The "Design and Build" or "Turnkey" Contract	9–014
(iii) Management Contracts	9–016
2. Duties	9–017
(a) Duties to Client	9–017
(i) Contractual Duties	9–017
(ii) Duties Independent of Contract	9–039
(b) Duties to Third Parties	9–060
(i) The Definition of the Type of Loss	9–066
(ii) Recovery by Third Parties in respect of Personal Injury and Damage to "Other Property"	9–073
(iii) The General Exclusionary Rule adopted in England with regard to the Recovery of Economic Loss	9–082
(iv) The English Exceptions to the General Exclusionary Rule	9–086
(v) The Position in Other Jurisdictions	9–112
(vi) Problems of Scope of Duty	9–118
(c) Other Torts	9–125
(d) The Standard of Care and Skill	9–126
(i) The Ordinary Competent and Skilled Practitioner	9–126
(ii) General Practice and Knowledge as Evidence of the Standard	9–137
(iii) Expert Evidence	9–144
(iv) *Res Ipsa Loquitur*	9–150
(v) Codes of Practice and Legislation	9–152
(vi) Knowledge of the Law	9–156
(vii) Not Every Error is Negligence	9–160

	Para.
(viii) The Specialist Practitioner	9–163
(ix) Special Steps and Warranty of Reasonable Fitness	9–165
(x) Reliance upon Specialists and Delegation to them	9–172
3. Liability for Breach of Duty	9–177
(a) Examination of Site	9–178
(b) Cost Estimates and Budgets	9–189
(c) Compliance with Legislation, Planning and Building Control Requirements and Codes of Practice	9–196
(d) Design and Specification	9–199
(e) Preparation of Bills of Quantities	9–218
(f) Selection of Contractor and the Tender Process	9–219
(g) Advice on Choice and Terms of a Building Contract	9–222
(h) Administration of the Building Contract	9–226
(i) Supervision or Inspection of the Works	9–236
(j) Certification	9–254
(k) Specialist Survey	9–261
(l) Investigation of Defects	9–264
4. Damages	9–265
(a) The Scope of the Duty	9–266
(b) Remoteness	9–272
(i) Causation	9–273
(ii) Foreseeability	9–284
(c) The Measure of Damages	9–289
(d) Heads of Damage	9–293
(i) Costs of Rectification	9–294
(ii) Diminution in Value	9–306
(iii) Wasted Expenditure	9–308
(iv) Excess Expenditure	9–309
(v) Underpayment	9–310
(vi) Consequential Losses	9–311
(vii) Liability to Third Parties	9–314
(viii) Personal Injuries	9–315
(ix) Inconvenience, Distress and Loss of Amenity	9–316
(e) Mitigation of Loss	9–319
(f) Abatement of Fees	9–322

[43]

9-002 CHAPTER 9—CONSTRUCTION PROFESSIONALS

5. Shared Responsibility .... 9-324 (b) Contributory Negligence 9-347
■ (a) Apportionment of Liability .... 9-324 ■ 6. Adjudication 9-351

1. INTRODUCTION

(a) *The Construction Professionals*

9-002 Add: The Architects' Registration Board exercises a disciplinary jurisdiction over registered architects and its decisions are amenable to judicial review; see, for an example, *Vranicki v Architects Registration Board* [2007] EWHC 506 (Admin).

9-006 Add to NOTE 17: For a case where loss adjusters were held liable to their instructing insurers for breach of duty in managing remedial works, see *AXA Insurance UK Plc v Cunningham Lindsey United Kingdom* [2007] EWHC 3023 (TCC).

(b) *Claims against Construction Professionals*

9-007 Add to NOTE 22: In *Cundall Johnson and Partners LLP v Whipps Cross University Hospital NHS Trust* [2007] EWHC 2178 (TCC), Jackson J. held that a disputed claim for professional fees made by a firm of consulting engineers was within the scope of the protocol.

Add to NOTE 25: An action was stayed pending completion of the protocol procedures in *Cundall Johnson and Partners LLP v Whipps Cross University Hospital NHS Trust* [2007] EWHC 2178 (TCC), but a stay was refused in *Orange Personal Communications Services Ltd v Hoare Lea* [2008] EWHC 223 (TCC). In *TJ Brent v Black & Veatch Consulting Ltd* [2008] EWHC 1497 (TCC), Akenhead J. rejected the argument that a claimant had failed to comply with the pre-action protocol and so refused the defendant's application for costs; the judge suggested *obiter* that such an application could not succeed without evidence that there was a realistic prospect that settlement would have been achieved had there been compliance with the protocol.

9-008 Add to NOTE 26: For guidance on the procedure for transferring cases to the TCC, see *Brynley Collins v Raymond J Drumgold* [2008] EWHC 584 (TCC).

2. DUTIES

(a) *Duties to Client*

(i) *Contractual Duties*

9-020 Add to NOTE 61: In *Oxford Architects Partnership v Cheltenham Ladies College* [2006] EWHC 3156 (TCC), it was held that a similar clause in an earlier edition of the RIBA standard form (CE/95) was effective to shorten the time within which a claim might be brought but otherwise did not affect the operation of the Limitation Act 1980. Certain claims referred to arbitration were within the contractual time limit but were nevertheless statute-barred.

Add to NOTE 10: See also *London Fire and Emergency Planning Authority v Halcrow Gilbert Associates Ltd* [2007] EWHC 2546 (TCC) (defendant engineers' original design for a facility where fire fighters could train in simulated operational conditions was not negligent, given that this was an unique and innovative project, but they were in breach of a duty to review that design when the facility caught fire). **9–038**

(ii) *Duties Independent of Contract*

Add to NOTE 10: For a further example, see *Oxford Architects Partnership v Cheltenham Ladies College* [2006] EWHC 3156 (TCC). **9–039**

Add: With effect from April 6, 2007, the 1994 Regulations were revoked and replaced by the Construction (Design and Management) Regulations 2007 (SI 2007/320). The new regulations apply to a wider range of construction projects, although domestic projects remain exempt. **9–048**

(b) *Duties to Third Parties*

Add: The existence of a collateral warranty will mean that breach of a single obligation creates liability to two parties, but double recovery in respect of the same loss will not be permitted. For a discussion of the ways in which a professional may protect himself against double recovery, see *Biffa Waste Services Ltd v Maschinenfabrik Ernst Hese GmbH* [2008] EWHC 6 (TCC) at [127]–[135]. **9–060**

(ii) *Recovery by Third Parties in respect of Personal Injury and Damage to "Other Property"*

Add: One principle identified in *Baxall Securities Ltd v Sheard Walshaw Partnership* (discussed in the main work) was that where it is reasonable to expect that a subsequent occupier will inspect a property before entering into occupation, a person responsible for the design of the property will not owe a duty of care to the occupier in respect of any defect that such an inspection should reveal. This principle was doubted *obiter* by the Court of Appeal in *Pearson Education Ltd v The Charter Partnership Ltd* [2007] EWCA Civ 130, although it had no direct application on the facts of that case. The defendant architects were responsible for the design of a rainwater drainage system at a warehouse. The system was defectively designed, leading to flood damage to books stored there. Loss adjusters for the occupier's insurers discovered the defects in the system but did not inform the occupier and the defects were not rectified. The claimant was a subsequent, different occupier which suffered property damage during a second flood. It was held that the loss adjusters' discovery did not prevent the architects owing a duty of care to the claimant. **9–078**

9–111 CHAPTER 9—CONSTRUCTION PROFESSIONALS

(iv) *The English Exceptions to the General Exclusionary Rule*

9–111 Add: Despite extensive liaison in the pre-contract period between a design and build contractor and consulting engineers retained by a subsidiary of the employer, it was held in *Galliford Try Infrastructure Limited v Mott Macdonald Limited* 2008 [EWHC] 1570 (TCC) that the engineers did not owe a duty of care to the contractor in producing their concept design. In tendering for the contract, the contractor had not relied upon any statement or conduct by the engineers (it had retained its own design consultant) and the engineers' designs had been produced subject to a disclaimer of responsibility to any party other than their client.

(v) *The Position in Other Jurisdictions*

9–115 Add: The approach in *Woolcock Street Investments v CGD Pty Ltd* was followed in *Rickard Constructions Pty Ltd v Rickard Hails Moretti Pty Ltd* [2006] NSWCA 356 (designing engineer alleged to owe duty of care to subsequent purchaser) and in *Aquatec-Maxcon Pty Ltd v Barwon Regional Water Authority (No.2)* [2006] VSC 117 (designing engineers alleged to owe duties of care to parties higher up in the contractual chain). In each case, no duty of care was owed because the claimant lacked the required element of "vulnerability", that is, the inability to protect itself against the consequences of breach of duty by the defendant.

(vi) *Problems of Scope of Duty*

9–121 Add to NOTE 65: Similarly, the insurance provisions of a contract did not prevent the recovery of damages for negligently caused loss in *Biffa Waste Services Ldt v Maschinenfabrik Ernst Hese GmbH* [2008] EWHC 6 (TCC) or in *Tyco Fire & Integrated Solutions (UK) Ltd v Rolls-Royce Motor Cars Ltd* [2008] EWCA Civ 286. The duration of the obligation to take out joint insurance may be important. Under the JCT Standard Form of Building Contract for Minor Works (1993 edn) it endures only until practical completion of the works: *TFW Printers Ltd v Interserve Project Services Ltd* [2006] EWCA Civ 875.

(d) *The Standard of Care and Skill*

(ix) *Special Steps and Warranty of Reasonable Fitness*

9–170 Add to NOTE 6: For a case where, on the facts, a designer was held not to owe a duty to provide a design which was fit for purpose, see *Roger Benfield (trading as Autoroute Circuits) v Life Racing Limited* [2007] EWHC 1505 (TCC).

3. LIABILITY FOR BREACH OF DUTY

(d) *Design and Specification*

9–203 Add to NOTE 77: See also *London Fire and Emergency Planning Authority v Halcrow Gilbert Associates Ltd* [2007] EWHC 2546 (TCC) (engineers commissioned to design a facility where firefighters could train in simulated operational conditions had met the required professional standard, given that this was a unique and innovative project).

(i) Supervision or Inspection of the Works

Replace the reference in NOTE 60 to para.**9–236** with a reference to para.**9–244**.   **9–236**

Add: Similarly, in *McGlinn v Waltham Contractors Ltd* [2007] EWHC 149 (TCC), Judge Coulson Q.C. considered that if an inspecting professional identifies a defect and draws it to the attention of the contractor, he is obliged to monitor the progress of the rectification work until either it is done or the value of the work has been deducted from the contractor's account.   **9–239**

Add: On the facts in *McGlinn v Waltham Contractors Ltd* [2007] EWHC 149 (TCC), the architect's monthly inspections were too infrequent and represented too rigid a programme, since the timing of the inspections was not sensitive to the progress of the works.   **9–241**

Add: If an engineer employed by a building owner in respect of permanent works observes a state of temporary works which is dangerous and causing immediate peril to the permanent works, he owes an obligation in contract to take steps to obviate that danger: *Hart Investments Ltd v Fidler* [2007] EWHC 1058 (TCC). The judge also considered *obiter* that in the special circumstances of that case, the engineer would have owed a duty of care to the owner in tort even if there had been no contractual obligation and notwithstanding that the loss caused by collapse of a wall which formed part of the permanent works was pure economic loss.   **9–249**

Add to NOTE 12: In *McGlinn v Waltham Contractors Ltd* [2007] EWHC 149 (TCC), Judge Coulson Q.C. also approved paras.**8–236** to **8–249** of the fifth edition of the main work and provided a summary of the legal principles relating to an architect's duty to inspect.   **9–253**

(k) *Specialist Survey*

Add: In *Charlton v Northern Structural Services Limited* [2008] EWHC 66 (TCC), a structural engineer engaged to carry out a structural survey on a house was in breach of duty when he advised the prospective purchasers to fell four trees close to the property, rather than to carry out a phased programme of lopping, pruning and root curtailment. The sudden removal of the trees caused rehydration and clay heave in the sub-soil, which destabilised the property.   **9–262**

4. DAMAGES

(b) *Remoteness*

(i) *Causation*

Add: The factual analysis necessary to determine whether a professional's breach of duty has caused delay to construction works is often complex. In   **9–279**

Mirant Asia-Pacific Construction (Hong Kong) Ltd v Ove Arup & Partners International Ltd [2007] EWHC 918 (TCC), Judge Toulmin CMG Q.C. held that the movement of foundations (for which the designers had been held responsible: see para.**9–186** of the main work) was not the dominant cause of the delay to the project and did not even contribute materially to the loss arising out of delay to the project. The judgement includes consideration of the difficulty of accurate analysis of causation of delay to construction works and of the evidential requirements and limitations of the technique known as critical path analysis.

9–281   Add to NOTE 85: In *Pearson Education Ltd v The Charter Partnership Ltd* [2007] EWCA Civ 130 the Court of Appeal doubted this aspect of the decision in *Baxall Securities Ltd v Sheard Walshaw Partnership* (discussed in the main work).

(d) *Heads of Damage*

(i) *Costs of Rectification*

9–299   Add: Similarly, in *London Fire and Emergency Planning Authority v Halcrow Gilbert Associates Ltd* [2007] EWHC 2546 (TCC), the facts that the claimant did not intend to reinstate a training facility which had been damaged by fire and that it would not be reasonable to do so were fatal to the claim for damages based on the cost of reinstatement.

9–304   Add: However, the overriding principle which operates where the cost of repair or reinstatement is the appropriate basis of damages is that it must be both reasonable to reinstate and the amount awarded must be objectively fair as between the claimant and the defendant. It follows that while reliance on non-negligent expert advice is a highly significant factor in any assessment of loss and damage, it is not sufficient in every case to show that the claimant has acted reasonably. Judge Coulson Q.C. so held in *McGlinn v Waltham Contractors Ltd* [2007] EWHC 149 (TCC). In that case, the claimant sought to recover the cost of demolition and rebuilding of a substantial residential property from various professional defendants who had been involved in its construction. By the time of trial, the property had been demolished but not rebuilt; and there was no clear prospect that it would be rebuilt even if the claimant recovered the damages sought. Although the claimant had received expert advice that demolition was appropriate and it was not suggested that this advice was negligent, the claimant recovered only the cost of repair of certain defects of which he complained. The decision in *The Board of Governors of the Hospitals for Sick Children v McLaughlin & Harvey plc* (discussed in the main work) was distinguished on the facts but the judge considered that, in any event, the principles referred to above precluded recovery of the costs of demolition and rebuilding against all or any of the defendants. The decision to demolish rather than repair the property had more to do with the claimant's residual dissatisfaction with the general design of the house than with the defects alleged or the advice which he received. Most importantly, the defects alleged against each of the defendants were different. Even if, cumulatively, those defects might have justified demolition and rebuilding, no defects alleged against any one defendant could justify it. Accordingly, it was not reasonable or fair to award the cost of demolition against any one defendant and there was no principled way in which the demolition cost could be apportioned between them. As against each defendant which was held liable for specific defects, the claimant was entitled to recover only the cost of repair of those defects. In *AXA Insurance UK Plc v Cunningham Lindsey United Kingdom* [2007] EWHC 3023 (TCC), Akenhead J. followed the approach adopted in *McGlinn* and held that the claimant's reliance on non-negligent expert advice in deciding which remedial works should be carried out was not, of itself, sufficient to render the claimant's expenditure reasonable and recoverable.

(ii) *Diminution in Value*

Add to NOTE 66: Damages for diminution in value may also be recovered when remedial works are neither necessary nor appropriate, but it has become known that a building is susceptible to structural damage: see, e.g. *Charlton v Northern Structural Services Limited* [2008] EWHC 66 (TCC). **9–306**

(ix) *Inconvenience, Distress and Loss of Amenity*

Add to NOTE 98: For examples of the modest awards made for the inconvenience of living with defects and with subsequent remedial works, see *Eile v London Borough of Southwark* [2006] EWHC 1411 (TCC), *Iggleden v Fairview New Homes* [2007] EWHC 1573 (TCC) and *Charlton v Northern Structural Services Limited* [2008] EWHC 66 (TCC). In *AXA Insurance UK Plc v Cunningham Lindsey United Kingdom* [2007] EWHC 3023 (TCC), Akenhead J. held that general damages for physical inconvenience, distress and discomfort caused by breaches of contract will not normally exceed £2,500 per person per year (as at the end of 2007). **9–318**

(e) *Mitigation of Loss*

Add to NOTE 1: In *Iggleden v Fairview New Homes* [2007] EWHC 1573 (TCC), a building contract dispute, the defendant builder's conduct since the defects were discovered meant that the claimants reasonably refused to allow it to carry out the necessary remedial works and so were entitled to the rectification cost as damages. Cf. *City Access Ltd v Jackson* [1998] 64 Comm. L.R. 84 , where the refusal was unreasonable but the remedial works were not substantial. **9–320**

(f) *Abatement of Fees*

Add: In *Multiplex Constructions (UK) Ltd v Cleveland Bridge (UK) Ltd* [2006] EWHC 1341 (TCC), Jackson J reviewed the law on abatement and concluded that abatement is not available as a defence to a claim for payment in respect of professional services. This conclusion was *obiter* (since the claim concerned abatement as a defence to a claim under a building contract). The decision in *Turner Page Music Ltd v Torres Design Associates Ltd* (see text of main work) was apparently not cited but Jackson J.'s conclusion is respectfully regarded as a correct statement of the general principle. **9–323**

5. Shared Responsibility

(a) Apportionment of Liability

9–334 Add to Note 28: The duration of the obligation to take out joint insurance may be important. Under the JCT Standard Form of Building Contract for Minor Works (1993 edn) it endures only until practical completion of the works: *TFW Printers Ltd v Interserve Project Services Ltd* [2006] EWCA Civ 875. For cases where an insurance obligation did not prevent the recovery of damages, see *Biffa Waste Services Ltd v Maschinenfabrik Ernst Hese GmbH* [2008] EWHC 6 (TCC) and *Tyco Fire & Integrated Solutions (UK) Ltd v Rolls-Royce Motor Cars Ltd* [2008] EWCA Civ 286.

9–340 Add to Note 34: The principles considered in this section will apply also when a claimant seeks to recover, as a head of consequential loss, sums paid in settlement of its alleged liability to a third party. See, for an example, *Mirant Asia-Pacific Construction (Hong Kong) Ltd v Ove Arup & Partners International Ltd* [2007] EWHC 918 (TCC) (global settlement of a liability alleged to have been occasioned by engineers' breach of duty was unrecoverable because the project would have been delayed in any event and, further, no causal link was demonstrated between the amount paid in settlement and the engineers' breach).

9–343 Add: However, it is not necessary to prove that the third party's claim would probably have succeeded in order to show that settlement of that claim was reasonable. An argument that a settlement was unreasonable because the claimant had no liability to the third party will not succeed unless the claim was so weak as to be obviously hopeless, since the settlement of a weak claim in order to avoid the uncertainties and expenses of litigation may well be reasonable: see *F Hunt Demolition Limited v ASME Engineering Ltd* [2007] EWHC 1507 (TCC). In *AXA Insurance UK Plc v Cunningham Lindsey United Kingdom* [2007] EWHC 3023 (TCC), Akenhead J. agreed with the judge's analysis of authority and statement of the law relating to the recovery of sums paid in settlement of third-party claims in *Hunt v ASME* and provided (at [273]) a statement of the relevant principles.

6. Adjudication

9–351 Add to Note 59: The assignee of a party to a construction contract has a right to refer disputes to adjudication, but only if any contractual requirements for assignment have been met: *Rok Build Ltd v Harris Wharf Development Co Ltd* [2006] EWHC 3573 (TCC).

9–354 Add to Note 63: Cf. *Treasure & Son Ltd v Dawes* [2007] EWHC 2420 (TCC) (oral variation of a contract will not undermine the jurisdiction of an adjudicator in cases where the right to adjudicate is purely contractual). In *Hart Investments Ltd v Fidler* [2006] EWHC 2857 (TCC), letters of intent were held not to amount

ADJUDICATION 9–362

to a construction contract for the purposes of s.107 of the Housing Grants, Construction and Regeneration Act 1996; see also *Mott Macdonald Ltd v London & Regional Properties Ltd* [2007] EWHC 1055 (TCC), and *Mast Electrical Services v Kendall Cross Holdings Ltd* [2007] EWHC 1296 (TCC). The existence of a cogent argument that a term of the construction contract had not been evidenced in writing prevented enforcement of the adjudicator's decision in *Lead Technical Services Ltd v CMS Medical Ltd* [2007] EWCA Civ 316. The exchange of the parties' written submissions may amount to written evidence of a construction contract: see s.107(5) of the 1996 Act and *ALE Heavy Lift v MSD (Darlington) Ltd* [206] EWHC 2080 (TCC).

Add to NOTE 68: In certain circumstances, an adjudication agreement will lead to a stay of litigation or arbitration proceedings to allow adjudication to take place: see *DGT Steele & Cladding Ltd v Cubitt Building & Interiors Ltd* [2007] EWHC 1584 (TCC); *Cubitt Building and Interiors Ltd v Richardson Roofing (Industrial) Ltd* [2008] EWHC 1020 (TCC). 9–356

Add: Since failure to comply with an adjudicator's decision is a breach of contract, the court has a discretion to award statutory interest on the sum payable from the date of the failure: *Ringway Infrastructure Services Ltd v Vauxhall Motors Ltd* [2007] EWHC 2507 (TCC). 9–357

Add to NOTE 74: Although the question will rarely arise directly in cases concerning professional liability, for further consideration of the circumstances in which a defendant may set off sums due to him under the contract against sums due from him in compliance with an adjudicators' decision, see *Balfour Beatty Construction Ltd v Serco Ltd* [2004] EWHC 3336 (TCC), *William Verry Ltd v Camden London BC* [2006] EWHC 761 (TCC) and *RJ Knapman Ltd v Richards* [2006] EWHC 2518 (TCC). 9–359

Add: By contrast, it seems that errors made by the adjudicator within his jurisdiction are reviewable when the adjudication agreement is "purely contractual" in the sense that, in the absence of the express provision for adjudication, such provision would not be implied under the Housing Grants, Construction and Regeneration Act 1996: *Domsalla v Dyason* [2007] EWHC 1174 (TCC) (concerning a building contract incorporating the JCT Agreement for Minor Building Works (1998 edn) but made with a residential occupier). Where the adjudicator's decision properly addresses more than one dispute, a successful challenge to that part of the decision which addresses one such dispute will not necessarily prevent enforcement of the part of the decision which addresses the remaining dispute(s): *Cantillon Ltd v Urvasco Ltd* [2008] EWHC 282 (TCC). 9–360

Add to NOTE 82: In *AMEC Civil Engineering Ltd v Secretary of State for Transport* [2005] EWCA Civ 291, the Court of Appeal approved seven propositions concerning the meaning of the word "dispute"; for a review of the authorities, see *Ringway Infrastructure Services Ltd v Vauxhall Motors Ltd* [2008] EWHC 2421 (TCC). In *Cantillon Ltd v Urvasco Ltd* [2008] EWHC 282 9–362

9–362   (TCC), the court declined to follow the approach adopted in *Edmund Nuttall Ltd v RG Carter Ltd* [2002] EWHC 400 (TCC) (discussed in the main work).

9–363   Add: However, an adjudicator's failure to *make* his decision within the time period prescribed by the statutory scheme does invalidate his decision: see *Epping Electrical Company Ltd v Briggs and Forrester (Plumbing Services) Ltd* [2007] EWHC 4 (TCC); *Aveat Heating Ltd v Jerram Falkus Construction Ltd* [2007] EWHC 131 (TCC); and *Mott Macdonald Ltd v London & Regional Properties Ltd* [2007] EWHC 1055 (TCC).

Add to NOTE 88: Failure to meet the requirement of s.108 of the Housing Grants, Construction and Regeneration Act 1996 that a referral notice be served within seven days of the notice of adjudication deprived the adjudicator of jurisdiction in *Hart Investments Ltd v Fidler* [2006] EWHC 2857 (TCC). On the need to follow the contractual procedure for appointment of an adjudicator, see *Lead Technical Services Ltd v CMS Medical Ltd* [2007] EWCA Civ 316. The decision in *Quietfield v Vascroft Contracts Ltd* was upheld on appeal: [2006] EWCA Civ 1737; and, on the non-binding effect of a subsequent adjudication of the same dispute, see also *HG Construction Ltd v Ashwell Homes (East Anglia) Ltd* [2007] EWHC 144 (TCC).

9–364   Add: But in *Carillion Construction Ltd v Devonport Royal Dockyard* [2005] EWCA Civ 1358 the Court of Appeal emphasised that the courts will refuse to enforce an adjudicator's decision on grounds of a breach of natural justice only in the plainest cases: see the passage quoted at para.**9–360** of the main work. For an example of the application of this approach, see *Kier Regional Ltd v City & General (Holborn) Ltd* [2007] EWHC 848 (TCC), where it was held that an adjudicator's failure to consider part of the evidence lodged by one party was an error of law within his jurisdiction and so did not impede the enforcement of his decision. However, if such failure is a result of a serious breach of the rules of natural justice, enforcement will be refused on the latter ground: *Humes Building Contractors Ltd v Charlotte Homes (Surrey) Ltd*, unreported, January 4, 2007.

Add to NOTE 90: The decision in *Carillion Construction Ltd v Devonport Royal Dockyard* was upheld on appeal: [2005] EWCA Civ 1358.

9–365   Add to NOTE 93: The adjudicator's failure to allow the parties an opportunity to make submissions on an argument which he had introduced led to the court's refusal to enforce his decision in *Humes Building Contractors Ltd v Charlotte Homes (Surrey) Ltd* (unreported) January 4, 2007. Guidance as to the manner in which parties and nominating institutions should approach unilateral contact with adjudicators was given in *Makers UK Ltd v Camden London Borough Council* [2008] EWHC 1836 (TCC).

9–367   Add to NOTE 4: In *ALE Heavy Lift v MSD (Darlington) Ltd* [2006] EWHC 2080 (TCC), an application for a stay of execution failed on similar grounds to those in *Herschel Engineering Ltd v Breen Property Ltd* (discussed in the main work).

Add to NOTE 5: In *McDonnell Dowell Constructors (Aust) Pty Ltd v National Grid Gas plc* [2007] EWHC 2551 (TCC), a stay of execution was refused in the light of the claimant's offer to provide a bond to protect the defendant's position in the event that it clawed back in litigation or arbitration the sum due under an adjudicator's decision.

CHAPTER 10

SURVEYORS

	PARA.		PARA.
1. General	10–001	(iv) Limited Survey	10–097
(a) Bases of Liability	10–007	(v) Failing to Recognise	10–099
(b) Duties to Client	10–019	(d) Failing to Make Sufficient Inquiries	10–100
(i) Contractual Duties	10–019	(e) Failing to Make a Proper Appraisal	10–104
(ii) Duties Independent of Contract	10–032	(f) Inadequate Report	10–107
(c) Duties to Third Parties	10–033	3. Damages	10–110
(i) General Principles	10–033	(a) Has the Claimant Sustained the Loss Claimed?	10–112
(ii) Knowledge of Reliance	10–040	(b) Is the Loss Claimed within the Scope of the Defendant's Duty?	10–113
(iii) Duty of Mortgagee's Valuer to Purchaser	10–044	(c) Remoteness	10–120
(d) The Standard of Care and Skill	10–052	(i) Causation	10–121
(i) Reasonable Standard	10–052	(ii) Foreseeability	10–126
(ii) General Practice and Knowledge as Evidence of the Standard	10–054	(d) Measure of Damages	10–129
(iii) Not Every Error is Negligence	10–058	(i) Negligent Survey or Valuation for a Purchaser who Completes a Purchase	10–131
(iv) The Relevance of "the bracket"	10–059	(ii) Negligent Survey or Valuation for a Purchaser who Withdraws from Purchase before Completion	10–151
(v) Onus of Proof	10–062		
(e) Limitation of Liability	10–063		
(f) Mutual Valuer	10–074		
2. Liability for Breach of Duty	10–075		
(a) Failing to Carry Out Instructions	10–077	(iii) Negligent Survey or Valuation for Lender	10–152
(b) Insufficient Knowledge or Experience	10–079	(iv) Overvaluation for Vendor	10–177
(c) Failing to Inspect Properly	10–082	(v) Undervaluation for Vendor	10–178
(i) Failing to Inspect Particular Parts	10–083	(vi) Other Work	10–181
(ii) Failing to Uncover and Open Up	10–084	(vii) Inconvenience and Discomfort	10–184
(iii) Failing to Observe	10–090	(viii) Incidental Expenses	10–193

1. GENERAL

(a) *Bases of Liability*

Add new NOTE 51a at end of paragraph: A recent example of the benefits of an action in deceit can be seen in the case of *Cheshire Building Society v Dunlop Haywards* [2008] P.N.L.R. 549 where the claimant building society advanced an initial £10.5 million followed by a further £1 million against the security of a property which had recently been sold for £1.4 million. The claimant sought summary judgment, in deceit, against the employers of the valuer who, in turn, **10–011**

10–011 CHAPTER 10—SURVEYORS

brought the valuer himself in as a Part 20 Defendant. The court emphasised the need for caution in granting summary judgment but nonetheless was prepared to do so in the exceptional circumstances of the case.

(b) *Duties to Client*

(i) *Contractual Duties*

Add new para.**10–019A**:

10–019A   It is plainly possible for a surveyor, as for any other person, to warrant a state of affairs rather than merely assert that he has undertaken reasonable skill and care in relation to an aspect of his retainer. The consequence of such a warranty are, however, far-reaching. Aside from the obvious fact that liability can exist without negligence, no defence of contributory negligence will be available. Furthermore professional indemnity policies often contain exclusions in relation to contractual obligations which are assumed in circumstances where there would not be liability in the absence of negligence. In *Platform Funding Limited v Bank of Scotland Plc* [2008] EWCA Civ 930, the Court of Appeal considered a case in which the only cause of action pleaded was the breach of a warranty that a surveyor had inspected a particular property. The surveyor had been instructed to value a property for lending purposes known as 1 Bakers Yard and provided a certificate which stated "I certify that the property offered as security has been inspected by me and that the above valuation is a fair indication of the current open market valuation for mortgage purposes". In fact, the borrower had deliberately misled the valuer. 1 Bakers Yard was one of five un-numbered plots and had a house in the early stages of construction upon it. The borrower induced the valuer to inspect another plot, number 5, where the house was almost completed. By a majority (Clarke M.R. dissenting), the Court of Appeal held that the wording of the surveyor's instructions and his certificate were so clear that the surveyor had, indeed, assumed an unqualified obligation to inspect and report upon the correct property. All the members of the court recognised that clear words were necessary. Thus Moore-Bick L.J. said:

> "... there is every reason to assume, in the absence of a term to the contrary, that a professional person has undertaken no more than to use reasonable skill and care in relation to matters calling for the exercise of his professional skill and expertise."

He went on to set out Lord Woolf's observations in *Midland Bank v Cox Mcqueen* (see para.**2–010** above) to the effect that if commercial institutions wished to impose absolute obligations they should do so in clear terms. Nevertheless it was held that the words were sufficiently clear. It is respectfully doubted that this is so. Obviously in the overwhelming majority of cases, a failure to inspect the right property will be negligent. However if a valuer does exercise reasonable skill and care, it is doubted that either a simple instruction in relation to a particular property or the wording of the certificate are sufficient to impose an absolute duty. It has not been suggested that the second half of the certificate imposes any such absolute duty—thus, for example if a valuer reasonably asserts that the value provided is "a fair indication for mortgage purposes" when it is not (perhaps because of a substantial defect of which the valuer was reasonably

GENERAL 10–053A

unaware), the certificate will not impose an absolute liability. It is suggested that the certificate, read in the commercial context in which it was provided, meant and would have been understood to mean no more than "I believe and have taken reasonable care to check that I have inspected the right property... ". Clarke M.R. pointed out (at paras [63] to [64]) how odd an agreement it would have been for the valuers to provide an absolute warranty in relation to inspection but only the usual obligation in relation to the assessment of value. It is suggested that this would, indeed, have been a very strange agreement.

Add: Note generally that the structure of the Manual has, again, been changed and reference should be made to the current edition of the Manual for details of the applicable practice. **10–023**

(c) *Duties to Third Parties*

(i) *General Principles*

Add: A recent example of the application of Barwick C.J.'s dictum is provided by the decision of the Court of Appeal of Victoria in *Derring Land Pty Ltd v Fitzgibbon* [2007] VSCA 79 where a valuer had been engaged by the vendor of land to carry out a valuation which, to his knowledge was to be used for the calculation of the amount of Goods and Services Tax to be payable by the purchaser of land on an increase in value between certain dates. The fee was payable by the purchaser and the valuer knew the purpose for which his valuation was being produced. In those circumstances the court found that a disclaimer was insufficiently clear to avoid the imposition of a duty of care in favour of the purchaser in relation to a negligent valuation. **10–038**

(d) *The Standard of Care and Skill*

(i) *Reasonable Standard*

Add new para.**10–053A**:

One matter which often arises is the relevance of a firm holding itself out as having particular expertise or being a large and substantial firm with access to specialist departments. In principle it is suggested that this matter should be approached as follows. **10–053A**

If a firm holds itself out as having a particular skill, it is to be judged by the standards of people holding that skill. A professional is, by definition, a specialist within a particular field but professions naturally depend to develop sub-specialisms over time. Very often such sub-specialisms are recognised in practice very substantially before they are recognised by any formal accreditation (if, indeed, such sub-specialisms are ever formally recognised). Thus if a particular field is recognised, in practice, as requiring specialist experience, a professional man who holds himself out as having such experience is to be judged by the standards of reasonably competent people with the appropriate experience.

Where a firm is large and substantial, the ordinary expectation will be that an individual will have recourse within such a firm to appropriate specialists if such specialism is required.

10–053A

It is likely, however, that the above discussion is somewhat academic. If a small firm is instructed in relation to a specialist matter, it should have sufficient experience to realise the need to inform the client of its lack of expertise and the need to take appropriate advice. If it does not do this it is likely to be held to be negligent for not having realised the limits of its own experience.

It is only if a warning is given by a small firm but a claimant nonetheless proceeds to instruct it (for example on grounds of cost), that there is likely, in practice to be a difference in result. In such a situation a defendant would in effect be stating, "I informed you that I did not have the relevant experience and that you should obtain specialist advice. In such circumstances I cannot be judged by reference to experience I did not claim".

The above questions were considered by Jack J. in *Earl of Malmesbury v Strutt & Parker* [2007] P.N.L.R. 570 where a major national firm of land agents were sued in respect of advising as to the terms which should be negotiated for leasing land to an airport operator. The claimants alleged that the "level of expertise to be expected was that of a major national firm of surveyors, which had expressly put itself forward as well suited to the task of advising on land value near an airport. In other words the expertise to be expected was the very highest within the profession of chartered surveyors". The defendants accepted merely that the claimants were entitled to "expect the standard of a competent surveyor negotiator advising on such development of land near an airport".

Jack J. held that the standard of professional skill and care was that to be expected of a major national firm and that the competence to be expected was that of the whole firm. If such competence in a particular area was not to be found within a firm, it might be necessary to go outside it. In saying this, it is slightly difficult to see how the position of a major national firm would be different from that of a small local firm.

The judge then referred to the well-known dictum of Lord Hobhouse in *Hall v Simons* [2002] A.C. 615 at 737 to the effect that in order to establish negligence a plaintiff was required to show that "the error was one which no reasonably competent member of the relevant profession would have made". He then added a gloss: "That is not intended to imply that the standard to be expected of a specialist Queen's Counsel is the same as that to be expected of a white-wigged junior". For the reasons set out above, it is submitted that this will only be true if the white-wigged junior has realised the limits of his own experience and advised the client to take advice elsewhere.

2. LIABILITY FOR BREACH OF DUTY

10–075

Add: In *Platform Funding Ltd v Bank of Scotland* [2008] EWCA Civ 930, the Court of Appeal considered the circumstances in which a valuer might owe an absolute duty to inspect the correct property rather than merely to exercise reasonable skill and care to ensure that the same occurred. The court thus emphasised that it is perfectly possible for a valuer to assume such an absolute duty. For the reasons set out at para.**10–019A** above, it is suggested that the court may have been too ready, on the facts of that case, to find that an absolute duty was imposed.

(d) *Failing to Make Sufficient Inquiries*

Add: In *PricewaterhouseCoopers Legal v Perpetual Trustees Victoria Ltd* [2007] NSWCA 388, the New South Wales Court of Appeal considered a claim brought by a lender against a valuer and solicitors based upon the facts that manufactured houses had not, under the relevant legislation, merged with the land upon which they were situated with the result that the lender had no security over them. The trial judge had found the valuer and the solicitors liable but had held that the solicitors were primarily to blame in the ratio 80:20. The Court of Appeal set this aside and held that both parties were equally to blame. The valuer had carried out insufficient investigations into the nature of the development and had failed to pass on doubts as to whether the houses had, in fact, merged with the land. The court held that there was no difference in terms either of causative potency or blameworthiness between the breaches by the solicitors and the valuer. **10–100**

Add: In *ADF Properties Pty Ltd and Kestrel Holdings (No.2)* [2007] FCA 1561, the Federal Court of Australia showed the need for care by valuers when relying on information from potential borrowers. The court held valuers liable for having failed to check information given to them by the borrower as to the amount of croppable land which was the subject of the valuation. Heerey J. held that while the valuers were entitled to rely upon what the borrower said, this was not to the exclusion of other material: **10–101**

"Owners of properties will usually want the highest valuation possible. Without going into issues of honesty or otherwise, owners seeking valuations are not objective, disinterested bystanders. It should not take much to put a reasonably competent valuer on enquiry as to what an owner tells him about croppable area . . . . As [the claimant's expert] said, 'information that can be checked should be checked . . . '."

3. DAMAGES

(b) *Is the Loss Claimed within the Scope of the Defendant's Duty?*

Add: In the Scottish case *Preferred Mortgages Ltd v Shanks* [2008] P.N.L.R. 562, Lord Drummond Young considered the difference between the liability of a solicitor and a surveyor where both were sued by a lender following the default by a borrower on the purchase of a block of 12 flats. The pursuer had alleged that the surveyor had negligently over-valued the development while the defendant solicitor had not pointed out difficulties with the title—in particular that there was no access to permit compliance with a planning condition. The surveyor settled the claim against him for £50,000 which the pursuer gave credit for in the claim against the solicitor. The solicitors maintained that the pleading was inappropriate as it necessarily meant that the pursuer was claiming damages for sums which were, in truth, the responsibility of the surveyor and beyond the scope of his duty. The judge did not accept this. He pointed out that the liability of valuers had been limited on the basis that they were merely providing information whereas solicitors had been held to be advising as to whether to enter **10–116** into the transaction (see para.**11–304** below). The judge held that the case was also be categorised as an "advice" case which meant that the solicitors were liable for the entirety of the loss—subject, of course, to the amount already received from the valuers:

> "In the course of argument counsel for the [solicitors] submitted that a solicitor's liability should be restricted to the losses that fall within the scope of the duty of care owed by the solicitor. No doubt that is true, but the important point is that the solicitor will normally advise a lender that the proposed security is good. In those circumstances the solicitor's advice is responsible for the very fact that the transaction goes ahead. That is the basis upon which the solicitor may be liable for the whole of the losses that result from the transaction."

(c) *Remoteness*

(i) *Causation*

Add new para.**10–122A**:

10–122A   In the ordinary course of events, a claimant will establish causation in relation to a negligent valuation by showing that he was induced to act differently in relation to it. In *Derring Land Pty Ltd v Fitzgibbon* [2007] VSCA 79 (see para.**10–038** above), the Court of Appeal of Victoria pointed out that inducement would not always be necessary to establish causation. In that case a claimant purchaser of land had bound himself to act upon a valuation prepared by the defendant valuers for the purposes of assessment of Goods and Services Tax (payable on the increase of land values between certain dates). The claim was bought in tort as the claimant was not the client of the defendant (although he did pay for the valuation). The court found that causation was sufficiently established by a commitment to act in accord with a valuation even if the claimant was bound so to act.

(d) *Measure of Damages*

10–129   Add: A recent example of the application of the doctrine of "loss of a chance" is provided by *Earl of Malmesbury v Strutt and Parker* [2007] P.N.L.R. 570 at [588] to [593] (see further paras **10–053A** above and **10–179** below). The judge held that the defendant land agents had been negligent in failing to advise the claimants to press for turnover rent on two fields which were leased to an airport in 2002 and 2003. He further held that had such advice been given, the claimant landowner would have pressed for such a rent. The judge accepted that there was a theoretical possibility of accepting different probabilities for different levels of turnover rent but came to the conclusion that the most satisfactory way in which to approach the problem was to decide what the most likely figure would have been for agreement and then to decide the chance of the same being agreed. His conclusion was that a modest turnover rent would have been agreed at a figure of 10 per cent and that there was no real risk of such negotiations failing, with the result that there was no deduction to reflect the risk of a failure of the negotiation.

DAMAGES

(iii) *Negligent Survey or Valuation for Lender*

Add at end of first paragraph: In *Earl of Malmesbury v Strutt and Parker* **10–170**
[2007] P.N.L.R. 570 at [588] to [593] (see further paras **10–053A** and **10–129**
above), Jack J. had to consider the proper basis upon which to assess damages
where he found that the defendant land agents had negligently failed to advise the
claimant landowner to seek a turnover rent on two fields which were let on long
leases to an airport. He found that, by reason of the negligence, the claimant had
lost the chance to obtain 10 per cent of turnover for car parks (let in 2002 and
2003 respectively) and had, instead, obtained a fixed rent of £9,000 (albeit
reviewable every five years in line with increases in car park prices). By the time
that the matter came to trial in 2007, it was possible to see what the rental
difference would have been over the four and five years respectively since the
leases had been entered into. The questions arose as to (a) whether it was
appropriate to assess damages by reference to the difference between the capital
value of the leases at the time they were entered into (the "valuation method")
or by reference to an assessment of the actual rents lost and (b) if the valuation
method were appropriate, the date for such valuation. The judge considered that
he was bound by the majority of the Court of Appeal in *County Personnel v
Pulver* [1987] 1 W.L.R. 916 to hold that the valuation method of assessing loss
was appropriate *unless* there were circumstances which showed that it would be
inappropriate to award such damages in relation to the overriding compensatory
rule. He came to the conclusion that there were no such special features with the
consequence that the valuation method should be applied. He went on to hold
that there was nothing which required him to depart from the usual rule that
damages should be assessed as at the date of breach. It is suggested that this may
represent an over-mechanistic approach to the assessment of damages: if a
claimant successfully establishes that a turnover rent should have been contended
for, this will probably be because the conventional assessment of rent (that is, the
value of the land) is too difficult accurately to assess and turnover rent is likely
to be more satisfactory to both parties. The claimant would, accordingly, have
shared in the reward of an increase in turnover. It will be the defendant's
negligence which has denied this reward. In such circumstances it would appear
inappropriate for the court to shut its eyes to the fact that, had the defendant not
been negligent, the rewards would, in fact, have been great. If the court had
stepped back and asked itself the question, "What has the Claimant really lost?"
it is suggested that the answer would have been that the claimant lost the
opportunity to share in the rents which were actually achieved. The difference in
the two approaches can be seen from Jack J.'s subsequent judgment [2007]
EWHC 2641, where he revealed that the Claimants' valuation of the relevant
land at the date of breach with the hypothetical rental provisions totalled between
£3.3 million to £3.9 million, while the defendant's valuation of the same land
with the same provisions was £327,500 to £432,500.

Add: For a recent example of a case where the Court of Appeal of New South **10–175**
Wales considered a valuer and solicitor to have been equally responsible for
losses suffered, see *PriceWaterhouseCoopers Legal v Perpetual Trustees* [2007]
NSWCA 388 discussed at para.**10–100** above.

Chapter 11

SOLICITORS

		Para.
■	1. General	11–001
	(a) Duties to Client	11–004
■	(i) Contractual Duties	11–004
■	(ii) Tortious Duties	11–013
■	(iii) Fiduciary Duties	11–016
■	(iv) Trust Duties	11–033
	(b) Duties to Third Parties	11–039
□	(i) General	11–039
■	(ii) Liability to Beneficiaries without Reliance	11–047
□	(iii) Duty of Care to the Other Side	11–055
■	(iv) Solicitors' Liability on Undertakings	11–065
	(v) Other Liabilities	11–075
	(c) The Standard of Skill and Care	11–080
□	(i) The Standard of Reasonableness	11–080
■	(ii) General Practice as Evidence of Reasonable Skill and Care	11–087
	(iii) The Specialist Solicitor and the Inexperienced Solicitor	11–096
	(iv) Mitigating Factors	11–099
■	(v) Aggravating Factors	11–101
	(vi) General Observations	11–107
	(d) Specific Defences to a Claim for Breach of Duty	11–110
	(i) Immunity	11–110
■	(ii) Abuse of Process	11–111
■	(iii) Acting on Counsel's Advice	11–118
	(iv) Acting on Client's Instructions	11–124
■	(e) Solicitor's Liability for Costs	11–126
□	(f) Exclusion or Restriction of Liability by Contract	11–142
	(g) Practice and Procedure	11–143
	(i) Expert Evidence	11–143
	(ii) Privilege	11–145
■	(h) Attribution and Vicarious Liability	11–147
	2. Liability for Breach of Duty	11–151
	(a) General	11–151

		Para.
	(b) Giving Wrong Advice	11–153
	(c) Failing to Give Advice	11–156
	(d) Misconduct of Litigation	11–176
	(e) Misconduct of Non-contentious Business	11–194
	(i) Conveyancing	11–195
	(ii) The Investment of Money and Claims by Lenders	11–208
■	(iii) Wills	11–220
	3. Damages	11–227
■	(a) Breach of Fiduciary Duty and Breach of Trust	11–228
	(b) Remoteness	11–235
	(i) Causation	11–236
	(ii) Foreseeability	11–244
□	(iii) The Scope of the Duty	11–248
	(c) Measure of Damages	11–254
■	(i) Date of Assessment	11–255
	(ii) Credit for Benefits	11–257
■	(iii) Evaluation of a Chance	11–261
	(d) Heads of Damage	11–269
	(i) Loss of Opportunity to Acquire or Renew an Interest in Property	11–270
	(ii) Difference in Value of Property	11–275
	(iii) Loss of Opportunity to Bring Proceedings	11–284
	(iv) Loss of Opportunity to Defend Proceedings	11–302
	(v) Losses on Loans Secured by Mortgage	11–303
	(vi) Loss of Some Other Financial Advantage	11–306
	(vii) Liability to Third Parties	11–312
	(viii) Criminal Liability	11–314
	(ix) Wasted Expenditure	11–315
	(x) Incidental Expenses	11–320
	(xi) Physical Injury, Inconvenience and Distress	11–321
	(e) Mitigation of Damage	11–326
	4. Shared Responsibility	11–333
	(a) Contributory Negligence	11–333
	(b) Apportionment of Liability	11–338

[63]

11–003 CHAPTER 11—SOLICITORS

1. GENERAL

11–003 Replace the third sentence with: The Council of the Law Society through the Legal Complaints Service (formerly the Consumer Complaints Service and the Office for the Supervision of Solicitors) is concerned with complaints about a client's solicitor, but professional misconduct is handled by the Solicitors Regulation Authority.

Add to NOTE 14: See now the Solicitors' Code of Conduct 2007.

Add to NOTE 18. From July 1, 2007 the *Guide* was replaced by the Solicitors' Code of Conduct 2007, which can be found on the Solicitors Regulation Authority's website at *http://www.sra.org.uk/solicitors/code-of-conduct.page* [accessed October 17, 2008].

(a) *Duties to Client*

(i) *Contractual Duties*

11–011 Add to NOTE 51: From July 1, 2007 the *Guide* was replaced by the Solicitors' Code of Conduct 2007, and the guidance to r.2 gives examples of good reasons.

11–012 Add to NOTE 57: Nor was there a continuing duty in *Winnote Pt Ltd v Page* [2006] 68 N.S.W.L.R. 531, NSW CA.

(iii) *Fiduciary Duties*

11–018 Add to NOTE 4: In *Ratiu v Conway* [2005] EWCA Civ 1302; [2006] 1 E.G.L.R. 125 the Court of Appeal commented (at [77] and [78]) that the question of whether a fiduciary duty might outlive a solicitor/client relationship was fact-sensitive, and that there were powerful arguments to lift the corporate veil where the facts required it to include those behind the company who in fact relied upon the fiduciary.

11–021 Add to NOTE 12: In *Ratiu v Conway* [2005] EWCA Civ 1302; [2006] 1 E.G.L.R. 125 the Court of Appeal held that a jury could find that there was a conflict of interest where the solicitor's retainer from the clients had concerned one property, and he then attempted to purchase a related property which his clients also wished to buy.

11–025 Add: *3464920 Canada Inc v Strother* (2007) 281 D.L.R. (4th) 640 illustrates another example of breach of fiduciary duty where the same result may not have been reached in England. Mr Strother, a solicitor, was a partner in Davis & Co, and acted for Monarch Entertainments Corporation in an investment scheme involving substantial tax benefits. The retainer ended in 1997 and was not renewed because it was thought that amendments to Canadian tax law defeated the benefits of the scheme. After 1997 the retainer only related to residual services. Mr Strother then acted for and obtained profits from Sentinel in a revised tax scheme. The Supreme Court of Canada, unlike the trial judge, held

GENERAL **11–045**

that there was a breach of the retainer by the firm (including Strother) in failing to offer advice about tax shelter opportunities. This breach caused no loss, as Monarch would not have been able to benefit from such opportunities. However, the Court also held that there was a breach of fiduciary duty by Strother as he had a personal financial interest in the business of Monarch's competitor, Sentinel. The firm was held to be vicariously liable for Strother's breach of fiduciary duty, although it knew nothing of his financial involvement in Sentinel, and the remedy granted was to disgorge the profits which Strother had made. For a critical commentary see J. Edelman "Unanticipated fiduciary liability" (2008) 124 L.Q.R. 21.

Add to NOTE 46: See now the Solicitors' Code of Conduct 2007, in particular para.40 of the guidance to r.4. **11–027**

Add after second sentence of NOTE 47: From July 1, 2007 the *Guide* was replaced by the Solicitors' Code of Conduct 2007. See now r.4 and the accompanying guidance at paras 32 et seq.

Add: the law in Hong Kong is similar to that in England: see *Wright v Hampton Winter & Glynn* [2008] 2 H.K.L.R.D. 341. **11–030**

Add to NOTE 52: *Chern v Chern* (2006) 263 D.L.R. (4th) 318, Alberta CA.

Add to NOTE 59: From July 1, 2007 the *Guide* was replaced by the Solicitors' Code of Conduct 2007. Paragraphs 10 to 20 of the guidance to r.4 sets out the exceptions to the duty not to disclose confidential information. **11–031**

Add to NOTE 62: In *Kallinicos v Hunt* [2005] NSWSC 1181; (2006) 64 N.S.W.L.R. 561, Brereton J. held that the Court would, under its inherent jurisdiction, restrain a solicitor from acting when the proper administration of justice requires it, such as where the solicitor was a witness on controversial issues of substance and his own, his client's and the Court's interests might conflict. **11–032**

(iv) *Trust Duties*

Replace reference with [1996] 1 A.C. 421 at 436. **11–034**

(b) *Duties to Third Parties*

(i) *General*

Add: In *Reader v Molesworths Bright Clegg Solicitors* [2007] P.N.L.R. 22 the Court of Appeal held that solicitors acting for a claimant in a personal injury action who suddenly died owed no duty of care to his widow or children, and the retainer did not automatically pass to the client's personal representatives. In that case, the solicitors had discontinued proceedings, but the widow's and children's claims under the Fatal Accidents Act were conceptually distinct and remained intact. **11–045**

11-048 CHAPTER 11—SOLICITORS

(ii) *Liabilities to Beneficiaries without Reliance*

11-048 Add to NOTE 46: To similar effect, in *Matthews v Hunter & Robertson Ltd* [2007] CSOH 88; [2008] S.L.T. 634; [2008] P.N.L.R. 35, Lord Brodie held that no duty of care was owed to an executor in Scottish law. Both decisions may be difficult to reconcile with *Carr-Glynn v Frearsons* [1999] Ch. 327 (see para.**11-049** below) and *Otter v Church, Adams Tatham & Co* [1953] Ch. 280. In *Rind v Theodore Goddard (A Firm)* [2008] EWHC 459 (Ch); [2008] P.N.L.R. 24, Morgan J. held that it was not clear whether the estate, which had had to pay substantial tax as a result of negligent tax advice given by a solicitor to the deceased, had a remedy in substantial damages against the solicitors. Relying in part on that conclusion, the judge refused to strike out a claim by a disappointed beneficiary where it was claimed that there would otherwise have been double recovery (see para.**11-052** below).

(iii) *Duty of Care to the Other Side*

11-055 Add to NOTE 83: From July 1, 2007 the *Guide* was replaced by the Solicitors' Code of Conduct 2007. r.1.02 requires a solicitor to act with integrity, and r.10.01 requires a solicitor not to take unfair advantage of a third party.

11-058 Add to NOTE 92: Cf. *Mantella v Mantella* (2006) 267 D.L.R. (4th) 532, Ontario Superior Ct, where it was held that the wife's lawyer owed no duty of care to the husband. Both the husband's and the wife's lawyers had attested in the separation agreement that they had explained to their client the meaning and implications of each provision of the agreement.

11-062 Add to NOTE 9: A similar result was reached in *Young v Borzoni* (2007) 277 D.L.R. (4th) 685, British Columbia CA, and a claim for intentional infliction of nervous shock was struck out as the pleaded facts did not warrant it.

(iv) *Solicitors' Liability on Undertakings*

11-065 Add to NOTE 17: From July 1, 2007 the *Guide* was replaced by the Solicitors' Code of Conduct 2007. r.10.05 and the accompanying guidance concern undertakings.

Add to NOTE 19: Similarly a claim on an undertaking will not be an abuse of process because there had been an earlier deed of compromise, see *Commissioner of Inland Revenue v Bhanabhai* [2007] 2 N.Z.L.R. 478, NZCA.

11-068 Add to NOTE 44: The principle that ambiguous undertakings are construed in favour of the recipient was applied in *Templeton Insurance Ltd. v Penningtons Solicitors LLP* [2006] EWHC 685 (Ch); [2007] W.T.L.R. 1. Lewison J. construed an undertaking to apply monies for the express purpose of completion of the purchase of particular property in the same way as an undertaking to apply monies for that sole or exclusive purpose.

Add to NOTE 45: In *Commissioner of Inland Revenue v Bhanabhai* [2007] 2 N.Z.L.R. 478, NZCA, an undertaking was construed to be personal, although it

GENERAL   11–116

depended on matters beyond the control of the solicitors, because of the context of the undertaking.

Add to NOTE 72: In *Bank of Ireland Mortgage Bank v Coleman* [2006] IEHC **11–072**
337; [2007] P.N.L.R. 16, the High Court of Eire refused to order the defendant solicitor to compensate the plaintiff bank for failing to provide security over the relevant property, as the overall purpose of the detailed undertakings, which were in essence to provide such security, were still capable of being fulfilled.

Add to NOTE 89: See now the Solicitors' Code of Conduct 2007, para.30 of the **11–074**
Guidance to r.10.

(c) *The Standard of Skill and Care*

(i) *The Standard of Reasonableness*

Add to NOTE 15: The standard of reasonable care and skill is not the same as **11–080**
the lower standard of whether the lawyer has made an egregious error, see *Ristimaki v Cooper* (2006) 268 D.L.R. (4th) 155, Ontario CA.

(ii) *General Practice as Evidence of Reasonable Skill and Care*

Add to NOTE 51: In *Heibei Enterprises Ltd v Livasiri & Co* [2007] 3 **11–091**
H.K.L.R.D. 723, the Hong Kong Court of Appeal distinguished *Wong*. For the facts, see para.**11–202** below.

Add to NOTE 60: From July 1, 2007 the *Guide* was replaced by the Solicitors' **11–094**
Code of Conduct 2007. r.2 and the accompanying guidance concern client relations.

Add to NOTE 62: Cf. *Thai Trading Co v Taylor* [1998] Q.B. 781 at 785H, **11–095**
where the Court of Appeal observed that the fact that a professional rule prohibits a practice does not itself make the practice contrary to law.

Replace NOTE 65: This became para.**12–005** in the 8th edn, 1999. The Solicitors' Code of Conduct 2007 does not have this rule.

(v) *Aggravating Factors*

Add to NOTE 91: The Solicitors' Practice Rules 1990 and the *Guide* have been **11–103**
replaced from July 1, 2007 by the Solicitors' Code of Conduct 2007. r.3 concerns conflicts of interest, and sets out rules and guidance about acting for two clients, including buyers and sellers of property.

(d) *Specific Defences to a Claim for Breach of Duty*

(ii) *Abuse of Process*

Add: However, the decision was reversed by the Court of Appeal: see [2006] **11–116**
EWCA Civ 1749; [2008] 1 W.L.R. 484. It would not be manifestly unfair to the claimants if the issues as to the defendant's dishonesty had to be relitigated, as

11–116

they could plead and prove specific examples of dishonest conduct, it would not bring the administration of justice into disrepute to permit such relitigation, and it was not the defendant who initiated the proceedings. In *Laing v Taylor Walton (A Firm)* [2008] EWCA Civ 1146; [2008] P.N.L.R. 11, the claimant sued a lender about the terms of a loan he had entered and lost. He then sought to sue the solicitors who had drafted the loan agreement, and the Court of Appeal held that in order to succeed in that claim he would have to show that the Judge in the claim against the lender was wrong. The Court held that this collateral challenge to the original decision was an abuse of process.

Add to NOTE 56: In such cases the claim should only be struck out as abusive if its advancement was manifestly unfair to the other side, and the burden is a heavy one, see *Nesbitt v Holt* [2007] EWCA Civ 249; [2007] P.N.L.R. 24, CA. In that case the claimant sought to reopen industrial tribunal proceedings on the basis that his lawyer did not have any authority to settle them, but failed to do so. His subsequent claim against his lawyer was not struck out because the tribunal's conclusion that the lawyer was acting within his actual authority was not necessary to its decision which was based on ostensible authority, and as a result of further disclosure the evidence may have been different.

11–117 Add to NOTE 61: The strength or weakness of a claim and the delays in bringing it are generally not relevant to whether it is an abuse of process because it should have been included in earlier proceedings: see *Stuart v Goldberg Linde (a firm), The Times*, January 23, 2008, CA.

(iii) *Acting on Counsel's Advice*

11–121 Add to NOTE 72: *Regent Leisuretime Ltd v Skerrett* [2006] EWCA Civ 1184; [2007] P.N.L.R. 9, CA (solicitors entitled to rely on Counsel's view that two individuals' counterclaim for deceit against a bank should be pursued despite the problems caused by the reflective loss principle, but there were good reasons why their company should not sue); *Fennell v Johns Elliott (A Firm)* [2008] P.N.L.R. 8, Northern Ireland QBD (appropriately reasoned advice had been obtained from counsel and the solicitors had satisfied themselves that it was properly tenable).

(e) *Solicitor's Liability for Costs*

11–126 Add to NOTE 91: Note that solicitors may be liable to pay the other side's costs as a non-party who substantially controlled the proceedings or stood to benefit from them. Thus in *Myatt v National Coal Board* [2007] EWCA Civ 307; [2007] P.N.L.R. 25 the Court of Appeal ordered solicitors to pay 50 per cent of the costs of an appeal about the enforceability of conditional fee agreements, as they would only recover their profit costs if the appeal succeeded.

11–133 Add to NOTE 24: In *R. (on the application of Hide) v Staffordshire CC* [2008] EWHC 2441 (Admin); [2008] P.N.L.R. 13, Wyn Williams J. did not make a wasted costs order against a solicitor because there was a significant risk that she

Thank you for purchasing the 2nd supplement to the 6th edition of Jackson & Powell on Professional Liability.

☑ Don't miss important updates

So that you have all the latest information, Jackson & Powell on Professional Liability is supplemented regularly. Sign up today for a Standing Order to ensure you receive the updating supplements as soon as they publish. Setting up a Standing Order with Sweet & Maxwell is hassle-free, simply tick, complete and return this FREEPOST card and we'll do the rest.

You may cancel your Standing Order at any time by writing to us at Sweet & Maxwell, PO Box 2000, Andover, SP10 9AH stating the Standing Order you wish to cancel.

Alternatively, if you have purchased your copy of Jackson & Powell on Professional Liability from a bookshop or other trade supplier, please ask your supplier to ensure that you are registered to receive the new supplements.

All goods are subject to our 30 day Satisfaction Guarantee (applicable to EU customers only)

Yes, please send me new editions of **new supplements** of Jackson & Powell on Professional Liability to be invoiced on publication, until I cancel the standing order in writing.

☐ All new supplements to the 6th edition

Title   Name

Organisation

Job title

Address

Postcode

Telephone

Email

S&M account number (if known)

PO number

All orders are accepted subject to the terms of this order form and our Terms of Trading. (see www.sweetandmaxwell.co.uk). By submitting this order form I confirm that I accept these terms and I am authorised to sign on behalf of the customer.

Signed   Job Title

Print Name   Date

Goods will normally be dispatched within 3-5 working days of availability. The price charged to customers, irrespective of any prices quoted, will be the price specified in our price list current at the time of dispatch of the goods, as published on our website, unless the order is subject to a specific offer or discount in which case special terms may apply. Delivery Charges are not made for titles supplied in the UK. For deliveries in Europe the following charges apply: £7/€10 for first item, £2.50/€4 for each additional item. For deliveries outside Europe please add £30/€42 for first item, £15/€21 for each additional item.

UK VAT is charged on all applicable sales at the prevailing rate (currently 17.5%) except in the case of sales to Ireland where Irish VAT will be charged at the prevailing rate. Customers outside the EU will not be charged UK VAT. UK VAT Number: GB 900 5487 43. Irish VAT Number: IE 9513874E. For customers in an EU member state (except UK & Ireland) please supply your VAT Number. VAT No [   ]
Thomson Reuters (Legal) Limited (Company No. 1679046.
Registered in England & Wales. Registered Office and address for service: 100 Avenue Road, London NW3 3PF) trades using various trading names, of which a list is posted on its website at www.sweetandmaxwell.co.uk, and is part of Thomson Reuters.
"Thomson Reuters" and the Thomson Reuters logo are trademarks of Thomson Reuters and its affiliated companies.

SWEET & MAXWELL   **THOMSON REUTERS**

NO STAMP REQUIRED WITHIN U.K.

SWEET & MAXWELL

FREEPOST

PO BOX 2000

ANDOVER

SP10 9AH

UNITED KINGDOM

would become bankrupt as a result, which he considered would be a disproportionate consequence of her negligence.

Add to NOTE 34: In *Mitchells (A Firm) v Funkwerk Information Technologies York Ltd* [2008] P.N.L.R. 29, the Employment Appeal Tribunal set aside a wasted costs order against a solicitor in part because the tribunal had failed to consider whether there was any causation between the alleged negligence and the claimed loss. **11–135**

Add to NOTE 42: But see *Myatt v National Coal Board* [2007] EWCA Civ 307; [2007] P.N.L.R. 25, noted at para.**11–126** NOTE 91 above. **11–136**

Add to NOTE 44: In *Koo Golden East Mongolia v Bank of Nova Scotia* [2008] EWHC 1120 (QB); [2008] P.N.L.R. 32, Silber J. held that solicitors who had pursued the Central Bank of Mongolia, which had state immunity, did not act unreasonably or negligently, as the claim for relief could not be said to be doomed to failure. **11–137**

Add to NOTE 57: In *Hedrich v Standard Bank London Ltd* [2007] P.N.L.R. 31, Field J. did not make a wasted costs order against solicitors who failed to obtain a crucial CD-ROM from their clients, as it was not culpable conduct to fail to do so on taking instructions. They were later entitled to rely on their clients' assurance that the files had been lost, and while they should have obtained the files when they learnt of their existence during the trial, it was not proved that any costs were wasted as a result. **11–140**

Add to NOTE 61: In *Re Boodhoo* [2007] EWCA Crim 14; [2007] P.N.L.R. 20 the Court of Appeal set aside a wasted costs order against a solicitor who had withdrawn from a criminal trial when his client deliberately failed to appear, as the solicitor was entitled to conclude that he could not properly represent his client. **11–141**

(f) *Exclusion or Restriction of Liability by Contract*

Add to NOTE 65: See A. Horrocks and S. Brake, "Limitations of liability in solicitors' retainers" (2007) 23 P.N. 108. **11–142**

Add to NOTE 67: From July 1, 2007 the *Guide* was replaced by the Solicitors' Code of Conduct 2007. r.2.07 permits limitation of civil liability to now below the minimum level of insurance cover; see also the accompanying guidance.

(h) *Attribution and Vicarious Liability*

Add to NOTE 90: In *Zurich GSG Ltd v Gray & Kellas* [2007] CSOH 91; [2008] P.N.L.R. 1 a solicitor acting for an executor signed a form which stated that there was no claim or dispute affecting the estate, but he did not know that the representation was false. A partner in the defendant firm had notice of a claim against the estate. The knowledge of a partner is attributed to the firm by s.16 of **11–147**

11–147 CHAPTER 11—SOLICITORS

the Partnership Act 1890. However, Lord Brodie struck out a claim in negligence against the firm based only on such attributed knowledge.

Add to NOTE 92: It had been held by the Supreme Court of Canada under the equivalent provision in British Columbia that such liability extends to disgorgement of profits although such profits were unauthorised by the partners: see *3464920 Canada Inc. v Strother* (2007) 281 D.L.R. (4th) 640. See further para.**11–025** above, and for criticism see Edelman J. "Unanticipated fiduciary liability" (2008) 124 L.Q.R. 21.

2. LIABILITY FOR BREACH OF DUTY

(c) *Failing to Give Advice*

11–159   Add: The Solicitors' Practice Rules 1990 and the *Guide* have been replaced from July 1, 2007 by the Solicitors' Code of Conduct 2007. r.2.02(1) requires that the client is given a clear explanation of the issues involved and the options available to him, and that he is kept informed of progress unless otherwise agreed.

11–162   Add to NOTE 52: For an illustration of this principle, see *Heritage Developments Ltd v Davis Blank Furniss (A Firm)* [2007] EWCA Civ 765, CA, where developers instructed solicitors that the proposed development was not to concern certain land held on possessory title, and the solicitors therefore had no duty to advise that the licence provisions of a development agreement should be extended to enable development of part of that land.

11–165   Add to NOTE 64 after first sentence: See now para.55 of the guidance to r.3 of the Solicitors' Code of Conduct 2007, which has replaced the *Guide*.

11–166   Add to NOTE 71: And see *Gallop v Abdoulah* [2006] 8 W.W.R. 220, Saskatchewan CA, where the solicitor failed to warn of the risks of assuming a mortgage, and that a side-letter from the client's uncle to repurchase the property may be unenforceable.

11–167   Add to NOTE 80: This does not appear in the Solicitors' Code of Conduct 2007, which has replaced the *Guide*.

11–170   Add to NOTE 97: *Football League Ltd. v Edge Ellison (A Firm)* is now reported at [2007] P.N.L.R. 2. Cf. *Littler v Price* [2004] QCA 383; [2005] 1 Qd.R. 275, Queensland CA, where the solicitors did have an obligation to advise lay clients with respect to a lease where the proposed lessee was a $3 company. They should have advised as to the absence of any protection if the lessee was unable to meet its obligations and to secure the position by a guarantee if possible, see [29].

11–175   Add to NOTE 15 after the first sentence: This does not appear in the Solicitors' Code of Conduct 2007, which has replaced the *Guide*.

Add to NOTE 17: In *Phelps v Stewarts (A Firm)* [2007] EWHC 1561 (Ch); [2007] P.N.L.R. 32, QBD, a solicitor failed to advise a client that any payment above the inheritance tax nil rate band into a discretionary trust, in which the client may place his personal injury damages, was subject to an immediate tax charge at the rate of 20 per cent. The duty to give this advice would only have been discharged if it had been confirmed in writing.

(d) *Misconduct of Litigation*

Add to NOTE 18: The *Sarwar* test has been qualified in *Garrett v Halton Borough Council* [2006] EWCA Civ 1017; [2007] 1 W.L.R. 554, where the Court emphasised that what it laid down was guidance only, and the suggestion that the client should be invited to bring any relevant policy to a first interview had no application in high volume low value litigation conducted on referral by claims management companies. There is an obligation to explain a costs agreement even if there is no formal retainer yet: see *McNamara Business & Property Law v Kasmeridis* [2007] SASC; (2007) 97 S.A.S.R. 129, South Australia CA. In *David Truex (A Firm) v Kitchin* [2007] EWCA Civ 618; [2007] P.N.L.R. 33, CA, solicitors were told by their client that she had no money and was borrowing from her parents, and they were negligent in failing to advise her that she may be eligible for public funding.   **11–176**

Add: It will generally be impracticable and inappropriate for a solicitor to prepare a client for every conceivable line of cross-examination: see *Fennell v Johns Elliott (A Firm)* [2008] P.N.L.R. 8; Northern Ireland QBD.   **11–184**

Add to NOTE 92: From July 1, 2007 the *Guide* was replaced by the Solicitors' Code of Conduct 2007, which is to similar effect.   **11–193**

(e) *Misconduct of Non-contentious Business*

(i) *Conveyancing*

Add to NOTE 35: In *Heibei Enterprises Ltd v Livasiri & Co* [2007] 3 H.K.L.R.D. 723, the Hong Kong Court of Appeal distinguished *Wong*. The claimants entered a joint venture project with third parties to acquire and redevelop property. The claimants' solicitors transferred monies to the third parties' solicitors, as agreed, on those solicitors undertaking to use the money to purchase the property. The third parties' solicitors stole the money. The claimants' solicitors were not liable for failing to obtain greater security for their clients' monies, as the only method suggested, a bank account to hold the contributions, would not have achieved anything.   **11–202**

Add to NOTE 37: In *Heslop v Cousins* [2007] 3 N.Z.L.R. 679, Chisholm J. held solicitors liable for failing to advise their clients not to permit the purchasers to take possession of the property without suitable undertakings.   **11–203**

Add to NOTE 61: From July 1, 2007 the *Guide* was replaced by the Solicitors' Code of Conduct 2007. Rules 3.16 to 3.22, and the accompanying guidance at paras.82 to 89, concern acting for lenders and borrowers.   **11–207**

(iii) *Wills*

11-221 Add to NOTE 43: From July 1, 2007 the *Guide* was replaced by the Solicitors' Code of Conduct 2007. Rule 2.01(1)(c) requires that the instructions are checked with the client when given by someone else.

11-226 Add to NOTE 67: From July 1, 2007 the *Guide* was replaced by the Solicitors' Code of Conduct 2007; rule 3.04 is to similar effect.

3. DAMAGES

(a) *Breach of Fiduciary Duty and Breach of Trust*

11-228 Add to NOTE 74: In *3464920 Canada Inc v Strother* (2007) 281 DLR (4th) 640, the Supreme Court of Canada ordered a disgorgement of profits; see further para.**11-025** above.

(b) *Remoteness*

(i) *Causation*

11-236 Add to NOTE 3: Also reported at [2006] 1 P.&C.R. DG13. For the decision on the assessment of damages, see [2007] P.N.L.R. 8.

11-239 Add to NOTE 10: Cf. *Redbus LMDS Ltd v Jeffrey Green & Russell (a firm)* [2007] EWHC 2938 (Ch); [2007] P.N.L.R. 12, QBD, where it was held that a solicitor's negligence, in failing to make clear in drafting articles of association of a company that sub-licences of a licence which it owned could be granted without consent, was the effective cause of subsequent litigation costs between the two groups which controlled the company, as it allowed arguments to be run regarding the wording of the licence.

11-241 Add to NOTE 18: See further the discussion in *Luke v Kingsley Smith & Co (A Firm)* [2004] P.N.L.R. 12.

(iii) *The Scope of the Duty*

11-252 Add to NOTE 52: Cf. *Watts v Bell & Scott, WS* [2007] CSOH 108; [2007] S.L.T. 665; [2007] P.N.L.R. 30, OH, where compensation for loss of profits from the proposed development was awarded where solicitor had failed to intimate an offer for the purchase of property.

(c) *Measure of Damages*

(i) *Date of Assessment*

11-255 Add to NOTE 58: In *Veitch v Avery* [2007] EWCA Civ 711; [2008] P.N.L.R. 7, solicitors wrongly advised a client who owned a hotel that he was in default under a loan agreement and he did not defend possession proceedings. The Court of Appeal held that whether the loss should to be assessed at the date of breach depended on the circumstances, but as the judge had rightly found that there was no prospect of the claimant trading out of his financial difficulties, damages were correctly assessed at the date of breach, and were nominal.

(iii) *Evaluation of a Chance*

Add: In *Perkins v Lupton Fawcett (A Firm)* [2008] EWCA Civ 418; [2008] P.N.L.R. 30, the claimants sold their interest in a business which had substantial book debts. The claimants gave the purchasers a warranty that the book debts were recoverable. They and their solicitors mistakenly thought that the purchasers had to take proceedings against individual debtors before pursuing the claimants on their warranty, but in fact the purchasers only had to take reasonable steps to recover the debts. As a result, the claimants incurred substantial liabilities to the purchasers. The Court of Appeal held that if the claimants had been properly advised, there was a 20 per cent chance of the purchasers agreeing the warranty in the form the claimants had wanted.

11–264

Add to NOTE 84: *Football League Ltd v Edge Ellison (A Firm)* [2007] P.N.L.R. 2, Rimer J. (70 per cent chance of obtaining guarantees to £160 million, and 50 per cent for remaining £155 million); *Newline Corporate Name Ltd v Morgan Cole (A Firm)* [2007] EWHC (Comm) 1628; [2008] P.N.L.R. 2, Simon J. (solicitors negligently failed to advise underwriters that they were not liable because cover was excluded if the loss was covered by other insurance; damages reduced by 15 per cent because the other insurers may have continued to contest indemnity).

Add to NOTE 97: Similarly, in *Veitch v Avery* [2007] EWCA Civ 711; *The Times*, August 29, 2007, the Court of Appeal held at [26] that the judge was entitled to assess on the balance of probabilities the prospect of the claimant's father supplying further monies to support his son's business.

11–266

(d) *Heads of Damage*

(ii) *Difference in Value of Property*

Add to NOTE 35: At least where the complaint is that the solicitor's negligence caused the claimant to enter a transaction on worse terms than it would have done if properly advised, he will have to prove that the such negligence caused him to extricate himself from the transaction to obtain damages for such extrication, as the claimant did in *Funnell v Adamas and Remer (A Partnership)* [2007] EWHC 2166 (QB); [2008] 1 P.&C.R. DG5, Wilkie J.

11–279

Add to NOTE 47: See also *Watts v Bell & Scott, WS* [2007] CSOH 108; [2007] S.L.T. 665; [2007] P.N.L.R. 30, OH, where compensation for lost profits was awarded where the solicitors were aware of the pursuer's intentions for the premises and that he would lose the development potential if he failed to purchase them.

11–281

Add to NOTE 57: *Fulham Leisure Holdings Ltd v Nicholson Graham & Jones (a firm) (No.2)* is more fully reported at [2007] P.N.L.R. 5. The Court of Appeal

11–283

11-283 CHAPTER 11—SOLICITORS

reversed the finding of liability, and did not consider the issue of damages: see [2008] EWCA Civ 84; [2008] P.N.L.R. 22.

(iii) *Loss of Opportunity to Bring Proceedings*

11–289   Add to NOTE 82: *Dudarec v Andrews* is reported at [2006] 1 W.L.R. 3002.

11–293   Add to NOTE 97: In *Miller v Garton Shires (a firm)* [2006] EWCA Civ 1386; [2007] P.N.L.R. 11, CA, the claimant's claim against the lawyers for allowing his personal injury claim to become statute-barred was struck out, as the original claim would have failed, and thus the claimant had suffered no loss.

11–294   Add to NOTE 5: a similar result was reached, *obiter*, by Saunders J. in *Nicholson v Knox Ukiwa & Co (a firm)* [2008] EWHC 1222 (QB); [2008] P.N.L.R. 33.

11–297   Add to NOTE 18: In *Phillips & Co (a firm) v Whatley* [2007] UKPC 28; [2007] P.N.L.R. 27 the Privy Council discounted the full quantum of a lost personal injury litigation by 30 per cent for the prospect of failing to succeed in an action, and by a further 60 per cent because the original defendants were insolvent and reputable insurers may have relied on a breach of condition from late notification of the claim, so that 28 per cent of the value of the claim was recovered.

11–298   Replace NOTE 25 with: [2000] Lloyd's Rep. P.N. 89. The primary reason for the judge's conclusion at [116] col.2 was that if a later authority laid down the law in a way which was not intended to be a departure from the past, that authority should be applied in any event. See **para.10–292** for the facts of the case. For an apparent exception, see *Cohen v Kingsley Napley (A Firm)* [2005] EWHC 899 (QB); [2005] P.N.L.R. 37, where Tugendhat J. held that the prospects of any action being struck out should be assessed by reference to subsequent law, not the law as it then stood, although in fact there was no difference between the two.

11–299   Add: In *Whitehead v Hibbert Pownall & Newton* [2008] EWCA Civ 285; [2008] P.N.L.R. 25, CA, PM gave birth to a child with spina bifida, and claimed that this should have been diagnosed antenatally and she would have had a termination. The claim was progressed negligently slowly by the defendant solicitors, and PM committed suicide after the time at which the claim should have been brought to trial. In a claim brought by the estate, the Court of Appeal held that there would be a windfall if PM's death was ignored, and the court should not proceed to assess damages on that footing.

Add to NOTES 28 and 29: *Dudarec v Andrews* is reported at [2006] 1 W.L.R. 3002. For commentary see T. Dugdale, "Chance, Certainty and Risk" (2007) 23 P.N. 43, and more generally H. Evans "Lost litigation and later knowledge" (2007) 23 P.N. 204.

11–300   Add: In *Nicholson v Knox Ukiwa & co (a firm)* [2008] EWHC 1222 (QB); [2008] P.N.L.R. 33 Saunders J. held, obiter, that judgment rate was appropriate in that case where the delay was some fifteen years, as it compensated in part for the fact that the claimant would have obtained a compound return on his losses, whereas only simple interest was awarded by the courts.

(v) *Losses on Loans Secured by Mortgages*

Add to NOTE 45: Similarly, in *Preferred Mortgages Ltd v Shanks* [2008] CSOH 23; [2008] P.N.L.R. 20, OH, the solicitors failed to advise that title to property was seriously defective, and they were liable for the whole loss. **11–304**

(vi) *Loss of Some Other Financial Advantage*

Add to NOTE 61: See further J. Lee Suet Lin "Barring recovery for diminution in value of shares on the reflective loss principle" [2007] C.L.J. 537. **11–311**

(ix) *Wasted Expenditure*

Add to NOTE 89: The decision in *Hextall Erskine* has been followed in a number of decisions, including *Redbus LMDS Ltd v Jeffrey Green & Russell (a firm)* [2007] EWHC 2938 (Ch); [2007] P.N.L.R. 12. Damages on a standard basis can be recovered for reasonable mitigation, but not damages for pursuing a wholly unreasonable claim: see *Sifri v Clough Willis (a firm)* [2007] EWHC 985 (Ch); [2008] W.T.L.R. 1453. **11–319**

4. SHARED RESPONSIBILITY

(a) *Contributory Negligence*

Add to NOTE 38: For another illustration see *Football League Ltd v Edge Ellison (A Firm)* [2007] P.N.L.R. 2, Rimer J. The defendant solicitors were not negligent in failing to raise the issue of a parent company guarantee, but if they were, the claimant would have been contributorily negligent in not considering it, as it was a commercial aspect of the transaction. **11–333**

(b) *Apportionment of Liability*

Add to NOTE 74: The principles of that case were applied by Morgan J. in *Pulvers (A Firm) v Chan* [2008] EWHC 2406 (Ch); [2008] P.N.L.R. 9. There were a series of mortgage frauds orchestrated by S, the solicitors' employee W was a knowing participant in them, and third parties were also involved. The solicitors paid the lenders' losses and obtained 100 per cent recovery from W. As against other parties, the solicitors (who were affixed with the conduct of W) had to share liability equally with S and anyone else liable in respect of a given loss. **11–342**

CHAPTER 12

BARRISTERS

	PARA.		PARA.
1. General	12–001	(f) Abuse of Process	12–010
(a) The Function of a Barrister	12–001	(g) Liability for Costs	12–011
(b) Duties to Clients	12–004	■ 2. Liability for Breach of Duty	12–023
(c) Duties to Third Parties	12–006	3. Damages	12–042
☐ (d) The Standard of Skill and Care	12–008	4. Shared Responsibility	12–046
☐ (e) Immunity	12–009	■ (a) Apportionment of Liability	12–046

1. GENERAL

(d) *The Standard of Skill and Care*

Add: The test for negligence has been expressed as whether the advice fell within the range of that to be expected of reasonably competent counsel of the defendant's seniority and experience: see *Moy v Pettman Smith* [2005] 1 W.L.R., HL 581 at [62] and *Jassi v Gallagher* [2006] EWCA Civ 1065; [2007] P.N.L.R. 2, CA at [42]. **12–008**

(e) *Immunity*

Replace first sentence with: For commentary see H. Evans *Lawyers' Liabilities* (2nd edn, 2002) Ch.5. The abolition of immunity is retrospective until at least 1991: see *Awoyomi v Radford* [2007] EWHC 1671 (QB), [2007] P.N.L.R. 34 Lloyd Jones J. **12–009**

Add to NOTE 41: Also reported at [2007] P.N.L.R. 7. For commentary, see G. Gordon, "Not Yet Dead: *Wright v Paton Farrell* and Advocates' Immunity in Scotland" (2007) 70 M.L.R. 471.

Add to NOTE 42: *Lai* is reported at [2007] 2 N.Z.L.R. 7.

Add to NOTE 44: Also reported at (2005) 223 C.L.R. 1.

2. LIABILITY FOR BREACH OF DUTY

Add: Successful appeals from findings that a barrister has or has not been negligent will be rare, if the judge has properly recognised the applicable standard by which conduct is to be judged: see *Jassi v Gallagher* [2006] EWCA Civ 1065; [2007] P.N.L.R. 2, CA at [42] and [58]. **12–023**

12-033 CHAPTER 12—BARRISTERS

12-033   Add to NOTE 33: In *Jassi v Gallagher* [2006] EWCA Civ 1065; [2007] P.N.L.R. 2 a tenant owned the long lease of a house and served a notice in 1994 seeking enfranchisement. The defendant barrister advised him in 1997 and 1998 that he had a strong case, but the claim failed at trial because the notice was invalid as the tenant did not occupy the house as his main residence for part of the time and he had other residences. The Judge held that the barrister was not negligent in failing to advise that a fresh notice should be served in 1997 or 1998, as new notices would be difficult to draft to comply with the relevant Act, and may have disadvantaged the tenant's credibility and reduced his chances of winning on the basis of the 1994 notice. The Court of Appeal upheld that finding.

12-037   In *Prichard Joyce & Hinds (A Firm) v Batcup* [2008] EWHC 20 (QB); [2008] P.N.L.R. 18, Underhill J. held that two barristers negligently failed to advise of the time limits in relation to a potential claim against the clients' former solicitors W. That claim would have concerned a failure to advise the clients of a time limit against another firm LL for allegedly negligent advice losing the opportunity of a favourable settlement of a dispute about property in Spain. While the barristers were instructed in relation to the ongoing claim against LL, which was in fact statute-barred, the question of the time-limit in any proceedings against W were so closely related to the limitation issue in the claim against LL that by necessary implication it fell within the scope of the instructions of the barristers.

4. SHARED RESPONSIBILITY

(a) *Apportionment of Liability*

12-046   Add to NOTE 65: In *Prichard Joyce & Hinds (A Firm) v Batcup* [2008] EWHC 20 (QB); [2008] P.N.L.R. 18, Underhill J. ordered leading and junior counsel to pay a 75 per cent contribution, because their relationship was of the conventional kind where solicitors looked to counsel for authoritative guidance on the major strategic questions in litigation. For the facts see para.**12-037** above.

CHAPTER 13

MEDICAL PRACTITIONERS

	PARA.		PARA.
1. General	13–001	(e) Failure of Communication Between Hospitals or Medical Practitioners	13–088
(a) Duties to Patient	13–003		
(i) Contractual Duties	13–003		
(ii) Statutory Duties	13–005	(f) Failing to Explain Treatment or Warn of Risks	13–089
■ (iii) Common Law Duty of Care	13–006	3. Damages	13–105
(b) Duties to Third Parties	13–013	■ (a) Scope of Duty	13–106
□ (i) The "Nervous Shock" Cases	13–014	■ (b) Remoteness	13–111
□ (ii) Duty to Prevent Injury to Third Parties	13–017	□ (i) Causation	13–112
		(ii) Loss of a chance	13–126
■ (iii) Unborn Children	13–020	(iii) Warnings	13–134
■ (iv) "Wrongful Life"	13–021	□ (iv) The Application of the Bolam Test in Causation—Bolitho	13–139
■ (c) The Standard of Skill and Care	13–022		
(d) General and Approved Practice	13–032	(v) Intervening Events	13–142
(i) Acting in Accordance with General and Approved Practice	13–032	(vi) Contributory Negligence	13–143
		(vii) Causation in Wrongful Birth and Wrongful Conception Claims	13–144
(ii) Departing from General and Approved Practice	13–034	■ (c) Foreseeability	13–149
■ (e) Expert Evidence	13–037	(d) Measure of Damages	13–155
□ (f) Res Ipsa Loquitur	13–039	(i) Damages for Personal Injury	13–155
(g) Consent to Treatment	13–043		
(i) Limits to Consent	13–044	(ii) Reduced Damages Due to Successive Events	13–156
(ii) Voluntary Consent	13–045		
(iii) Informed Consent	13–046	(iii) Aggravated Damages	13–157
■ (iv) Capacity to Consent	13–047	(iv) Damages in Wrongful Birth and Wrongful Conception Claims	13–158
□ (h) Allied Professions	13–058		
(i) Hospitals and Health Authorities	13–059	(v) Impact of the Human Rights Act 1998	13–168
□ (j) Apportionment of Liability	13–064	(vi) Claims by Unwanted Disabled Child	13–169
2. Liability for Breach of Duty	13–066		
(a) Failing to Prevent Illness	13–067		
(b) Failing to Attend or Examine a Patient	13–069	(vii) Proportionate Damages in *Fairchild* Exception Cases	13–170
(c) Wrong Diagnosis	13–073		
(d) Error in the Course of Treatment	13–077		

1. GENERAL

(a) *Duties to Patient*

(iii) *Common Law Duty of Care*

13–006 Add a new NOTE 32A: For the interrelationship between private and public healthcare and the desire of the courts to ensure that a duty of care exists in

[79]

13–006   CHAPTER 13—MEDICAL PRACTITIONERS

circumstances where NHS responsibilities are contracted out to private providers see *Farraj v King's Healthcare NHS Trust* [2006] EWHC 1228; [2006] 2 F.C.R. 804; (2006) 90 B.M.L.R. 21 (private laboratory engaged by hospital trust to culture sample for testing owed duty of care to claimants following incorrect test result).

13–011   **Economic Losses.** Add the following sentence after the end of the first paragraph: For a fuller discussion of this issue see para.**13–109** below.

Add at the end of NOTE 55: See also *Meadow v General Medical Council* [2006] EWCA Civ 1390; [2007] Q.B. 462, CA in which it was stated that there was no basis for extending the common law immunity of a witness from civil suit to all fitness to practice proceedings since their purpose was to protect the public. If the conduct of an expert witness raised the question of whether the expert was fit to practise in his particular field, the regulatory authorities should be entitled and might be bound to investigate.

(b) *Duties to Third Parties*

(i) *The "Nervous Shock" Cases*

13–014   Add a new NOTE 76A: For a recent application of this principle see *Farmer v Outokumpu Stainless Ltd* LTL 31/8/06 (wife of accident victim had to demonstrate that she was close to the accident in time and space and that the accident was communicated to her through sight or hearing of the event or its immediate aftermath). If the patient was merely receiving emergency first aid at the scene of an accident or even at hospital and the patient was essentially in the same state as immediately after the accident, that would constitute the immediate aftermath.

13–016   Add to NOTE 87: Contrast the approach taken by the Australian courts in *Halech v State of South Australia* [2006] S.A.S.C. 29 (son of a deceased victim of a car accident suffered major depressive disorder as a result of the misidentification of his mother which led to her being buried as opposed to cremated. The police officers were held by the Supreme Court of South Australia to owe no duty of care to the son as the imposition of such a duty would be inconsistent with the public interest).

(ii) *Duty to Prevent Injury to Third Parties*

13–019   Add to NOTE 2: See also *Ellis v Counties Manukau District Health Board* [2007] 1 N.Z.L.R. 196 in which the High Court in Auckland struck out a claim by a mentally disordered claimant against District Health Board arising out of his release and subsequent murder of his father on the grounds that he had been a voluntary outpatient and no duty arose to detain him against his wishes so as to prevent him causing harm to others.

Add to NOTE 4: For an example of a successful claim see *Stefaniu v Ahmed et Al* (2007) 275 D.L.R. (4th) 101 in which a successful claim in Ontario was brought against a psychiatrist who released a mental patient from hospital who then went on to murder his sister. The patient had previously been held as an involuntary patient and the Ontario Court of Appeal upheld the jury's finding that the psychiatrist had acted negligently in changing the patient's status from that of a voluntary patient to an involuntary one shortly before his release.

(iii) *Unborn Children*

Add to the end of the paragraph: See also (2006) *Bovingdon et al v Hergott* 275 D.L.R. (4th) 168 in which a successful negligence claim was brought against a physician who failed to warn a mother of the risks associated with a fertility drug, and in particular failed to warn her that it increased the risk of twin births which in turn caused the children's disabilities. **13–020**

(iv) *"Wrongful Life"*

Add at the end of NOTE 8: Cf. the decision in (2006) *Bovingdon et al v Hergott* 275 D.L.R. (4th) 168 in which the Ontario Superior Court of Justice upheld a successful negligence claim against a physician who failed to warn a mother of the risks associated with a fertility drug, and in particular that it increased the risk of twin births which in turn caused the children's disabilities. The case was stated to not be a case for wrongful life but rather one in which the damages were caused by the wrongful act of the physician in respect of which the ordinary principles of negligence applied providing that the children were born alive. It was emphasised that in such a case there was no conflict between the duty to warn the mother and the duty to the children. In *Hibbert Pownall & Newton (a Firm) and another v Eric Whitehead (Administrator of the Estate of Paula McLeish, deceased* [2008] EWCA Civ 285; (2008) P.N.L.R. 25 the Court of Appeal dismissed a claim against solicitors in respect of allegedly negligently conducted litigation concerning a mother's "wrongful birth" clinical negligence claim on the grounds that such losses were not recoverable. **13–021**

(c) *The Standard of Skill and Care*

Add: For a recent example of the Court of Appeal overturning a first instance decision as a result of insufficient logical analysis see *Smith v Southampton University Hospital NHS Trust* [2007] EWCA Civ 387. The court emphasised that even if there was a substantial amount of agreement between two experts in relation to the surgical technique under discussion, a judge was still required to explain why she rejected the evidence of one expert and it was not sufficient simply to say that the other expert was representative of a responsible body of medical opinion and that, as a consequence, there had been no negligence. **13–024**

(e) *Expert Evidence*

Add at the end of NOTE 74: The importance of expert evidence is illustrated by the decision in *Lennie v Royal Victoria Infirmary & Associated Hospitals NHS Trust* [2006] EWCA Civ 975 where an appeal in respect of alleged clinical negligence arising from the circumstances surrounding the birth of a baby with cerebral palsy was dismissed. The principal reason for the failure of the appeal **13–037**

13–037

was that it was not open to the claimant to change his key allegations on appeal where evidence was not adduced to meet those allegations at trial and where the defendant had no notice nor had been given any opportunity to muster any further evidence that it might otherwise have wished to adduce in order to rebut them.

13–038 Add after the end of the first paragraph: This can be contrasted with the Court of Appeal's refusal to set aside a judgment on the grounds of an expert witness's failure to disclose a potential conflict of interest (membership of the Cases Committee of the Medical Defence Union) in *Toth v Jarman* [2006] EWCA Civ 1028. The Court of Appeal stated that the key question to be considered was whether or not the expert's opinion was independent and gave guidance as to duties of expert witnesses in such circumstances.

Add at the end of NOTE 84: For a recent application of the Bolitho test, see *Cowley v Cheshire and Merseyside Strategic Health Authority* [2007] EWHC; (2007) 94 B.M.L.R. 29 in which the claimant's claim failed as the overwhelming weight of the evidence was that the health authority's policy on the administration of antenatal cortico-steroids was within the reasonable range of policies for the management of premature labour and the treating clinician had followed that guidance.

(f) *Res Ipsa Loquitur*

13–042 Add to NOTE 16: This analysis of *Lillywhite* is taken from Robert Francis Q.C.'s update to the PNBA Clinical Negligence Seminar on September 10, 2006.

(g) *Consent to Treatment*

(iv) *Capacity to Consent*

13–047 Add at the end of the paragraph a new paragraph: The principles governing compulsory treatment and s.58 of the Mental Health Act 1980 were recently reviewed by the Court of Appeal in *R. (on the application of B) v Dr SS* [2006] EWCA Civ 28; (2006) 90 B.M.L.R. 1. B was a patient detained at Broadmoor who had been diagnosed as suffering from Bipolar Affective Disorder but who had not received any medication since 2003. His responsible medical officer believed that B's condition was deteriorating and wished to treat him with an anti-psychotic medication, administered by injection and a mood stabilizer. B sought to argue that treatment without his consent would infringe his rights under the European Convention on Human Rights and sought to challenge the validity of compulsory treatment. The Court of Appeal upheld the judge's findings that such treatment could be lawfully administered on the grounds that: (i) a patient would plainly lack capacity to consent if he was not able to appreciate the likely effects of receiving treatment and the judge had found that B did not accept that he might be mentally ill and therefore in need of treatment, (ii) it was objectively in B's own interests that he should accept the medication and ensuring that he received treatment was justified as this was necessary for the health and safety of the patient or for the protection of others. Articles 3, 8 and 12 of the European Convention on Human Rights had not been breached, (iii) on the evidence the judge was entitled to find that the treatment was in B's best interests and it had been convincingly shown that it was a medical necessity.

Withdrawal of Treatment from Insensate Patients. Add to NOTE 81: See further the consideration of *Bland* in *An NHS Trust v MB (a child represented by CAFASS as Guardian Ad Litem)* [2006] EWHC 507; [2006] F.L.R. 319 discussed at para.**13–056** below. For a recent application of the decision in *Bland*, see *A Hospital v W* [2007] EWHC 425; [2007] LS Law Medical 273. Sir Mark Potter, the President of the Family Division, confirmed that while a medical practitioner had a duty to act in the best interests of a mentally incapacitated patient, he was under no duty to continue to treat such a patient where there was a large body of informed, responsible medical opinion that continuance would be of no benefit, as would be the case where the patient was in a persistent vegetative state with no prospect of recovery. Withdrawal of hydration and nutrition in these circumstances was also confirmed not to be a breach of Arts 2 and 3 of the European Convention on Human Rights.

13–054

Add at the end of the paragraph a new paragraph: The issue of withdrawal of treatment from a child suffering from a degenerative and progressive condition, namely a very severe form of spinal muscular atrophy was considered by the Court of Appeal in *An NHS Trust v MB (a child represented by CAFASS as Guardian Ad Litem)* [2006] EWHC 507; [2006] F.L.R. 319. The child was not in a persistent vegetative state but had become unable to move save for the movement of his eyes and possible slight movement of his eyebrows, corner of his mouth, thumb and toes or feet. His treating doctors considered that his quality of life was so low and the burdens of living so great that it was unethical to continue artificially to keep him alive and that his endotracheal tube should be removed. However his parents did not consent to this. The Court of Appeal held that:

13–056

(a) although the concept of "intolerability" had been described as an invaluable guide, it really meant no more than that the conclusion that it was in the best interests of the patient to be allowed to die should only be reached in a clear and strong case;

(b) there was no legal distinction between withholding or withdrawing life support and the best interests test applied equally to both situations;

(c) the drawing up of a list specifically identifying the benefits or advantages or the burdens and disadvantages of continuing or discontinuing the treatment in question had proved an enormously useful discipline;

(d) it was not in the best interests of the child to discontinue ventilation with the inevitable result that he would immediately die. Further it was in his best interests to continue with the continuous pressure ventilation, with the nursing and medical care that properly went with it although no declaration to that effect could or would be made. Notwithstanding the burdens of discomfort, distress and pain, the child had the benefits of age appropriate cognition and continued to have a relationship of value to him with his family and to gain other precious and real pleasures from touch, sight and sound;

(e) however it would be in the child's best interest to withhold those procedures which went beyond maintaining ventilation which required the positive infliction of pain, the need for such procedures itself being an indicator that the child had moved towards death despite ventilation.

13–057 **Children.** Add to NOTE 87: For a recent application of the *Gillick* case see *R. (Axon) v Secretary of State for Health (Family Planning Association intervening)* [2006] EWHC 37 (Admin); [2006] Q.B. 539. The *Gillick* case was stated to remain authoritative on the lawfulness of the provision by health care professionals of confidential advice and treatment on contraception to young people under the age of 16 without parental knowledge or consent and provided appropriate guidelines on proposed and actual provision of advice and treatment on all sexual matters, including abortion, without parental knowledge or consent. The Department of Health's guidance on such issues was found to be both in accordance with the decision in *Gillick* and Art.8 of the ECHR.

(h) *Allied Professions*

13–058 Add at the end of the paragraph a new paragraph: For duties owed by pharmacists see *Horton v Timothy Evans and Lloyds Pharmacy Ltd* [2006] EWHC 2808; (2007) P.N.L.R. 17. On the facts of that case a failure by the pharmacist to question the correctness of a prescription of a different strength and dose to that previously prescribed with either the prescribing doctor or the patient was held to be conduct which fell below the standard to be expected of a reasonably competent and careful pharmacist.

(j) *Apportionment of Liability*

13–065 **Apportionment between medical practitioners and pharmacists.** Add to NOTE 26: For a recent application of *Dwyer* see *Horton v Timothy Evans and Lloyds Pharmacy Ltd* [2006] EWHC 2808; [2007] P.N.L.R. 17.

2. LIABILITY FOR BREACH OF DUTY

(f) *Failing to Explain Treatment or Warn of Risks*

13–100 **Risk of disability of unborn baby.** Add to the end of this paragraph: See also *Lillywhite v University College London Hospitals' NHS Trust* [2005] EWCA Civ 1466 discussed at para.**13–042**.

DAMAGES 13–114

3. DAMAGES

(a) *Scope of Duty*

Add at end of paragraph a new paragraph: The Court of Appeal dismissed the club's appeal, holding (on different grounds and rejecting the judge's reliance on the lack of intent to create legal relations) that there was no contract between the defendant surgeon and the club because there was no need to imply such a contract with the club (rather than the footballer), and for a contract to be implied the test was necessity: see *Baird Textile Holdings Ltd v Marks & Spencer Plc* [2001] EWCA Civ 274; [2002] 1 All E.R. (Comm) 737 at [62]. There was no duty of care on the defendant surgeon to the club not to cause it financial loss. Indeed if there were such a duty a conflict of interest would arise because the defendant surgeon's concern had to be exclusively his patient's well being, not the financial circumstances of the club. Rix L.J. and Mummery L.J. (with whom Mr Justice Peter Smith agreed) found none of the necessary elements for liability in tort to be present. The nearest authority on the facts, *Islington v UCL Hospital* [2005] Lloyd's Rep. Med. 386 (a case where negligent medical advice by the defendant hospital resulted in a patient suffering a stroke and requiring residential care from her local authority, the claimant) resulted in no duty of care to the claimant health authority—the duty of medical care to the patient was not accompanied by a duty of care not to cause financial loss to a third party. This case was unfavourable to the club's position. If insurance was a relevant consideration (for determining whether or not a duty of care was owed) the club, and not the surgeon, would be expected to insure itself against suffering loss of this kind. Reported at [2006] EWCA Civ 1299; [2007] P.I.Q.R. P7; (2006) 92 B.M.L.R. 179.

13–109

(b) *Remoteness*

(i) *Causation*

Add to NOTE 48: See also *Holt v Edge* [2007] EWCA Civ 602 (unreported elsewhere), where the defendant's admitted breach by failure to carry out a telephone triage (by means of which the claimant's case would be allocated an appropriate priority) did not cause the claimant's additional suffering (it was not contended on appeal that an earlier admission or diagnosis would have made any difference to the claimant's outcome—the claim was for her additional suffering) as the key symptoms of a subarachnoid haemorrhage (pounding headache and vomiting) were absent at the time of the telephone call, and so the correctly carried out triage would not have resulted in an earlier admission to hospital. The court further held that although the defendant, when visiting the claimant subsequently, should have asked about vomiting there was no evidence that had he done so the claimant would have given an answer which would have resulted in her immediate referral to hospital. The claimant's appeal was dismissed. See also *NDRI v Moorfields Eye Hospital NHS Trust* [2006] EWHC 3652, QBD (unreported elsewhere) where the court indicated that even had the claimant established breach, she would have failed on causation because she could not prove, on the balance of probabilities, that the defendant's alleged breach (failing to

13–114

13–114

decontaminate the donor tissue with antiseptic and not merely antibiotics) was the source of the bacteria which led to the claimant's loss of sight in her eye following a corneal graft procedure. The defendant's experts suggested a credible alternative source, for the bacterial, namely internal origin. Reported at (2007) 97 B.M.L.R. 74.

13–115 **Material contribution.** Add at end of paragraph: The Court of Appeal in *Bailey v Ministry of Defence* [2008] EWCA Civ 883 again reviewed the cases where there are cumulative causes. Waller L.J.'s speech culminated in the following summary at para.46:

> "In my view one cannot draw a distinction between medical negligence cases and others. I would summarise the position in relation to cumulative causes cases as follows. If the evidence demonstrates on a balance of probabilities that the injury would have occurred as a result of the non-tortious cause or causes in any event, the claimant will have failed to establish that the tortious cause contributed. *Hotson* exemplifies such a situation. If the evidence demonstrates that 'but for' the contribution of the tortuous cause the injury would probably not have occurred, the claimant will (obviously) have discharged the burden. In a case where medical science cannot establish the probability that 'but for' an act of negligence the injury would not have happened but can establish that the contribution of the negligent cause was more than negligible, the 'but for' test is modified, and the Claimant will succeed."

(ii) *Loss of a chance*

13–133 **Evidence of culpable delay.** Add to NOTE 11: See also *Demery v Cardiff and Vale NHS Trust* [2006] EWCA Civ 1131, where the Court of Appeal allowed the claimant's appeal holding that the judge should have considered whether the culpable delay in treatment had rendered the operation less likely to succeed. See para.**13–130** above.

(iv) *The application of the* Bolam *Test in Causation*—Bolitho

13–139 Add to NOTE 38: See *Michelle Zarb v Odetoyinbo* [2006] EWHC 2880, QBD: it was not the case that no surgeon of ordinary skill would have failed to admit and operate on the claimant immediately, and therefore the defendant could not have been negligent for failing to refer the claimant immediately. Cf. *Sutcliffe (by his wife and litigation friend Julie Sutcliffe) v BMI Healthcare Ltd* [2007] EWCA Civ 476: a nurse's decision to leave the claimant to sleep (he sustained severe brain damage following aspiration of vomit) rather than carrying out observation of pulse, temperature and blood pressure, had a logical basis and the judge was right to accept this.

13–141 Add to NOTE 44: In *Gouldsmith v Mid Staffordshire General Hospitals NHS Trust (2007)* [2007] EWCA Civ 397 (unreported elsewhere), the Court of Appeal found that the judge had failed to follow the correct approach to causation as set out in *Bolitho*, when considering whether the defendant trust's breach of duty by failing to secure specialist medical attention for the claimant, had caused the claimant's injuries.

DAMAGES 13-154

(c) *Foreseeability*

13-149 Add new NOTE 79a at end of paragraph: In *Farraj v King's Healthcare NHS Trust* [2006] EWHC 1228, QBD; [2006] P.I.Q.R. 470; (2006) 90 B.M.L.R. 21, on a preliminary issue the court held that it was foreseeable that if a tissue culture lab carried out its work in a substandard manner, the defendant trust's analysis of the cultured tissue would be compromised with the risk of producing a misleading result leading to the birth of a child suffering from a condition that the tissue culturing and analysis had been intended to detect.

13-154 **Psychiatric injury.** Add to end of paragraph: By contrast, there is no cause of action in respect of anxiety or psychiatric illness caused by the apprehension of the risk of a future illness which has not yet, and may never, be suffered. This was decided unanimously by the House of Lords in the conjoined appeals *Johnston v NEI International Combustion Ltd; Rothwell v Chemical & Insulating Co Ltd; Topping v Benchtown Ltd (formerly Jones Bros Preston Ltd); Grieves v FT Everard & Sons* [2007] UKHL 39 reported at [2007] 3 W.L.R. 876. The Claimants had developed pleural plaques, which were symptomless but indicated past exposure to asbestos, which brought with it a 1 to 5 per cent risk of developing asbestosis or pleural thickening and mesothelioma (respectively). The plaques themselves were not compensatable damage and the risk of future illness was not itself damage, accordingly even by "aggregating" these matters there was no cause of action.

One of the appellants, Mr Grieves, had actually developed psychological symptoms and a depressive illness when he was told he had pleural plaques. Nevertheless his claim failed and *Page v Smith* was distinguished on grounds including that in this case there was an intervening causative event (namely being told of the presence of the plaques discovered upon a chest X-ray examination) and that therefore Mr Grieves' illness was not an immediate response to an unpleasant past event with no time to prepare himself (such as the car accident which caused the psychiatric injury in *Page v Smith*) but his reaction in contemplation of a risk that something unpleasant might happen in the future. It was also held that his employers (unlike the defendants in *Creutzfeldt-Jakob Disease Litigation Group B Plaintiffs v Medical Research Council* [2000] Lloyd's Rep. Med. 161) did not owe him a duty of care not to cause him psychiatric harm as a result of learning he was at risk of developing asbestosis/pleural thickening or mesothelioma.

The correctness of the decision in *Page v Smith* (and in particular whether the correct test should be foreseeability of psychiatric injury in order to recover damages for psychiatric injury) was questioned, but this was left for decision on another day. For the present time *Page v Smith* remains the law.

[87]

CHAPTER 14

REGULATION OF FINANCIAL SERVICES

	PARA.
1. General	14–001
(a) The FSA	14–004
(b) The General Prohibition	14–006
(c) The Financial Promotion Restriction	14–008
(d) Authorised Persons	14–010
(e) Approved Persons	14–012
(f) Exempt Persons	14–013
(g) Appointed Representatives	14–014
(i) Status Requirements	14–015
(ii) Liability of Principal under FSMA	14–016
(h) Members of Professions	14–017
(i) European Aspects	14–019
(j) Human Rights Law	14–020
2. Application of the FSMA Regulatory Regime	14–021
(a) Regulated Activities	14–022
(b) Financial Promotion	14–025
(c) Investment	14–027
(d) Nature of the Services	14–029
(e) Status of Provider of Financial Services	14–030
(f) Status of Recipient of Financial Services	14–031
3. Duties and Liabilities under FSMA	14–032
4. Regulatory Rules and the FSA Handbook	14–033
(a) General	14–033
(b) FSA Handbook	14–034
(i) Sourcebooks	14–035
(ii) Glossary	14–037
(iii) Rules	14–039
(iv) Guidance	14–040
(v) Treatment	14–041
(c) Principles for Business	14–042
(d) Statements of Principle and Code of Practice for Approved Persons	14–043
(e) "Conduct of Business" Sourcebook ("COB")	14–044
(i) Arrangement	14–045
(ii) Scope	14–046
(iii) Rules of General Application to all Firms Conducting "Designated Investment Business"	14–047
(iv) Financial Promotion	14–049

	PARA.
(v) Accepting Customers	14–051
(vi) Advising and Selling	14–054
(vii) Product Disclosure	14–059
(viii) The Customer's Right to Cancel and Withdraw	14–060
(ix) Dealing and Managing	14–061
(x) Reporting to Customers	14–067
(f) The "Client Assets" Sourcebook ("CASS")	14–068
5. FSMA Imposed Regulatory Liabilities	14–069
(a) Liabilities Related to Lack of Authorisation	14–070
(i) Liability for Contravention of General Prohibition	14–071
(ii) Liability for Contravention of the Financial Promotion Restriction	14–072
(b) Liabilities related to Authorised Persons	14–073
(i) "Private Person"	14–074
(ii) Liability for Acting outside Permission	14–075
(iii) Liability for Employment of Certain Persons	14–076
(iv) Authorised Persons' Liability for Contravention of FSA Rules	14–077
(c) Liabilities related to EEA Firms	14–080
(d) Liabilities related to Listing Particulars and Prospectuses	14–081
6. FSMA Remedies	14–083
(a) Remedies Available to Regulators	14–083
(i) Grounds for Application to Court	14–084
(ii) Persons against whom Order Available	14–087
(iii) Orders Available	14–089
(iv) The FSA's Extra-judicial Power to Require Restitution	14–094
(v) The FSA Regulatory Guide	14–095
(b) Remedies Available to Private Litigants	14–096

[89]

14–004   Chapter 14—Regulation of Financial Services

- (i) Recovery of Money or Property Paid under Agreements Made by or Through Unauthorised Persons............................ 14–097
- (ii) Damages or Compensation.................................. 14–102
7. The Ombudsman Scheme................ 14–103
- (a) Introduction 14–103
- (b) Compulsory, Consumer Credit and Voluntary Jurisdiction 14–105
  - (i) The Compulsory Jurisdiction 14–105
- (ii) The Consumer Credit Jurisdiction 14–106
  - (iii) The Voluntary Jurisdiction.................................. 14–107
- (c) Complaint Handling Procedures for Firms..................................... 14–108
- (d) Jurisdiction of the FOS............. 14–109
- (e) Complaints Handling Procedures of the FOS....................... 14–113

- (f) The Investigation....................... 14–114
- (g) The Award................................ 14–118
- (h) Limited Immunity 14–124
8. Compensation Scheme 14–125
   - (a) Introduction 14–125
   - (b) Purpose 14–126
   - (c) Structure 14–127
   - (d) Qualifying Conditions for Compensation............................. 14–128
     - (i) Eligible Claimants........... 14–129
     - (ii) Protected Claims 14–130
     - (iii) Relevant Persons............. 14–131
     - (iv) Default by Relevant Persons................................... 14–132
     - (v) Assignment of Rights 14–133
   - (e) Compensation............................. 14–134
     - (i) Offers of Compensation.. 14–134
     - (ii) Acceptance of Offers of Compensation.................. 14–137
     - (iii) Insurance 14–138
     - (iv) Challenging the FSCS..... 14–139

1. General

(a) *The FSA*

14–004   Add to Note 10: And see the Regulatory Reform (Regulatory Functions) Order 2007, SI 2007/3544 (made under the Legislative and Regulatory Reform Act 2006), which requires the FSA to have regard to the "five principles of good regulation".

(c) *The Financial Promotion Restriction*

14–009   Add to Note 39: And see the exceptions in the FPO, Arts 12, 20B and 30–33. (As to the FPO, see para.**14–026**, below.)

(d) *Authorised Persons*

14–010   Add to Note 43: The Markets in Financial Instruments Directive ("MiFID") came into force (and replaced the Investment Services Directive) on November 1, 2007.

14–011   Delete last sentence (referring to "AUTH", which has been deleted from the FSA Handbook).

GENERAL

(g) *Appointed Representatives*

(i) *Status Requirements*

In NOTE 66 replace first sentence with: RAO, Arts 25, 25A, 25B, 25C, 39A, 40, 52B, 53, 53A, 53B, 53C and 64. **14–015**

(i) *European Aspects*

Add to NOTE 88: The Transparency Obligations Directive was implemented on January 6, 2007. **14–019**

In NOTE 92 replace existing text with: The Markets in Financial Instruments Directive ("MiFID") came into force (and replaced the Investment Services Directive) on November 1, 2007.

(j) *Human Rights Law*

In NOTE 95, for the second sentence, substitute: See the modules in the FSA Handbook relating to Market Conduct ("MAR"), Decision Procedure and Penalties Manual ("DEPP") and Enforcement Guide ("EG"). **14–020**

2. APPLICATION OF THE FSMA REGULATORY REGIME

(a) *Regulated Activities*

In NOTE 5 after the reference to *Smith v Anderson* add: and, more recently, *GE Capital Ltd v Rushton* [2005] EWCA Civ 1556. **14–022**

For penultimate sentence substitute: Further amendments were made (with effect from April 6, 2007) to facilitate so-called "Islamic mortgages" and (with effect from November 1, 2007) to give effect to MiFID.9 **14–023**

Add: Additional "regulated activities" that have been added to the RAO are (a) operating a multilateral trading facility, a "MTF" (RAO, art.25D, inserted as a result of MiFID) and (b) activities (arranging, advising, entering and administering) in relation to "regulated home purchase" and "regulated home reversion" plans (RAO, arts.25B, 25C, 53B, 53C, 63B, 63F—inserted in part to cater for Islamic mortgages). **14–024**

Add to NOTE 18: See *Inertia Partnership LLP, Re* [2007] EWCA 539 (Ch) on the meaning of "arrangements" in the RAO, Art.25.

(b) *Financial Promotion*

Add to NOTE 35: SI 2007/1083 and SI 2007/2615. **14–026**

[91]

14–027 CHAPTER 14—REGULATION OF FINANCIAL SERVICES

(c) Investment

14–027 Add: Rights under "regulated home purchase plans" and "regulated home reversion plans" have been added to the RAO (Art.63F and 63B) and FPO (Sch.1, 26A and 26B) as investments.

14–028 In NOTE 65 for *FSA v Fradley* [2004] EWHA 3008, substitute: *FSA v Fradley* [2005] EWCA 1183.

(f) Status of Recipient of Financial Services

14–031 Delete from penultimate sentence: e.g. private customer, as defined

Add before last sentence: The status now reflects the Markets in Financial Instruments Directive ("MiFID") which requires clients of authorised persons to be classified into: "retail clients", "professional clients" or "market counterparties".

4. REGULATORY RULES AND THE FSA HANDBOOK

(b) FSA Handbook

(i) Sourcebooks

14–035 Add: The content of the Handbook has been amended, in part as a result of a move towards more "principles-based" regulation by the FSA. Reference should be made to the FSA website (see NOTE 4 under para.**14–004**) to ascertain the most up-to-date contents.

(ii) Glossary

14–038 Delete the antepenultimate sentence beginning "There are two types . . . " and substitute: As a result of the Markets in Financial Instruments Directive ("MiFID"), there are three types of client: "retail client", "professional client" and "market counterparty".

(iv) Guidance

Add new para.**14–040A**:

14–040A The FSA has embarked on a revision of its sourcebooks in implementation of a more "principles-based" approach to regulation (so-called "PBR"). Thus it is reducing the number of detailed prescriptive rules (in particular in "COB", the Conduct of Business Sourcebook, which has been rewritten and is now designated "COBS") and replacing them by more general "principles" which are amplified by more "guidance".

(v) Treatment

14–041 For both occurrences of "COB", substitute: "COBS"

REGULATORY RULES AND THE FSA HANDBOOK   14–081A

(c) *Principles for Businesses*

Add new NOTE 2a after item 6, **Customers' interests**: This principle is the basis of the FSA's so-called TCF ("Treating Customers Fairly") initiative.   14–042

(e) *"Conduct of Business" Sourcebook ("COB")*

Add new para.**14–044A**:

Note that from November 1, 2007, "COB" was replaced by the new conduct of business sourcebook, "COBS". This is available on the FSA website at *http://www.fsa.gov.uk/pubs/hb-releases/rel71/rel71cobs.pdf* [accessed October 17, 2008]. Hence paras.**14–045** to **14–067** will be applicable only to business conducted **before** that date. The text in the main work has been retained given its applicability to current claims.   14–044A

5. FSMA IMPOSED REGULATORY LIABILITIES

(b) *Liabilities Related to Authorised Persons*

Add to NOTE 41: See *Re Whitely Insurance Consultants* [2008] EWHC 1782 (Ch) for a consideration of such a right of action in the context of the liquidation of an insurer acting in breach of their Part IV permission (which only extended to acting as an intermediary and not effecting or carrying out insurance contracts).   14–073

(iv) *Authorised Persons' Liability for Contravention of FSA Rules*

Delete the sentence that begins with "Secondly" and substitute: Secondly, the so-called "Part 6 rules", i.e. rules (for example, listing rules) made under Part 6 of the Act, made by the FSA as "competent authority"[66] are excluded.[67]   14–077

Delete the penultimate sentence.

Add to NOTE 63: ; *Shore v Sedgwick Financial Services* [2007] EWHC 3054; [2008] P.N.L.R. 10. See also *Spreadex Ltd v Sekhon* [2008] EWHC 1136 (Ch) (a successful s.150 claim, reduced by contributory negligence of claimant).

Add to NOTE 73: See *Spreadex Ltd v Sekhon* [2008] EWHC 1136 (Ch) (a successful s.150 claim, reduced by contributory negligence of claimant).

(d) *Liabilities related to Listing Particulars and Prospectuses*

Add new para.**14–081A**:

Similar liabilities are imposed by FSMA s.90A[93a] in relation to statements in various publications issued in compliance with the Transparency Obligations Directive.[93b]   14–081A

14–081A CHAPTER 14—REGULATION OF FINANCIAL SERVICES

Add to NOTE 88: Further amendments were made by the Companies Act 2006 s.1272 and Sch.15, paras 4 and 5 on November 8, 2006.

Add new NOTE 93a: Added by the Companies Act 2006 s.1270, but the relevant secondary legislation has not yet been made.

Add new NOTE 93b: Directive 2004/109/EC which imposes continuing obligations to make disclosures in relation to "securities" traded on "regulated markets" (as therein defined). See also s.90B, enabling the Treasury by regulation to extend such liability, and see the Consultation Paper, "Extension of the statutory regime for issuer liability" (HMT, July 2008).

6. FSMA REMEDIES

(a) *Remedies Available to Regulators*

14–083 Add to NOTE 5: See *FSA v Fradley* [2004] All E.R. (D) 297 (Martin Q.C.); *FSA v Matthews* [2004] EWHC 2966; *FSA v Martin* [2004] EWHC 3255 (Ch); [2005] 1 B.C.L.C. 495.

14–086 Add to NOTE 20: The 2003 Regulations were replaced on December 15, 2007 by the Money Laundering Regulations 2007, SI 2007/2157, amended by SI 2007/3299.

(ii) *Persons against whom Orders Available*

14–088 Add to NOTE 26: See also *FSA v Martin* [2004] EWHC 3255 (Ch); [2005] 1 B.C.L.C. 495 (a decision under FSMA 2000).

Add to NOTE 28: See also *FSA v Fradley* [2004] All ER (D) 297 per Martin Q.C. and *FSA v Martin* [2004] EWHC 3255 (Ch); [2005] 1 B.C.L.C. 495 (decisions under FSMA 2000).

(iii) *Orders Available*

14–091 Add to NOTE 33: See *FSA v Martin* [2004] EWHC 3255 (Ch); [2005] 1 B.C.L.C. 495.

14–093 In NOTE 50, after first sentence, add: See also *FSA v Matthews* [2004] EWHC 2966.

14–095 Change sub-heading to:

(v) *The FSA Regulatory Guide*

Delete "manual" and substitute: Regulatory Guide

[94]

FSMA Remedies

(b) *Remedies Available to Private Litigants*

(ii) *Recovery of Money or Property Paid under Agreements Made by or Through Unauthorised Persons*

Add to NOTE 56: See now *Re Whitely Insurance Consultants* [2008] EWHC 1782 (Ch). **14–097**

Add to NOTE 63: See *Re Whitely Insurance Consultants* [2008] EWHC 1782 (Ch), where s.28(3) was considered, in general terms, in the context of the liquidation of an unauthorised insurer. Richards J. opined that although the fact that the unauthorised persons knew he was contravening the general prohibition was not conclusive against the exercise of the discretion (as it was under the predecessor ss.5(3) and 132(3) of the Financial Services Act 1986), "it is nonetheless a weighty factor against the grant of relief". **14–098**

Add after second sentence: In *Re Whitely Insurance Consultants* [2008] EWHC 1782 (Ch), Richards J. opined that the "loss sustained" referred to "loss in fact sustained . . . rather than a notional loss" and held that persons who had paid over premiums for insurance policies could not recover interest on those sums as (it was assumed) they would have parted with the same amounts to another insurer. **14–099**

7. THE OMBUDSMAN SCHEME

(a) *Introduction*

In NOTE 82, for the last sentence substitute: The jurisdiction came into force in April 2007. **14–104**

For NOTE 86 substitute: This came into force in April 2007.

(b) *Compulsory, Consumer Credit and Voluntary Jurisdiction*

(ii) *The Consumer Credit Jurisdiction*[93]

In NOTE 93, for the last sentence substitute: The jurisdiction came into force in April 2007. See the Financial Services and Markets Act 2000 (Ombudsman Scheme) Order 2007, SI 2007/383. **14–106**

(f) *The Investigation*

Add to NOTE 34: See now *R (on the application of Heather Moor and Edgecomb Ltd) v Financial Ombudsman Service Ltd* [2008] EWCA 642, confirming that the FOS did not have to decide cases according to common law principles. **14–116**

14–117 CHAPTER 14—REGULATION OF FINANCIAL SERVICES

14–117 In line 2, for "only" substitute: usual
After the second sentence, add: However, a challenge (on grounds that would give rise to a judicial review) can also be asserted by way of defence in an action to enforce a direction by the Ombudsman.[36a]

Add to NOTE 36: *Financial Ombudsman Service Ltd v Heather Moor and Edgecomb Ltd* [2008] EWCA 643 (fee-charging regime whereby all firms, even those where complaints were dismissed, had to pay fees to FOS) was upheld as not irrational; *R. (on the Application of Keith Williams) v Financial Ombudsman Services* [2008] EWHC 2142 (Admin). For a successful challenge see: *Garrison Investment Analysis v FOS* [2006] EWHC 2466 (Admin): decision quashed as being "irrational" in that it was based on an assumption that was unsupported by the evidence.

Add new NOTE 36a: See *Bunney v Burns Anderson Plc* [2007] EWHC 1240 (Ch), Lewison J.

(g) *The Award*

14–122 Delete second sentence, and delete NOTE 46.

Add new para.**14–123A**:

14–123A In *Bunney v Burns Anderson Plc* [2007] EWHC 1240 (Ch) (Lewinson J.) the Ombudsman made a "direction" (to undertake loss assessment to discover whether the claimant had suffered loss and to make good that loss) which entailed payment in excess of the cap imposed on the "money award". First, it was confirmed that the two possible determinations (a "money award" and a "direction") were not mutually exclusive and that a determination may "include" both a money award and a direction. Second, it was held that "whether a determination is a money award or a direction depends on the substance of the decision and not on the form in which it is expressed". Hence if the determination required the payment of money it was a "money award" and subject to the cap and so the Ombudsman could not by "direction" require the payment of more than the statutory cap. If a "direction" entailed costs of compliance which were unknown at the time of the direction, then it was "subject to an implicit limitation that it will not be enforced beyond the statutory cap, once reached". Thus in so far as making good the loss exceed the cap, this excess was not recoverable.

8. COMPENSATION SCHEME

(d) *Qualifying Conditions for Compensation*

(v) *Assignment of Rights*

14–133 Add: In *FSCS Ltd v Abbey National Treasury Services Plc* [2008] EWHC 1897 (Ch), Richards J. held that (a) the rules in COMP that gave the FSCS express power, on making compensation, to take a legal assignment of the claims that those it compensated had, were not ultra vires the powers of the FSA to make compensation rules under FSMA 2000 and (b) as assignee, the FSCS did not have to give credit for the compensation received by the assignors when recovering (as assignee) for the loss they had suffered.

CHAPTER 15

FINANCIAL PRACTITIONERS

	PARA.		PARA.
1. General	15–001	(b) Misleading Promotion	15–045
(a) Scope	15–001	(i) Old Prospectus Cases	15–045
(b) The Financial Sector	15–004	(ii) Financial Promotional Documents	15–046
(c) Regulation	15–007	(iii) Customer Classification	15–047
(d) Raising Standards	15–009	(iv) Advising and Selling	15–048
2. Duties and Liabilities	15–010	(v) Dealing and Managing	15–053
(a) Sources	15–010	4. Defences and Relief	15–058
(b) Relevant Approach	15–011	(a) General	15–058
(c) The FSMA Regime	15–012	(b) Limited Immunity of the FSA from Liability in Damages	15–059
(d) The Misrepresentation Act 1967	15–013	(c) Restriction of Liability by Contract	15–060
(i) Relevance	15–013	(d) Statutory Relief	15–062
(ii) Representations as to Suitability	15–014	5. Remedies Including Damages	15–063
(iii) False in Material Respect	15–015	(a) General	15–063
(iv) Comparison with Common Law	15–016	(b) Remedies Available to Regulators	15–064
(e) Contractual Duties	15–017	(c) Remedies Available to Private Litigants	15–065
(i) Relevant Contracts	15–017	(i) Rescission of Contract Induced by Misrepresentation	15–066
(ii) Regulatory Requirements as to Terms of Business and Customer Agreements	15–018	(ii) Recovery of Money Paid or Property Transferred Under Agreements Made by or Through Unauthorised Persons	15–067
(iii) Incorporation of Regulatory Duties in Contract	15–019	(iii) Damages or Compensation	15–068
(iv) Duty of Care and Skill	15–020	6. Shared Responsibility	15–079
(v) Agency	15–023	(a) Contributory Negligence	15–079
(f) Tort-based Duties	15–025	(b) Contribution	15–080
(i) Deceit or Fraudulent Misrepresentation	15–025	7. The Process of Resolving Claims	15–081
(ii) Misfeasance in Public Office	15–031	8. Parallel Proceedings	15–082
(iii) Negligence	15–032		
(g) Fiduciary Duties	15–041		
3. Breach of Duty	15–044		
(a) General	15–044		

2. DUTIES AND LIABILITIES

(b) *Relevant Approach*

15–011 Add after final sentence: While plainly a matter of fact for consideration in each case, increasingly courts are reluctant to find the existence of a common law duty of care whose scope exceeds the obligations imposed by statute: see for example *Walker v Inter-Alliance Group Plc (In Liquidation)* [2007] EWHC 1858 (Ch), per Henderson J. at [40].

[99]

15-014   CHAPTER 15—FINANCIAL PRACTITIONERS

(d) *The Misrepresentation Act 1967*

(ii) *Representations as to Suitability*

15-014   Add to NOTE 6: In *IFE Fund SA v Goldman Sachs International* [2007] EWCA Civ 811 the claimant alleged that it had been induced to purchase certain bonds and warrants as a result of information contained in a Syndicate Information Memorandum ("SIM") prepared by the defendant. It claimed that by the time that the SIM had been provided to it by the defendant, the defendant had become aware of information that cast doubt on the correctness of its contents yet had not sought to correct or qualify the SIM in any way. Toulson J. concluded that there had been no representation of fact to the effect that the defendant knew nothing to suggest that the information contained in the SIM was or might be materially incorrect. The Court of Appeal dismissed the claimant's appeal against that finding. While accepting that "someone may make a statement which is not a representation of fact but which by implication carries with it a representation of fact i.e. in the case where the original representation is one of opinion that the representor is not aware of facts which make the statement of opinion untrue", the Court of Appeal agreed that on the facts of the case the SIM had carried with it no such implied representation of fact. In the absence of bad faith on the part of the defendant (i.e. proof that the defendant had had actual knowledge by the relevant time that the information in the SIM was inaccurate) the claim failed.

Add to NOTE 7: *Peekay Intermark Ltd v ANZ Banking Group Ltd* [2006] EWCA Civ 386 is now reported at [2006] 2 Lloyd's Rep. 511.

(iv) *Comparison with Common Law*

15-016   Add as NOTE 11A at the end of the first sentence: In *IFE Fund SA v Goldman Sachs International* (*supra*) the claimant's alternative claim based on an alleged breach of a common law duty of care by the defendant in failing to disclose certain material information failed on the basis that it would only be in exceptional circumstances that a party involved in negotiations towards a commercial venture might owe a positive duty of disclosure towards another prospective party.

(e) *Contractual Duties*

(i) *Relevant Contracts*

15-017   Add as NOTE 13A at the end of the first sentence: That will not however always be the case. For an example of a case in which a provider of financial services had no contractual relationship with the recipient see *Walker v Inter-Alliance Group Plc (In Liquidation)* [2007] EWHC 1858 (Ch) considered further at para.**15-023** below.

Add new para.**15-017A**:

15-017A   The contractual documentation agreed between parties will frequently be the starting point for any analysis of the extent of the rights and obligations that exist between them: see by way of example *JP Morgan Chase v Springwell Navigation Corporation* [2008] EWHC 1186 (Comm). Such documentation is capable of excluding parallel or free-standing common law duties of care: see *IFE Fund v Goldman Sachs International* (above).

(iv) *Duty of Care and Skill*

Add at the end of NOTE 28: For a helpful summary of the principles governing the admissibility and relevance of expert evidence in a claim for *inter alia* negligent investment advice see *JP Morgan Chase Bank v Springwell Navigation Corp* [2006] EWHC 2755 (Comm), per Aikens J.

15–020

(v) *Agency*

Add as NOTE 32A at the end of the paragraph: The importance of ascertaining the authority or otherwise of the individuals responsible for providing advice is illustrated by *Walker v Inter-Alliance Group Plc (In Liquidation)* [2007] EWHC 1858 (Ch). In that case the claimant had attended meetings at which he had received advice from both an IFA and a representative of Scottish Equitable Plc, a product provider. While the IFA was authorised under the FSA 1986 and the PIA to provide investment advice, the representative of Scottish Equitable was not; his authority was confined to providing factual information about Scottish Equitable products. Since the Scottish Equitable representative had in fact provided investment advice within the meaning of para.15 of Sch.1 to the FSA 1986, Scottish Equitable was found to have acted in breach of s.62 of the FSA 1986.

15–023

Add new para.**15–032A**:

The inter-relationship of contractual and tortious duties obligations was considered at length by Gloster J. in *JP Morgan Chase Bank v Springwell Navigation Corporation* [2008] EWHC 1186 (Comm). In that case the claimant, an investment vehicle for a group of companies controlled by wealthy Greek shipowners, brought a raft of claims against the JP Morgan Chase Group arising out of the collapse of investments in Russia. While the case was factually complex at its heart lay the nature of the relationship between the claimant and the defendant—in particular, did the defendant owe duties to provide investment advice to the claimant in relation to its Russian investments? Gloster J. found that although no advisory agreement had been entered into between the parties and there existed no express contractual duty to advise, such matters were not determinative of whether the defendant owed tortious duties to advise to the claimant. The absence of any such contractual obligations was however a factor to be given considerable weight when considering the existence or otherwise of a tortious duty to advise. Other factors identified by the judge as being relevant to the existence or otherwise of such a tortious duty to advise included (i) the factual matrix of the relationship between the parties—what was said between them at the outset of the relationship, what roles each played during the relationship and the like; (ii) the extent of the defendant's financial experience and sophistication; (iii) the extent of the claimant's reliance on the defendant and the foreseeability of such reliance; and (iv) the regulatory background to the relationship.

15–032A

(g) *Fiduciary Duties*

15–043 Add after final sentence: In *JP Morgan Chase Bank v Springwell Navigation Corporation* (above) the claimant sought to argue that, although the relationship of investment adviser and client was not one of the categories of relationship where a fiduciary relationship was presumed by law, there nonetheless existed such a relationship on the complex facts of that case. Gloster J. rejected the argument, finding that what was "essentially a commercial banking relationship" did not give rise to the extensive fiduciary obligations on the part of the defendant contended for by the claimant.

3. Breach of Duty

(b) *Misleading Promotion*

(ii) *Financial Promotion Documents*

15–046 Add to end of NOTE 99: *IFE Fund SA v Goldman Sachs International* [2007] EWCA Civ 811 (allegedly incomplete and misleading statements in a Syndicate Information Memorandum).

(iv) *Advising and Selling*

Add new para.**15–049A**:

15–049A In *Walker v Inter-Alliance Group Plc (In Liquidation)* [2007] EWHC 1858 (Ch) an issue arose as to the meaning of "investment advice" for the purposes of para.15 of Sch.1 of the FSA 1986. Henderson J. concluded that, while the giving of purely factual information could not properly be described as the giving of "investment advice", the provision of information in a context which involved "any element of comparison or evaluation or persuasion" would be likely to "cross the line". The judge acknowledged that frequently the line between providing "information" and "advice" would be a fine one.

(v) *Dealing and Managing*

Add new para.**15–056A**:

15–056A In *Spreadex Limited v Sekhon* [2008] EWHC 1136 (Ch) the claimant, a spread betting company, sued the defendant for losses on his account following a series of unsuccessful spread bets. The defendant defended the claim on the basis that, in contravention of COB 7.10.5R, the claimant had failed to close certain open positions held by him, and that the losses on his account would have been avoided had the claimant done so. He also counterclaimed for damages for breach of statutory duty to recover monies already paid over to the claimant towards his liabilities. Following a consideration of the statutory position under FSMA and the relevant Conduct of Business Rules, Morgan J. concluded that, by failing to close all of the defendant's open positions, the claimant had in fact contravened the mandatory provisions of COB 7.10.5R despite the fact that the positions had been left open at the express request of the defendant. The claimant

BREACH OF DUTY 15–070

was therefore unable to recover from the defendant those liabilities on his account that would have been avoided had the positions been closed promptly, and, subject to a discount for contributory negligence (see para.**15–079** below), the defendant was able to recover losses suffered by him as a result of the claimant's contravention.

4. DEFENCES AND RELIEF

(c) *Restriction of Liability by Contract*

Add at the end of the paragraph: Fourthly, in cases of misrepresentation it may be necessary to draw a distinction between statements which (on the one hand) seek to exclude liability for representations actually made and which (on the other hand) simply go to the scope of the representations being made: see *IFE Fund SA v Goldman Sachs International* (above). **15–061**

5. REMEDIES INCLUDING DAMAGES

(c) *Remedies Available to Private Litigants*

(iii) *Damages or Compensation*

Add at the end of NOTE 50: In *Andrews v Barnett Waddingham (A Firm)* [2006] EWCA Civ 93; [2006] P.N.L.R. 432 the claimant succeeded in demonstrating that advice given by the defendant as to the true construction of the Policyholders Protection Act 1975 had been negligent. He contended that as a result of that advice he had purchased a with-profits annuity policy from the Equitable Life Assurance Society which he would not otherwise have purchased, that had he been properly advised he would not have purchased the Equitable Life annuity, and that as a result of purchasing the Equitable Life annuity he had suffered loss. The Court of Appeal, reversing the findings of Cox J. ([2006] P.N.L.R. 2), dismissed the claimant's claim for damages. The losses sustained by the claimant were not losses which flowed from the defendant's breach of duty and were not losses which fell within the scope of the duty that the defendant was found to have owed to the claimant: to advise competently as to the true construction of the Policyholders Protection Act 1975. **15–069**

Add as NOTE 50A at the end of the first sentence: That remains the case whether the claim pursued is one for breach of a common law duty of care, for breach of a contractual term or for breach of statutory duty: see *Walker v Inter-Alliance Group Plc (In Liquidation)* (above). **15–070**

Add after final sentence: An interesting situation arose in *Walker v Inter-Alliance Group Plc (In Liquidation)* (above). The claimant had received investment advice in materially identical terms from an IFA retained by him and also from a representative of Scottish Equitable, the provider of the money-purchase pension product into which the claimant subsequently transferred his existing

15–070

occupational pension. That advice had been given at meetings attended by all three individuals. The Scottish Equitable representative was not authorised to provide investment advice and, when asked for advice (rather than simply information) by the claimant, ought to have declined to respond to the claimant's question. It was likely that, had the Scottish Equitable representative declined to respond to the claimant's requests for advice, the IFA would nonetheless still have advised in the same terms. Having analysed the relevant principles of causation, Henderson J. concluded that the advice given by the Scottish Equitable representation had nonetheless been an effective cause of the claimant's loss since, even though the claimant would have received the same advice from the IFA, he would not have been swayed by the IFA alone to exit his occupational pension scheme and transfer to the money-purchase scheme.

15–072 Add as NOTE 64A at the end of the final sentence: In *JP Morgan Chase Bank v Springwell Navigation Corp* [2006] EWCA Civ 161; [2006] P.N.L.R. 528 it was alleged that as a result of poor advice, the value of the investor's portfolio was some US$280 million less than it should have been. As well as seeking to recover that sum by way of damages from its adviser, the investor also sought to recover profits lost as a result of being unable to use that US$280 million to renew vessels in its fleet. The Court of Appeal refused to strike out the "lost profits" element of the claim. It was at least arguable that to recover both heads of loss would not provide the investor with "double recovery".

Add after final sentence: In *Bear Stearns Bank Plc v Forum Global Equity Ltd* [2007] EWHC 1576 (Comm) the claimant succeeded in demonstrating that it had entered into a binding contract with the defendant for the purchase of distressed debt by way of notes in Parmalat. Two issues arose on quantum: (i) whether the assessment should take into account a marginally-profitable contract into which the claimant had entered for the sale-on of 50 per cent of the notes, but which the claimant had been unable to fulfil; and (ii) the date at which damages should be assessed. As to (i), Andrew Smith J. concluded that the sale-on should be disregarded. It was not in the contemplation of the parties at the time of the contract that the claimant would enter into a contract which committed it to sell-on the very notes that it was purchasing. As to (ii), the claimant had for many months pursued a claim for specific performance against the defendant to compel delivery of the notes. When it was discovered that the defendant had in fact disposed of the notes, that claim was abandoned and a claim for damages for the value of the lost notes was pursued in its place. The judge concluded that that date, rather than the date of the defendant's breach of contract, was the date at which to assess loss so as to most fairly compensate the claimant.

6. SHARED RESPONSIBILITY

(a) *Contributory Negligence*

15–079 Add as NOTE 77A at the end of the final sentence: A case in which the defence did succeed is *Spreadex Limited v Sekhon* (above). In that case the claimant spread betting company was found to have acted in breach of statutory duty by failing to close certain open positions on the defendant's accounts, with the result that the defendant had suffered substantial losses on those accounts. However, Morgan J. concluded that the defendant had "wanted to keep his positions open" and had in fact "persuaded [the claimant] to permit him to do so". As a result, the defendant had "deliberately run the risk of harm through adverse market movement". In the light of such findings the judge discounted the damages recoverable on the defendant's counterclaim by 85 per cent to reflect the defendant's own contributory negligence. Similarly in *JP Morgan Chase Bank v Springwell Navigation Corporation* (above) Gloster J. concluded that, had the claimant in fact succeeded in demonstrating a breach of a duty of care on the part of the defendant, a substantial reduction in the damages recoverable would nonetheless have been appropriate to reflect the claimant's contributory negligence. The judge identified numerous factors which, she concluded, demonstrated a "clear disregard" by the claimant for its own interests in the pursuit of profit including (i) expecting a full advisory service from the defendant without ever requesting such a service; (ii) failing to query whether investments purchased on its behalf were consistent with its investment objectives; (iii) treating contractual documents "with contempt"; (iv) disregarding research communicated by the claimant or "any views that [the claimant] did not wish to hear"; (v) aggressively pursuing a strategy of high returns and opportunistic investments, including by way of large amounts of leverage, thereby assuming obvious risk; and (vi) ignoring concerns expressed by the defendant about the claimant's portfolio of investments and recommendations by the defendant to diversify.

Chapter 16

INSURANCE BROKERS

	Para.
1. General	16–001
(a) Duties to the Client	16–011
(i) Contractual Duties	16–011
(ii) Duties Independent of Contract	16–014
(b) Duties to Third Parties	16–017
(i) Duties to Insurers	16–018
(ii) Duties to Other Third Parties	16–026
(c) Sub-brokers	16–033
(d) The Standard of Skill and Care	16–036
2. Liability for Breach of Duty	16–040
(a) Failing to Effect Insurance	16–042
(b) Effecting Insurance, but not on the Terms Specified by the Client	16–047
(c) Effecting Insurance which does not meet the Client's Requirements	16–050
(d) Failing to Exercise Discretion Reasonably	16–066
(e) Failing to Act with Reasonable Speed	16–068
(f) Liability Arising out of Material Non-disclosure	16–069
(g) Making a Misrepresentation to the Insurers	16–080

	Para.
(h) Failing to keep the Client Properly Informed as to the Existence or Terms of Cover	16–085
(i) Failing to give Proper Advice	16–093
(j) Failings after the Risk has been Placed	16–098
(k) Failings Relating to Claims Against the Insurer	16–102
3. Damages	16–105
(a) Remoteness	16–106
(b) Causation	16–107
(i) Intervening Error or Omission of the Claimant	16–108
(ii) Where the Claimant would not have been Insured in any Event	16–117
(iii) Where the Required Insurance would not have been Granted if the Full Facts had been Known	16–129
(c) Foreseeability	16–133
(i) Measure of Damages	16–135
(ii) Contributory Negligence	16–148
(iii) Mitigation of Loss	16–154
4. Claims for Contribution	16–155

1. General

16–009 Add at end of paragraph: ICOB ceased to be in force from January 5, 2008, at which time it was replaced by a new sourcebook, namely the *Insurance: New Conduct of Business Sourcebook* ("ICOBS"). In the context of claims against brokers, the most important rules are those contained in Chs 5 and 6 of ICOBS, which respectively deal with "Identifying client needs and advising" and "Product Information."

16–015A   Chapter 16—Insurance Brokers

(a) *Duties to the Client*

(ii) *Duties Independent of Contract*

Insert new paragraph **16–015A**:

16–015A   It is common for a broker to act both for an insured in placing cover with an insurer, and also for that insurer in placing re-insurance cover. In such circumstances the broker owes a duty to both his clients, i.e. both the insured and the reinsured. The fact that this may give rise to a potential or actual conflict of interest does not alter the position (*HIH Casualty & General Insurance Ltd v JLT Risk Solutions Ltd* [2007] EWCA Civ 0710).

(c) *Sub-brokers*

16–033   Add to Note 91: In *Dunlop Haywards (DHL) Ltd v Erinaceous Insurance Services Ltd* [2008] EWHC 520 (Comm) Field J. held that the broker had a good arguable case that the sub-broker acted in breach of the terms of the sub-broking agreement between them and that the court should apportion the insured's loss between the broker and sub-broker having regard to the relative primacy of the obligations broken and the causative potency of the breaches committed by the broker and sub-broker. The broker may also bring a claim in negligence against the sub-broker: in *Fisk v Brian Thornhill & Son (A Firm)* [2007] EWCA Civ 152; [2007] P.N.L.R. 21 it was common ground that the Lloyd's sub-broker owed the producing broker a duty of care.

16–035   Add to Note 96: In *Fisk v Brian Thornhill & Son (A Firm)* [2007] EWCA Civ 152; [2007] P.N.L.R. 21 it was conceded that the Lloyd's sub-broker owed the insured a duty of care.

Add at end of paragraph: In *Fisk v Brian Thornhill & Son (A Firm)* [2007] EWCA Civ 152; [2007] P.N.L.R. 21 the Lloyd's sub-broker was found to have breached the duties he owed to both the producing broker and the insured: (i) by failing to advise either of them on renewal that cover was being placed with a new insurer on different terms; (ii) in providing warranties to the insurer without instructions or authority to do so; and (iii) in failing to obtain a new proposal form prior to placing cover.

Add to Note 1: In *Dunlop Haywards (DHL) Ltd v Erinaceous Insurance Services Ltd* [2008] EWHC 520 (Comm) Field J. held that the broker had a good arguable case that the Lloyd's sub-broker had assumed a responsibility to the insured, and would be liable to the insured if it failed to act with reasonable skill and care. The terms of the sub-broking agreement did not prevent the sub-broker owing a duty of care in tort to the insured.

2. Liability for Breach of Duty

(c) *Effecting Insurance which does not meet the Client's Requirements*

16–049   Insert at the end of the paragraph: However, if the cover which is needed by the client is not available, the broker must take care to ensure that the precise

LIABILITY FOR BREACH OF DUTY 16–058

nature of what is and is not covered is made entirely clear to the client: see *Standard Life Assurance Ltd v Oak Dedicated Ltd* [2008] EWHC 222 (Comm) (Tomlinson J.).

Add: More recently in *Standard Life Assurance Ltd v Oak Dedicated Ltd* [2008] EWHC 222 (Comm) Tomlinson J. held that the broker had acted negligently in arranging a policy which did not meet its client's requirements. The policy was unsuitable because the wording of the excess clause in the professional indemnity policy dramatically reduced the scope of cover. 16–053

Add at the end of NOTE 65: In *Standard Life Assurance Ltd v Oak Dedicated Ltd* [2008] EWHC 222 (Comm) Tomlinson J. stated that the broker would not be in breach of duty "in consequence alone of insurers putting forward a spurious construction of the cover". 16–054

Add at the end of the paragraph: These decisions were applied by Tomlinson J. in *Standard Life Assurance Ltd v Oak Dedicated Ltd* [2008] EWHC 222 (Comm) who stated: "it is the duty of the broker to obtain, so far as is possible, insurance coverage which clearly meets his client's requirements. Coverage is only clear in so far as it leaves no room for significant debate. The coverage will be unclear, and the broker in breach of duty, if the form thereof exposes the client insured to an unnecessary risk of litigation. Of course the risk of litigation can never be wholly avoided and the broker is not in breach of duty in consequence alone of insurers putting forward a spurious construction of the cover". The judge accepted the insurer's case on construction of the policy and that the broker was liable. However, the judge also stated that (even if he had found for the insured on the construction of the policy) he would still have found the broker liable because the policy wording was insufficiently clear and exposed the insured to the unnecessary risk that the insurer might dispute the proper meaning of the policy.

Add a new NOTE 69a at the end of the paragraph: For a further illustration, see *Ramco Limited v Weller Russell & Laws Insurance Brokers Ltd* [2008] EWHC 2202 (QB) in which David Donaldson Q.C., sitting as a Deputy High Court Judge, held that the broker was in breach of its obligation to obtain insurance which clearly and indisputably met its client's requirements owing to the existence of wording in the policy which introduced complications and was possibly fatal to the insured's entitlement to an indemnity from the insurer.

Add a new NOTE 72a at the end of the paragraph: In *Standard Life Assurance Ltd v Oak Dedicated Ltd* [2008] EWHC 222 (Comm) Tomlinson J. stated that, in relation to the preparation of the policy, "the broker must be careful to ensure that the policy language clearly encompasses the needs of the client". 16–055

Add at the end of the paragraph: A more recent example is provided by the decision in *Ramco Limited v Weller Russell & Laws Insurance Brokers Ltd* [2008] EWHC 2202 (QB) (David Donaldson Q.C., sitting as a Deputy High Court Judge). In that case the insured was a bailee. The broker arranged cover which was ineffective due to the terms on which the insured held the bailed 16–058 goods. The judge held that the broker was obliged to explore the nature of the insured's business so as to be able to advise properly what cover was or might be appropriate. The broker was found to have acted negligently in failing to investigate the terms on which the insured held the bailed goods, and in arranging insurance which, because of those terms, was unsuitable. In *Standard Life Assurance Ltd v Oak Dedicated Ltd* [2008] EWHC 222 (Comm) Tomlinson J. described the broker's duty as follows: "It is the duty of the broker to identify and advise the client about the type and scope of cover which the client needs and, in doing so, to match as precisely as possible the risk exposures which have been identified within the client's business with the coverage available".

(j) *Failings after the Risk has been Placed*

16–100 Add: The judge's decision was upheld on appeal ([2007] EWCA Civ 0710). Longmore L.J. (at [116]) described the nature of the duty on the broker as follows:

"an insurance broker who, after placing the risk, becomes aware of information which has a material and potentially deleterious effect on the insurance cover which he has placed is under an obligation to act in his client's best interest by drawing it to the attention of his client and obtain his instructions in relation to it."

3. DAMAGES

(b) *Causation*

(i) *Intervening Error or Omission of the Claimant*

Add new paragraph **16–116A**:

16–116A **Reinsurance.** In *HIH Casualty & General Insurance Ltd v JLT Risk Solutions Ltd* [2007] EWCA Civ 0710 (the facts of which are set out at para.**16–100** above) the reinsured's claim against the broker failed on the basis that the broker's negligence had not caused the reinsured's loss. It was held that the true cause of the reinsured's loss was the reinsured's own decision to pay the insured's claims when it had no legal liability to do so and when it knew that the reinsurers disputed the validity of the claims.

(ii) *Where the Claimant would not have been Insured in any Event*

Add new paragraph **16–128A**:

16–128A In *Philips & Co v Whatley* [2007] PNLR 27 (PC) the claimant's solicitors had negligently failed to issue proceedings against his employer prior to the expiry of the limitation period. The court therefore had to assess the value of the claimant's lost opportunity to sue his employer. One of the issues that arose was whether the employer's insurer would have satisfied any judgment the claimant obtained against his employer (given that the employer had gone into liquidation). The employer was in clear breach of a condition precedent requiring it to give notice of the claim to the insurer. The Privy Council held that the principle in *Armory*

DAMAGES   16–143A

v Delamirie (1722) 1 Strange 505 applied, because the solicitors' negligence meant that the actual prospects of recovery from the insurer were not known (and even though the solicitors were not responsible for the late notification to the insurer). The issue to be addressed was one of fact, namely what were the prospects that a reputably insurer would have relied on the breach of the condition precedent. The Privy Council assessed the claimant's prospects of making a recovery from the insurer at 40 per cent.

(c) *Foreseeability*

(i) *Measure of Damages*

Add at the end of the paragraph: In assessing the claimant's loss, the court is **16–135** not strictly concerned with what the insured was entitled to recover under the relevant policy of insurance. Instead, the court has to assess, on the balance of probabilities, what would have occurred had there been no breach of duty. Consequently, if the court finds that an insurer would or might have made a payment to the claimant but for the broker's negligence, then the claimant will recover damages even if (as a matter of law) the claimant would not have been entitled to any payment from the insurer (see also paras **16–127** and **16–128** above). The court will assess the likelihood that the claimant would have received a payment from the insurer. If, as a result of the broker's negligence, there is uncertainty as to the claimant's likely recovery from the insurer, then such uncertainty will be resolved in favour of the claimant (*Armory v Delamirie* (1722) 1 Strange 505 as applied in *Philips & Co v Whatley* [2007] PNLR 27 (PC) and *Ramco Limited v Weller Russell & Laws Insurance Brokers Ltd* [2008] EWHC 2202 (QB) (David Donaldson Q.C., sitting as a Deputy High Court Judge).

Add to NOTE 86: Further, the principle may fall to be reconsidered in the light **16–143** of the decision of the House of Lords in *Sempra Metals Ltd v IRC* [2007] UKHL 34; [2007] 3 W.L.R. 354.

Add new paragraph **16–143A**:

However, in *Arbory Group Ltd v West Craven Insurance Services (A Firm)* **16–143A** [2007] P.N.L.R. 23 (HHJ Grenfell, sitting as a Judge of the High Court) it was held that the *Ramwade* and *Verderame* decisions did not apply where there was a failure to receive a payment relating to business interruption insurance. The claimant had the benefit of business interruption insurance but, as a result of the broker's negligence, the amount of such insurance was too low. As a result, when a fire damaged the claimant's premises the amount the claimant received from the insurer in respect of business interruption was insufficient to re-establish the claimant's business and the claimant suffered on-going loss of profits. The insured claimed damages from the broker for both: (a) the amount that it would have received from the insurer in respect of its business interruption if it had not been under-insured; and (b) the consequential loss of profits it had suffered as a result of being under-insured. The judge held that business interruption insurance should be distinguished from other forms of insurance because it was designed to inject additional funds into a going concern in order to maintain it as a going

[111]

16–143A   Chapter 16—Insurance Brokers

concern. He held that the broker's duty was to ensure that sufficient business interruption cover was in place to enable the company to recover and to resume its pre-fire level of profitability at the earliest date, and that it was reasonably foreseeable that a failure to effect sufficient cover was likely adversely to affect the profitability of the insured's business. On that basis the judge held that the insured could recover damages for both: (a) the shortfall in the payment it received from the insurer due to the under-insurance; and (b) the loss of profits suffered by the insured as a result of that shortfall. The judge gave the broker permission to appeal, but the appeal was subsequently compromised.

16–144   Add a new Note 88a at the end of the second sentence: Where the client sues the insurer and succeeds, the client is likely to recover some but not all of its legal costs from the insurer. In such an event it may seek to recover the shortfall from its broker (i.e. the difference between its actual costs and the costs it recovered from the insurer) on the basis that, had the broker acted with due skill and care, it would not have become embroiled in a dispute with its insurer. Such a claim succeeded in *Ramco Limited v Weller Russell & Laws Insurance Brokers Ltd* [2008] EWHC 2202 (QB) (David Donaldson Q.C., sitting as a Deputy High Court Judge).

Add at the end of Note 89: For a further illustration see *Ramco Limited v Weller Russell & Laws Insurance Brokers Ltd* [2008] EWHC 2202 (QB) (David Donaldson Q.C., sitting as a Deputy High Court Judge) in which the insured unsuccessfully sued the insurer, unsuccessfully appealed, and then unsuccessfully petitioned the House of Lords. The insured recovered damages from the broker in respect of its own costs, and the costs it was ordered to pay the insurer, in respect of each of those steps. For criticism of the decision in *The Tiburon* see "Costs as Damages: The Flawed New Approach" (Professional Negligence Law Review, February 2008, Harvey McGregor Q.C.).

(ii) *Contributory Negligence*

16–150   Add at the end of the paragraph: In *Standard Life Assurance Ltd v Oak Dedicated Ltd* [2008] EWHC 222 (Comm) Tomlinson J. rejected an allegation that the claimant insurer was contributorily negligent in failing to notice that the wording of the excess clause in its professional indemnity insurance policy meant that the policy was unsuitable and did not meet its requirements.

4. Claims for Contribution

16–155   Add: Such a claim arose in *Fisk v Brian Thornhill & Son (A Firm)* [2007] EWCA Civ 152; [2007] P.N.L.R. 21. The trial judge held that the producing broker was solely responsible for the insured's loss. However, the Court of Appeal reversed that finding and held that the Lloyd's sub-broker was responsible for 25 per cent of the insured's loss.

CHAPTER 17

ACCOUNTANTS AND AUDITORS

	Para.
1. Introduction	17–001
2. Duties	17–006
(a) The Statutory Context	17–007
(i) Companies Legislation: the Company Audit	17–008
(ii) Regulatory Statutes relating to the Financial Sector	17–018
(iii) Whistle-blowing	17–019
(b) Duties to Client	17–020
(i) Contractual Duties	17–020
(ii) Duty in Tort	17–023
(iii) Fiduciary Obligations	17–024
(c) Duties to Third Parties	17–026
(i) Overview	17–026
(ii) *Caparo*	17–028
(iii) Factors which may be Relevant	17–030
(iv) Categories of Advisee	17–038
(v) Policy Considerations: Duplication of Remedies	17–046
(vi) The Contracts (Rights against Third Parties) Act 1999	17–047
(vii) The Human Rights Act 1998	17–048
(d) The Standard of Skill and Care	17–049
(i) General	17–049
(ii) Auditing	17–051
(e) Limitation of Liability	17–053
3. Liability for Breach of Duty	17–054
(a) Auditing	17–054

	Para.
(i) Planning, Control and Recording	17–055
(ii) Accounting and Internal Control Systems	17–056
(iii) Evidence	17–057
(iv) Reporting	17–059
(b) Other Breaches of Duty	17–060
4. Damages	17–063
(a) Remoteness	17–063
(i) Causation	17–063
(ii) Foreseeability	17–067
(b) Measure of Damages	17–068
(c) Heads of Damage	17–070
(i) Lost Investment or Advance	17–071
(ii) Overpayment	17–072
(iii) Moneys Wrongly Paid Out	17–073
(iv) Defalcations by Director or Employee	17–074
(v) Costs of Fresh Audit and Investigations	17–075
(vi) Tax Advice and Returns	17–076
(vii) Late Notices and Returns	17–077
(viii) Negligent Advice	17–078
(ix) Avoidance of Double Recovery	17–079
(d) Contributory Negligence and Contribution Proceedings	17–080
(e) Failure to Mitigate	17–082
(f) Statutory Relief	17–083

2. Duties

(a) *The Statutory Context*

(i) *Companies Legislation: the Company Audit*

17–008 Add: Part 15 of the Companies Act 2006 replaces the 1985 Act in relation to accounts and reports with effect from April 6, 2008 (SI 2007/3495).

17–013 Add: Part 16 of the Companies Act 2006 replaces the 1985 Act in relation to auditors. Sections 485–488 dealing with the appointment of auditors in a private company came into force on October 1, 2007 (SI 2007/2194). The remainder of

[113]

17–013

Pt 16 came into force on April 6, 2008 (SI 2007/3495). Because of the inevitable time-lag between the introduction of any new rules and the bringing of a claim against an auditor for alleged failure to follow such rules, it is unlikely that the new provisions will affect negligence claims for some time to come. For a summary of the new provisions, see *Palmer's Company Law*, paras 9.500.1 to 9.500.7.

Of particular interest are ss.532–538, which provide that clauses exempting auditors from liability are void, subject to two exceptions. The first exception permits a company to agree to indemnify an auditor for his costs where the auditor is successful in his defence or obtains relief from liability. The second exception permits liability limitation agreements which: (i) are authorised by the company; (ii) are limited to one year at a time; (iii) comply with regulations (which have not yet been made); and (iv) are fair and reasonable.

(b) *Duties to Client*

(iii) *Fiduciary Duties*

17–024 Add: In *Simpson v Harwood Hutton* [2008] EWHC 1376 (QB) Judge Seymour Q.C. held that an accountant who was instructed by the partnership to value its assets on the retirement of one partner had not acted in breach of fiduciary duty by reason merely of the potential conflict of interests inherent in accepting the instructions, since all the partners had given their informed consent.

17–025 Add to NOTE 24: The HK Court of Final Appeal has allowed the appeal in *Nam Tai Electronics v PricewaterhouseCoopers* [2008] 1 H.K.L.R.D. 666. The court agreed with the courts below that an exception to the principle of confidentiality would be made where there was a legitimate self-interest to be protected, but only so far as proportionate to the protection of that interest. The court was prepared to assume that PwC had a legitimate interest: (i) in seeking appointment as liquidator; and (ii) in countering the suggestion by the parent company that PwC lacked impartiality because it had previously conducted the due diligence review of the company now in liquidation. However, on the facts, that legitimate interest did not make it necessary for PwC to disclose that it had advised against acquisition of the company in question.

(c) *Duties to Third Parties*

(i) *Overview*

17–027 Add: In *United Project Consultants Pte Ltd v Leon Kwok Onn* [2005] S.L.R. 214, D acted as auditor and tax agent for P Co. D filed an incorrect tax return despite having actual knowledge that the directors were under-declaring their fees. The CA of Singapore held that a tax agent was not a mere form-filler but had a duty of care to see that the return was accurate and that it was foreseeable that breach of that duty would cause P loss in having to pay penalties. The court left open the question whether there would have been a valid claim if D had merely been the auditor and not the tax adviser. The court was critical of the English courts for failing to propound a uniform test (this was before *Customs &*

DUTIES   17–059A

Excise v Barclays had reached the HL): "In contrast to the apparent uncertainty emanating from the UK Courts it would seem that the local approach is comparatively settled". The Singapore approach was a combination of proximity and policy (i.e. the 3-fold test). The court rejected a defence of illegality both on the facts and on the basis that this was the very thing which the auditor had been engaged to advise on (presumably subject to proof that P would have acted differently if properly advised: see **17–065** below). However, in *Stone & Rolls Ltd v Moore Stephens* the English C.A. said that the Singapore Court had been wrong to reject the defence of illegality as a matter of law (see paras **17–064** and **17–081** below).

Add to NOTE 34: for *MAN Nutzfahrzeuge AG v Freightliner Ltd* on appeal, see para.**17–064** below.

(iv) *Categories of Advisee*

Add to NOTE 9: for *MAN Nutzfahrzeuge AG v Freightliner Ltd* on appeal, see **17–039** para.**17–064** below.

Add to NOTE 18: for *MAN Nutzfahrzeuge AG v Freightliner Ltd* on appeal, see **17–040** para.**17–064** below.

(d) *The Standard of Skill and Care*

(ii) *Auditing*

Add: In *JSI Shipping (S) Pte Ltd v Teofoongwonglchong* [2007] 1 S.L.R. 821; **17–052** [2006] S.G.H.C. 223, H. Ct of Singapore relied on the principle that an auditor is not a bloodhound. In that case the company suffered loss through the fraud of a director who took excessive remuneration. The auditor had not seen the employment contract of the director in question but relied on the representation of another director as to its terms. It was held that the auditor had not been negligent since he was not obliged to verify every single representation made to him (it would have been different if he had not checked anything represented to him). (The case is under appeal.) See also *Gaelic Inns Pte Ltd v Patric Lee PAC* [2007] 2 S.L.R. 147, a case on the other side of the line.

3. LIABILITY FOR BREACH OF DUTY

(a) *Auditing*

(iii) *Evidence*

Add: For a recent case on enquiries of knowledgeable persons inside the entity, **17–057** see *JSI Shipping* (under para.**17–052** above).

(iv) *Reporting*

Add new para.**17–059A**:

The giving of a certificate. In *M&S Tarpaulins v Green*, [2008] 6MA 70030 **17–059A** (Lawtel May 2, 2008), an auditor was instructed to issue an audit certificate under

[115]

17-059A CHAPTER 17—ACCOUNTANTS AND AUDITORS

the Companies Act 1985 s.156 (a "whitewash" for the purpose of lawfully giving financial assistance). The auditor failed to prepare a cash flow analysis, sensitivity analysis or post-assistance balance sheet. HHJ Pelling Q.C. held that this amounted to a breach of duty to the company when issuing the certificate. The statutory purpose of a certificate under s.156 is to say whether the auditor is aware of anything which renders the director's opinion in the statutory declaration unreasonable. If the certificate is negligent, the loss is the entire assistance provided by paying the sum contemplated by the declaration. However, as between the directors and the auditors, the auditors should be liable for the true value of the shares at the date of completion and the directors should be liable for the windfall, i.e. the difference between the true value and the price paid.

4. DAMAGES

(a) *Remoteness*

(i) *Causation*

17-064 Add: In *Pearce v European Reinsurance* [2006] P.N.L.R. 8; [2005] EWHC 1493 (Ch), Hart J. held that it was arguable that the costs of a supervening bankruptcy petition were within the scope of the auditor's responsibility. This was a fact-sensitive enquiry and therefore not suitable for a strike-out.

The claim against the auditors in *MAN Nutzfahrzeuge AG v Freightliner Ltd* [2007] EWCA Civ 910; [2008] P.N.L.R. 6 (noted at NOTE 18), which was dismissed at first instance by Moore-Bick L.J., has also been dismissed on appeal. The issues on appeal were much narrower than at first instance and principally concerned the purpose for which the auditors had assumed a "special audit duty". MAN purchased the share capital of ERF from a vendor company whose liabilities were then taken over by Freightliner. The finance director of ERF falsified ERF's accounts and also made false oral representations about the accounts to the purchaser. Nobody else on the vendor's side was aware of the fraud. ERF's auditors, E&Y, were admittedly negligent in failing to uncover the falsity in the accounts. MAN sued Freightliner for (1) deceit (i.e. vicarious liability for the false representations), and (2) breach of warranty. Claim (1) succeeded but claim (2) failed on grounds specific to the terms of the share sale agreement. Freightliner brought a Pt 20 claim against the auditors but failed at first instance. On appeal, it was common ground that E&Y's client was ERF alone and that its parent company (the vendor) would not succeed unless E&Y owed it a special audit duty. The CA agreed with the trial judge that, in order to succeed, Freightliner had to show that E&Y assumed a duty to Freightliner in respect of the oral representations made by the finance director. This failed on the facts. E&Y might well have assumed a special audit duty in respect of reliance on the accounts for the purpose of the warranty, but that was not the ground on which Freightliner was liable to MAN. The case is an illustration of the importance of correctly identifying the purpose for which a responsibility has been assumed.

In *Stone & Rolls Ltd v Moore Stephens* [2008] EWCA Civ 644; [2008] P.N.L.R. 36, it was alleged that the claimant company was controlled by a fraud-

ster, who caused it fraudulently to receive and then pay out large sums. The company went into liquidation and the liquidator sued the auditor for failing to uncover the fraud. At first instance ([2008] P.N.L.R. 4) Langley J. had refused to strike out the claim on the ground that the detection of the fraud was the "very thing" for which the auditor was responsible, that there was no policy objection provided that the claim was brought for the benefit of the creditors, and that the court would ensure that the action was of no benefit to the fraudster. On appeal the CA struck out the claim, saying that even if the "very thing" for which the defendant owed a duty to save the claimant harmless included the commission of a criminal offence, this would not override the public policy defence of illegality (see para.**17–081** below).
See also *M&S Tarpaulins Ltd v Green* at para.**17–059A** above.

Add: *Floyd v John Fairhurst & Co* [2004] P.N.L.R. 41; [2004] EWCA Civ 604 at [66] is an example of a case where the claimant failed because he could not prove that he would have acted differently if properly advised that he could use certain tax reliefs.

17–065

(c) *Heads of Damage*

(ix) *Avoidance of Double Recovery*

Add: The principle of reflective loss was applied in [75] to [79] of *Floyd* (see para.**17–065** above): the CA held that, just as a shareholder cannot recover for loss which he merely reflects the company's loss, so too he must give credit for a gain which the company achieved as a result of the negligence.

17–079

(d) *Contributory Negligence and Contribution Proceedings*

Add to NOTE 79: See also *M&S Tarpaulins Ltd v Green* at para.**17–059A** above.

17–080

Add to NOTE 80: For *MAN Nutzfahrzeuge AG v Freightliner Ltd* on appeal, see para.**17–064** above.

Add to NOTE 87: In *Stone & Rolls Ltd v Moore Stephens* (see para.**17–064** above) the company's liquidator argued that detection of the company's fraud was the "very thing" for which the auditor had assumed responsibility. However, the CA held that, even if this were correct, it was trumped by the defence of illegality (i.e. *ex turpi causa*). *Barings* was not cited, but might be distinguishable on two grounds. First, Barings was merely vicariously liable for Leeson's fraud, whereas Stone & Rolls' fraud was that of the company's sole directing mind and will (i.e. it was therefore the fraud of the company itself). Secondly, Barings was the target or intended victim of Leeson's fraud, whereas Stone & Rolls merely became a secondary victim when the fraud in that case backfired.

17–081

Add to NOTE 91: In *Charter plc v City Index Ltd* [2007] EWCA Civ 1382; [2008] 2 W.L.R. 950, a director D misappropriated company money. D received the money with knowledge and was liable for knowing receipt. D sought

17–081

recovery from the company's auditors and other directors. On an application for summary judgment, the CA held: (1) Liability for "knowing receipt" is compensatory, not restitutionary, and is fault-based so as to fall within s.6 of the Civil Liability (Contribution) Act 1978; (2) There is no absolute rule that a wrongdoer who has received a benefit is unable to claim contribution from another wrongdoer who has not received a benefit. If the first wrongdoer has parted with the money, they will both be out of pocket if the liability is enforced against them. Hence the Pt 20 claim could not be decided without a full trial.

Add to the main text after item (5):

(6) Where the company is itself the perpetrator and not the victim of the fraud, the auditor will have a good defence of illegality if the company seeks to allege that the fraud was the "very thing" from which the auditor owed a duty to save the company harmless (see *Stone & Rolls Ltd v Moore Stephens* at para.**17–064** above).

CHAPTER 18

ACTUARIES

	PARA.		PARA.
1. Introduction	18–001	(ii) Duty in Tort	18–017
2. Duties	18–004	(iii) Fiduciary Obligations	18–018
(a) The Statutory Context	18–005	(c) Duties to Third Parties	18–023
(i) Pensions	18–005	(d) The Standard of Skill and Care	18–030
(ii) Life Insurance	18–010	(e) Limitation of Liability	18–037
(b) Duties to Client	18–013	3. Liability for Breach of Duty	18–038
(i) Contractual Duties	18–013	4. Damages	18–039

General Note:

The principal developments over the last two years have been the steps which continue to be taken to restructure the actuarial profession following the Morris Review. A number of new and revised Guidance Notes have been drafted or implemented, as well as revised Professional Conduct Standards which include sections on confidentiality and conflict of interest. In July 2008 the FRC's Board for Actuarial Standards published its "Scope and Authority of Technical Standards" (which can be viewed on the FRC website). Section 1274 of the Companies Act 2006 puts in place the necessary statutory framework to enable the Financial Reporting Council to become the body which oversees the profession.

CHAPTER 19

MEMBERS' AND MANAGING AGENTS AT LLOYD'S

	PARA.
1. General	19–001
(a) Lloyd's of London	19–001
(b) The Regulatory Regime	19–005
(c) Duties to Client	19–017
(i) Contractual Duties	19–017
(ii) Tortious Duties	19–021
(iii) Fiduciary Duties	19–024
(iv) Duties Imposed by the FSA	19–025
(d) Duties to Third Parties	19–026
2. The Standard of Care	19–030
3. Liability for Breach of Duty	19–033
(a) Members' Agent—Failure to Advise Adequately as to Syndicate Participation	19–035
(b) Managing Agent—Failure to Plan Properly	19–043
(c) Managing Agent—Unjustified Departure from Plan	19–051
(d) Managing Agent—Failure to Obtain Adequate Reinsurance	19–052
(i) Deciding what Reinsurance Cover to Seek	19–053
(ii) Choosing the Reinsurer	19–060
(iii) Maintaining Commercial Viability	19–065
(iv) Obtaining Valid Reinsurance	19–067

	PARA.
(e) Managing Agent—Negligent Underwriting of Individual Risks	19–069
(f) Managing Agent—Inadequate Supervision of Active Underwriter	19–074
(g) Managing Agent—Negligence in Relation to Reinsurance to Close	19–075
4. Damages	19–077
(a) Remoteness	19–078
(b) Causation	19–079
(i) Members' Agent—Consequences of Failure to Advise Adequately as to Syndicate Participation	19–080
(ii) Losses Caused by Negligent Underwriting	19–084
(c) Foreseeability	19–088
(d) Measure of Damages	19–089
(i) Members' Agents—Consequences of Failure to Advise Adequately as to Syndicate Participation	19–090
(ii) Losses Caused by Negligent Underwriting	19–094

1. GENERAL

(b) *The Regulatory Regime*

Add: The Lloyd's sourcebook ceased to be in force on December 30, 2006. Recently steps have been taken to simplify and rationalise the requirements for operating at Lloyd's. On January 1, 2008 all bar two of Lloyd's Codes of Conduct were revoked. The Codes were replaced with a Performance Framework. As a result 150 pages of codes of practice have been replaced by five pages of principles and standards. In addition, numerous byelaws have been revoked. **19–005**

Chapter 20

INFORMATION TECHNOLOGY PROFESSIONALS

	Para.
1. General	20–001
(a) Standard Software	20–002
(b) Bespoke and Modified Standard Software	20–004
(c) The Nature of Software	20–005
(d) Software as Services or Goods	20–007
(e) Implied Warranties at Common Law	20–009
2. Duties	20–010
(a) Duties to Client	20–010
(i) Bespoke Software: Warranties of Satisfactory Quality and Fitness for Purpose	20–010
(ii) Modified Standard Software	20–019
(iii) Communication of Client's Purpose	20–027
(iv) Implementation and Testing	20–032
(v) The Importance of Co-operation between the Parties	20–036
(vi) Duties of Support	20–042
(vii) Staff Training	20–044
(viii) User's Operation Manual	20–045
(ix) Implied Terms of Reasonable Skill and Care	20–046
(x) Common Law Duty of Care	20–050
(xi) Supply of Standard/Modified Standard Software: Consultant or Supplier?	20–051
(xii) Negligent Misstatements	20–054
(xiii) Collateral Contract	20–055
(xiv) Advice on Computer Systems	20–056

	Para.
(xv) Grant of Quiet Possession: "Time Bombs"	20–058
(b) Duties other than to Client	20–060
(i) Common Law Liability to third Parties	20–060
(ii) The Consumer Protection Act 1987	20–071
(iii) "Safety-Critical" Information	20–077
3. Standard of Care and Breach	20–078
(a) Standard of Care	20–078
(i) Contracts for Services	20–078
(ii) Contracts for Sale/Supply of Goods	20–081
(b) "Bugs" and "Bedding In"—Inevitable Defects and Software	20–085
(c) The Time when the Obligation of Fitness for Purposes Arises	20–090
(d) The Time when the Obligation Ceases	20–092
(e) "State of the Art" Defence	20–094
4. Causation	20–095
5. Remedies	20–098
(a) Contract	20–099
(b) Repudiation: When Possible?	20–100
(c) Acceptance: When Deemed?	20–101
(d) Time of the Essence?	20–102
(e) "Reliance Loss" and "Expectation Loss": Election Necessary?	20–106
(f) Quantum: Difficulties in Calculation	20–112
(g) Tort	20–116
6. Exclusion and Limitation of Liability	20–118
7. Mitigation	20–128
8. Contributory Negligence	20–130
9. Limitation	20–135

[123]

20–104 CHAPTER 20—INFORMATION TECHNOLOGY PROFESSIONALS

5. REMEDIES

(d) *Time of the Essence?*

20–104 Add new NOTE 73a after the antepenultimate sentence: In fact it now appears that the general position in relation to claims for wasted staff time is not as restrictive as the approach taken by Forbes J. in *Tate & Lyle* was previously perceived to be. A thorough review of the law relating to claims of this nature was undertaken by Wilson L.J. in the case of *Aerospace Publishing Ltd v Thames Water Utilities Ltd* [2007] EWCA 3; [2007] Bus. L.R. 726. At [79] to [86] of the judgment Wilson L.J. reviews the authorities in this area (including *Holman*) and concludes, at [86]:

> "I consider that the authorities establish the following propositions. (a) The fact and, if so, the extent of the diversion of staff time have to be properly established and, if in that regard evidence which it would have been reasonable for the claimant to adduce is not adduced, he is at risk of a finding that they have not been established. (b) The claimant also has to establish that the diversion caused significant disruption to its business. (c) Even though it may well be that strictly the claim should be cast in terms of a loss of revenue attributable to the diversion of staff time, nevertheless in the ordinary case, and unless the defendant can establish the contrary, it is reasonable for the court to infer from the disruption that, had their time not been thus diverted, staff would have applied it to activities which would, directly or indirectly, have generated revenue for the claimant in an amount at least equal to the costs of employing them during that time."

A significant award for lost staff time was upheld by the Court of Appeal. It seems that, provided some persuasive evidence is adduced that staff time was diverted towards remedying a problem caused by the defendant, and it is shown that this caused "significant disruption" to the claimant's business, then a claimant is likely to recover in damages at least the cost of employing the staff for the relevant period. A claimant need not go further and prove that the staff would have been employed more profitably elsewhere; the court will generally be prepared to infer that, employed in their usual roles, those staff members would generate profits for the company of at least the amount of their salary.